ATLAS OF MISSISSIPPI

ATLAS OF MISSISSIPPI

RALPH D. CROSS
Editor

ROBERT W. WALES
Co-editor

CHARLES T. TRAYLOR
Chief Cartographer

Cartographers

Deborah K. Moreland
Sophie K. Nagy
Mackie Odom

UNIVERSITY PRESS OF MISSISSIPPI
JACKSON, 1974

THIS VOLUME IS AUTHORIZED
AND SPONSORED BY THE
UNIVERSITY OF SOUTHERN MISSISSIPPI
HATTIESBURG, MISSISSIPPI

FOREWORD

In 1972, under the editorship of Dr. Ralph D. Cross, the University of Southern Mississippi undertook the task of compiling an atlas of the state of Mississippi. The Atlas was envisioned as serving two principal purposes. First, following the publication of the well-received, two-volume *History of Mississippi* edited by Dr. Richard A. McLemore, the projected book would be the vehicle whereby the present and future story of Mississippi could be told. Second, in view of the fact that the state is in the process of severing many of its traditional economic and social ties with the past while retaining the best of its cultural heritage, this work would further serve to inform the public of the changes occurring in one of the nation's most dynamic growth areas.

I believe the utility of this Atlas has been greatly increased through an expansion of descriptive and explanatory narrative information to complement the detailed maps and other graphics. Business and industrial leaders, schools and colleges, research and planning organizations, government agencies, and many others will find this work of considerable use.

The Atlas is neither a one-man nor a one-school undertaking. Contributions were made by individuals from a host of institutions, organizations, and agencies. This has not only lent expertise to the many subjects covered, but also has made the work a truly cooperative effort. I believe that the publication of this Atlas made a great step forward in Mississippi's growing effort toward self-analysis and self-judgment and toward her consequent progress.

Dr. William D. McCain,
President
University of Southern Mississippi
June 1, 1974

ACKNOWLEDGMENTS

The compilation of such a work as the Atlas of Mississippi necessitates drawing upon the expertise of many individuals. Foremost, our sincerest appreciation is extended to the members of the Atlas staff whose untiring work made the Atlas a reality. Charles "Tim" Traylor, chief cartographer, whose unparalleled knowledge of cartographic and publishing techniques made the Atlas the high quality product that it is. Deborah Moreland, Sophie Nagy, and Mackie Odom, cartographers, contributed their cartographic excellence and tireless efforts toward the real tedious work of scribing maps and peeling overlays, and whose long hours at the drafting table made it possible for us to meet deadlines. Laura Gail Bishop, project secretary, withstood our temperamental moods for two long years and wore out two typewriters typing and retyping edited manuscript.

Likewise, our heartfelt thanks go out to the many persons listed on the page opposite, who gave unselfishly of their time and knowledge to supply the narrative and the data which form the contents of the Atlas. We also owe a deep debt of gratitude to many people whose names do not appear in the List of Contributors, but who, nonetheless, lent their time and expertise when called upon. Among these are Dr. William D. McCain, president, University of Southern Mississippi, who was instrumental in securing funding for the Atlas; Dr. Charles W. Moorman, dean of the University, who contributed advice and assistance during some very trying times; Dr. Robert T. van Aller, dean of the Graduate School, who smoothed out many of our administrative problems with the project; Dr. Claude E. Fike, dean of the College of Liberal Arts, who provided his support throughout the entire project; Mr. Robert W. Galbraith, projects and grants officer, who was a tremendous help in budgetary matters; and Dr. John E. Gonzales who always had a ready answer when we needed to check the authenticity of data.

Moreover, there were several other individuals employed in other capacities who, likewise, contributed their efforts toward completion of the Atlas. These included: James "Fred" Wise, graduate student cartographer, who worked for several months scribing, peeling, and preparing color proofs of Atlas maps. Sharon Kuse, Carol Bryant, and Brenda Boro, Geography secretaries, who helped with manuscript typing when deadlines were near.

Finally, we wish to thank the many agencies which supplied data, pictures, and very welcome advice. Among these are the Research and Development Center, the Agricultural and Industrial Board, the Board of Water Commissioners, the Jackson office of the United States Geological Survey, the Division of Comprehensive Health Planning of the Office of the Governor, and the Southern Forest Experiment Station in New Orleans.

June 1, 1974

R.D.C.
R.W.W.

CONTRIBUTORS

DANIEL L. BERTELSON, Forester, Southern Forest Experiment Station, New Orleans, La.

RAYMOND L. BUSBEE, Chairman, Department of Recreation, University of Southern Mississippi, Hattiesburg, Ms.

GLORIA CHANNELL, Free–lance Artist, Jackson, Ms.

JOSEPH H. CLEMENTS, Professor of Finance, University of Southern Mississippi, Hattiesburg, Ms.

WALTER COOPER, Dean, School of Health, Physical Education, and Recreation, University of Southern Mississippi, Hattiesburg, Ms.

RALPH D. CROSS, Associate Professor of Geography, University of Southern Mississippi, Hattiesburg, Ms.

JAMES W. GLADDEN, JR., Assistant Professor of Geography, University of Southern Mississippi, Hattiesburg, Ms.

JOHN EDMOND GONZALES, The William D. McCain Professor of History, University of Southern Mississippi, Hattiesburg, Ms.

JOHN D. GUICE, Associate Professor of History, University of Southern Mississippi, Hattiesburg, Ms.

ERIC M. GUNN, Dean, College of Education and Psychology, University of Southern Mississippi, Hattiesburg, Ms.

STANFORD P. GWIN, Chairman, Department of Communications, University of Southern Mississippi, Hattiesburg, Ms.

JAMES A. HEAD, Special Projects Officer, Pat Harrison Waterway District, Hattiesburg, Ms.

RICHARD KAZELSKIS, Director, Bureau of Research and Education Programs, University of Southern Mississippi, Hattiesburg, Ms.

ARTHELL KELLEY, Professor of Geography, University of Southern Mississippi, Hattiesburg, Ms.

JOHN W. KILBURN, Head, Department of Geography, Jacksonville State University, Jacksonville, Ala.

BYRLE A. KYNERD, Director, State Historical Museum, Jackson, Ms.

CHARLES E. LINDLEY, Dean, College of Agriculture, Mississippi State University, Starkville, Ms.

CHARLES H. LYLES, Staff Marine Biologist, Gulf Coast Research Laboratory, Ocean Springs, Ms.

GARY W. MATTHEWS, Graduate Student, Department of Recreation, University of Southern Mississippi, Hattiesburg, Ms.

JESSE O. McKEE, Associate Professor of Geography, University of Southern Mississippi, Hattiesburg, Ms.

THOMAS D. McILWAIN, Staff Marine Biologist, Gulf Coast Research Laboratory, Ocean Springs, Ms.

JAMES M. McQUISTON, Assistant Professor of Economics, University of Southern Mississippi, Hattiesburg, Ms.

W. T. MEALOR, Assistant Professor of Geography, University of Southern Mississippi, Hattiesburg, Ms.

BARBARA MOORE, Assistant Director for Health Planning, Division of Comprehensive Health Planning, Jackson, Ms.

OSCAR L. PAULSON, Chairman, Department of Geology, University of Southern Mississippi, Hattiesburg, Ms.

KARL A. RIGGS, Assistant Professor of Geology, Mississippi State University, Starkville, Ms.

WILLIAM M. ROBERTS, Chairman, Department of Geography, University of Southern Mississippi, Hattiesburg, Ms.

E. J. SALTSMAN, Climatologist for Mississippi (ret.) Jackson, Ms.

DAVID G. SANSING, Assistant Professor of History, University of Mississippi, Oxford, Ms.

JOHN R. SKATES, Chairman, Department of History, University of Southern Mississippi, Hattiesburg, Ms.

HERBERT S. STERNITZKE, Principal Research Analyst, Southern Forest Experiment Station, New Orleans, La.

ANN TATALOVICH, Graduate Student, Department of Political Science, University of Southern Mississippi, Hattiesburg, Ms.

JOAB L. THOMAS, Dean of Students and Professor of Biology, University of Alabama, Tuscaloosa, Ala.

IRLYN C. TONER, Manager, Analysis and Forecast Branch, Research and Development Center, Jackson, Ms.

W. H. TURCOTTE, Chief, Game and Fisheries Division, Game and Fish Commission, Jackson, Ms.

H. B. VANDERFORD, Professor of Soils, Mississippi State University, Starkville, Ms.

F. JOHN WADE, Manager, Economic Analysis Division, Mississippi Research and Development Center, Jackson, Ms.

ROBERT W. WALES, Assistant Professor of Geography, University of Southern Mississippi, Hattiesburg, Ms.

L. DOW WELCH, Assistant Economist, Mississippi Agricultural and Forestry Experiment Station, Starkville, Ms.

LEON A. WILBER, Professor of Political Science, University of Southern Mississippi, Hattiesburg, Ms.

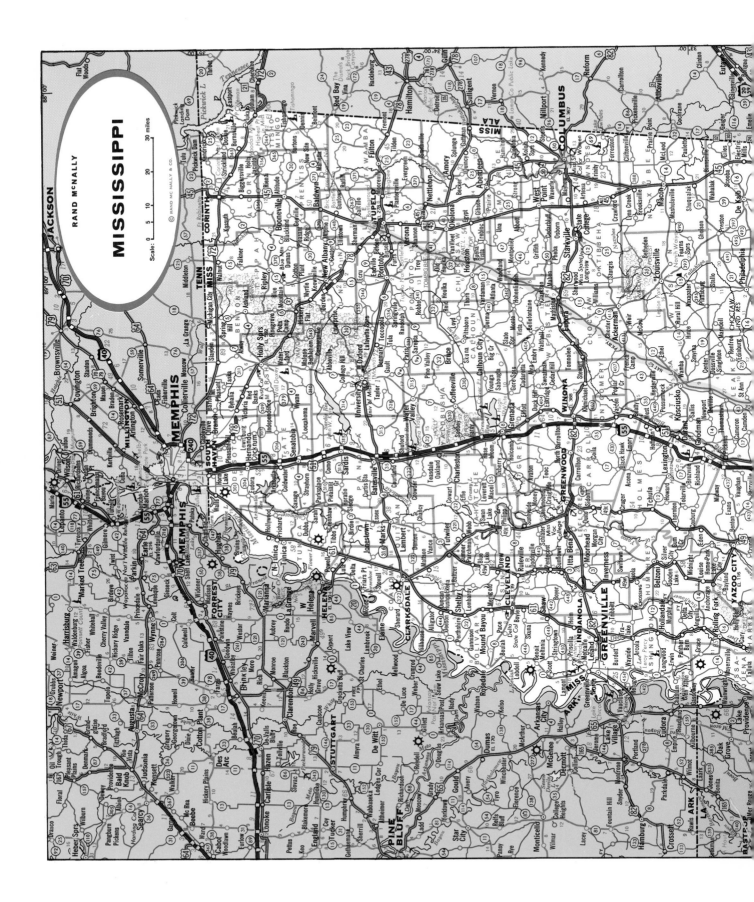

RAND MCNALLY

MISSISSIPPI

Scale:
0 5 10 20 30 miles

© RAND MC NALLY & CO.

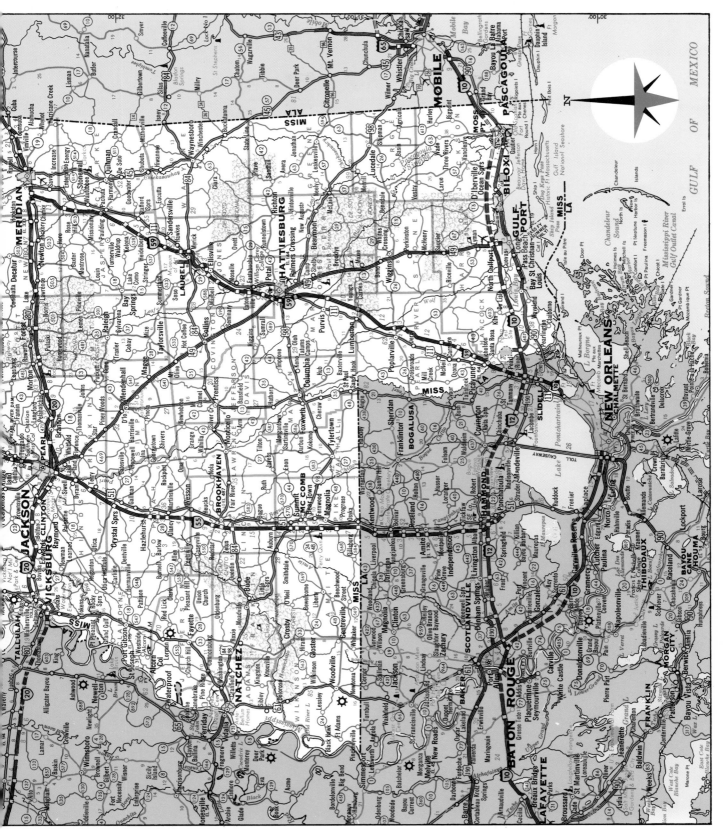

CONTENTS

INTRODUCTION

"The grave was dug through solid marble, but the marble headstone came from Vermont. It was in a pine wilderness, but the coffin nails, screws, and shovels came from Pittsburg. With hardwoods and metals abounding, the corpse was hauled on a wagon that came from South Bend, Indiana. A hickory grove grew near by, but the pick and shovels came from New York. The cotton shirt on the dead man came from Cincinnati; the coat and breeches from Chicago; the shoes from Boston, the folded hands were incased in white gloves from New York, and round the poor neck, that had borne all its living days the bondage of lost opportunity, was twisted a cheap cravat from Philadelphia." So read Henry Grady's famous obituary in the Atlanta *Constitution* in the mid-1880s, demonstrating the nature of the South's dependency on other regions of the country without real need.

Somehow, beyond the South, this concept of needless dependency, along with archaic views about the culture, tends to persist even to the present day. In spite of such a persistently unfavorable image, Mississippi has been working diligently to alter this illusion held in the minds of her countrymen. Mississippi reached a watershed in her historical development in the 1940s. Since that time the state has and is continuing to shed those customs which tend to cloud her image to the outside world, while retaining those which enhance her mien.

Mississippi's historical development is as unique as any other state's. Indigenously the home of the Choctaw, the Chickasaw, and the Creek, the lands called Mississippi passed through the hands of the French and Spanish before being organized and added to the United States by settlers of primarily British derivation.

She suffered through a lengthy period based on a one-crop economy—cotton. Slavery and tenancy tarnished her reputation. As a member of the Confederacy, she was ravished by the North both during and after the Civil War. Mississippi entered the twentieth century as an agrarian state still trying to live on cotton and riding the back of the tenant farmer. It was during this latter segment of the cotton era, between the closing of the nineteenth century and World War II, that Mississippi's reliance on others reached its peak. Stricken by the Great Depression, Mississippi struggled through what was probably her most trying economic period. She suffered through the second world war along with the remainder of the country, then began in earnest to alter her position as the dependent sister of the nation.

Today, Mississippi has made considerable progress toward curing the ills which have plagued her since the beginning of the century. Agriculture is still an important segment of the economy, but Mississippi can no longer be called an agrarian state. Manufacturing now leads the economy in most categories. Although she cannot be considered an industrial state in the same vein as several states of the North and East, she does offer a favorable environment for increasing industrial development. The people likewise are changing. For decades outmigration overshadowed natural increase, but thus far in the 1970s the state is showing an increase in population. This may indicate that many Mississippians are recognizing both the changes occurring around them and also the potentials that the state has to offer; instead of seeking their fortunes elsewhere, many of the people are staying home. The blacks have long been a suppressed majority in Mississippi. Although the black/white population ratio now has reversed itself, blacks are currently beginning to assume their rightful place in the state's society. Mississippi, so long an economically backward area, has seemingly forever had personal incomes below the national averages. Today, the mean and median incomes for most occupations and for the state as a whole are creeping up on the national averages.

Although Mississippi does not have an overabundance of natural resources, she does have a certain substantial reserve. Her forests, relatively clean waters, petroleum and natural gas reserves, and productive soils seem to offer the best potential for resource utilization in the near future. In many respects Mississippi is just coming of age. She has the opportunity to avoid the mistakes made by the highly developed states of the eastern seaboard. She is in a position to take advantage of their errors—to keep her environment free of pollution, yet to fully develop her potential; to manage her resources well, rather than to exploit them. For Mississippi the past is gone, the future is open.

Ralph D. Cross

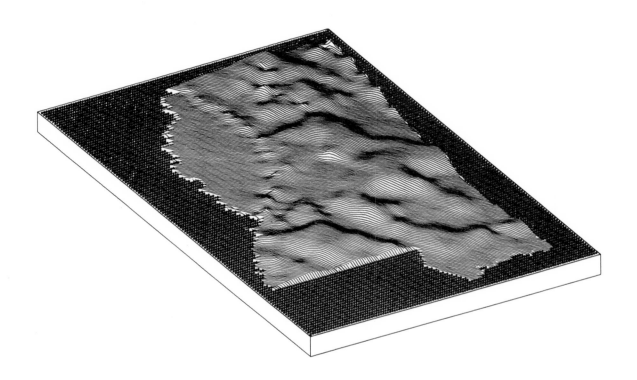

ELEVATION MAP OF MISSISSIPPI

NOTE: The three dimensional block diagram, located opposite the introduction to each major section in the atlas, represents a recently developed computer method for displaying spatially continuous data. An overview of total quantitative data is represented by "hills" and "valleys," which are proportional to data variation. Hence, spatial relationships among data are dramatically emphasized.

The data maps were produced by a computer driven pen plotter, using a modified version of SYMVU, a program originally developed by the Laboratory for Computer Graphics and Spatial Analysis, Harvard University, Cambridge, Massachusetts.

PHYSICAL FEATURES

Mississippi borders on the Gulf of Mexico, giving the state a somewhat unique character and providing for local diversity in its physical environment. The physical environment must naturally set limits for man based on the level of his technology. As man becomes more knowledgeable of his physical surroundings and as his technical expertise increases, the greater is his control over the environment. Hence, to better understand man's development of Mississippi and the current character of his existence within its boundaries, it is essential to understand the state's physical environment and to be aware of human–physical interaction occurring within it.

Rocks form the geologic foundation of any land area. In Mississippi most rock formations have developed from loose materials which were deposited by wind and water and subsequently cemented together. These sedimentary rock strata have been covered by unconsolidated sediments, partly from wind and water deposition and partly by rock decomposition in place. The sediments have changed in response to a number of variables to form various soil types.

The surface configuration reflects the underlying nature of the rocks. Mississippi is broadly classified as a belted coastal plain. The topography slopes generally from north to south, interrupted by three ridges with steeper slopes facing inland.

Climatically, Mississippi is situated in the humid subtropics. Precipitation tends to decrease northward, and annual totals range between 45 and 65 inches. Winter months experience the greatest rainfall, whereas fall is the driest season. Temperatures are mild. The annual average temperature varies from 61° F. in the north to 68° F. along the coast. Summer temperatures throughout the state reach the eighties and frequently the nineties but seldom exceed 100° F. Mississippi is susceptible to tornadoes, especially in the spring, to hurricanes during the summer and fall, and to thunderstorms throughout the year. Snow and ice storms occur infrequently in the south and more often in the north.

Natural vegetation develops largely in response to the climate and the surface materials of an area. Copious amounts of rainfall together with moderate temperatures provide conditions suitable for forest growth. The forests of Mississippi are largely composed of two types of trees, hardwoods such as oak and hickory and softwoods such as pine in pure or mixed stands. A few sporadic areas of grassland are also in evidence.

Ralph D. Cross

TOPOGRAPHY

Mississippi lies mostly within the East Gulf Coastal Plain physiographic region with small segments in the Interior Low Plateaus Province. The East Gulf Coastal Plain is a section of the larger Atlantic and Gulf Coastal Plain province which extends from New England into eastern Mexico. The East Gulf Coastal Plain is an elevated sea bottom with low topographic elevations and extensive tracts of marshy land. The elevations of this area are generally below 500 feet with a few minor exceptions.

Geologists estimate that the Gulf shoreline has been receding since the beginning of Cretaceous time when the coastal plain was elevated. The geologic formations are primarily sedimentary deposits representing the Cretaceous, Tertiary, and Quaternary geologic periods. These formations slope gently from the interior out toward the Gulf of Mexico. Paralleling the inner and outer edges of the plain are belts of uplands with gentle slopes seaward and much shorter, steeper slopes facing inland. These asymmetrical landforms are called cuestas. The Cretaceous formation forms an inland cuesta belt, the Tertiary an intermediate belt, and the Quaternary a coastal belt. Mississippi's position within the coastal plain accounts for the lack of extreme variation in the surface configuration of the area. However, variability of lithology produces notable differences in the erosibility of the rocks. As a consequence, the East Gulf Coastal Plain exhibits a series of lowlands separated by cuestas with escarpments facing inland, justifying the state's designation as a belted coastal plain. The topography varies from flat to undulating to steep eroded hills, and gives sufficient basis for dividing Mississippi into ten physiographic regions.

THE TENNESSEE RIVER HILLS

An area of rugged hill lands drained by the Tombigbee and Tennessee rivers lies in the northeastern part of the state and is known as the Tennessee River Hills. This region is part of the Fall Line Hills that constitute the innermost belt of the East Gulf Coastal Plain and is developed on rocks belonging to the Cretaceous, Tuscaloosa, and Eutaw formations. The drainage of the area is largely to the south and east; in the extreme northern part of the region drainage patterns trend northward. The tributary streams have cut narrow ravines in the uplands, and flow in short shift courses to the Tombigbee and Tennessee rivers. The

Tennessee River Hills area has an average elevation of 650 feet, rising to 806 feet at the highest point in Tishomingo County, whereas the local relief within the region may be as great as 200 to 250 feet.

BLACK PRAIRIE

Lying west of the Tennessee River Hills and stretching from Corinth to beyond Macon on the Alabama line is the crescent-shaped physical region known as the Black Prairie, one of the most famous areas of the Old South. The Black Prairie is an extension of the famous Black Belt of Alabama. The average width of the Black Prairie ranges from 20 to 25 miles, and it is situated from 200 feet to 300 feet below the uplands on the east and west of it. The surface is flat to gently undulating, and some areas are so lacking in relief that railways and highways have straight stretches for many miles. The Black Prairie derives its name from the dark color of the soil. The area is underlain by Selma chalk, a soft limestone deposit. The chalk has weathered into the dark, fertile, black to dark brown surficial deposits which make it distinct from surrounding areas. In places where erosion has been sufficient, huge outcroppings of crumbling rock have exposed the limestone at the surface. The Black Prairie is nearly devoid of trees, a condition which is somewhat of an enigma since precipitation in this area is sufficient to support tree growth.

PONTOTOC RIDGE

West of the Black Prairie and extending from the Tennessee line to a few miles north of West Point is an elevated land area, with heights reaching from 400 feet to 600 feet above sea level, known as Pontotoc Ridge. The flat to undulating prairies on the east and the level Flatwoods area on the west make the Pontotoc Ridge a prominent topographic feature of northern Mississippi. The ridge serves as the drainage divide between the Mississippi River basin to the west and the Tennessee–Tombigbee basins on the east. The ridge is formed by outcroppings of marls and sands of the Ripley cuesta. The marl and sand surficial materials have weathered into a reddish surface color, causing the formation to stand in sharp contrast to the dark tone of the prairie.

FLATWOODS

Immediately west of the Pontotoc Ridge and the

Black Prairie is the Flatwoods, a region of narrow breadth composed of level land. The width of the belt varies from six to twelve miles and extends from Kemper County to the Tennessee line. The region is formed from the Porter's Creek clay, accounting for the heavy clay texture of the soil and the resultant poor drainage.

NORTH CENTRAL HILLS

The North Central Hills physiographic region spans an area from Clarke County northwestward through Leake County, and north to the Tennessee line. The region is bordered on the east by the Flatwoods. The area is the most extensive upland in Mississippi, situated from 400 feet to 600 feet above sea level. Because of its elevation and because it is bounded by relatively flat areas on three sides, this region at one time was known as the North Central Plateau of Mississippi. The area is a part of the Red Hills section which extends eastward across southcentral Alabama. Along the south side of the North Central Hills in Lauderdale, Kemper, and Neshoba counties stands a ridge of the most rugged hills found in the coastal plain. This ridge is formed by the very resistant Tallahatta formation and is called the Buhrstone Cuesta. The local name of buhrstone (burrstone) derives from the presence in the formation of silliceous rocks suitable for use as millstones.

BROWN LOAM AND LOESS HILLS

West of the North Central Hills and stretching from the Tennessee line to Louisiana, is the Brown Loam and Loess Hills region. The western boundary is sharply defined as the loess hills drop off to the floodplain of the Yazoo and Mississippi rivers. The area receives its name from the color and character of the surface materials. The hills along the east side of the Mississippi River floodplain are covered with a thick layer of loess. Loess is a buff-colored material, exhibiting an angular structure, and it has a tendency to stand resistant to lateral erosion in vertical columns. The loess is material believed to have been transported by wind from glacial outwash material of Pleistocene age. The loess surface mantle thins eastward over a distance of twenty to forty miles until it blends into the central uplands.

Loess is calcareous and fertile but easily eroded in a direction perpendicular to the surface. The stream

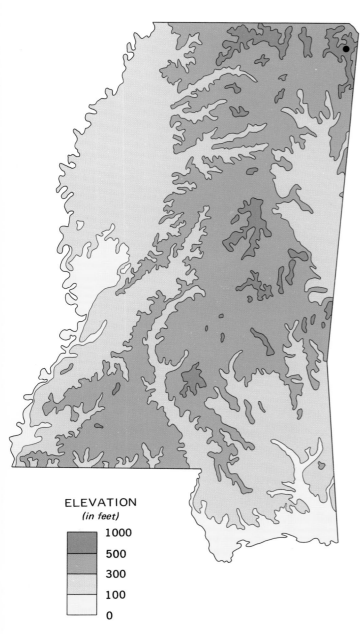

ELEVATION
(in feet)

1000
500
300
100
0

● Highest elevation:
Woodall Mountain - 806 feet

GENERAL ELEVATION

Source: U. S. Geological Survey

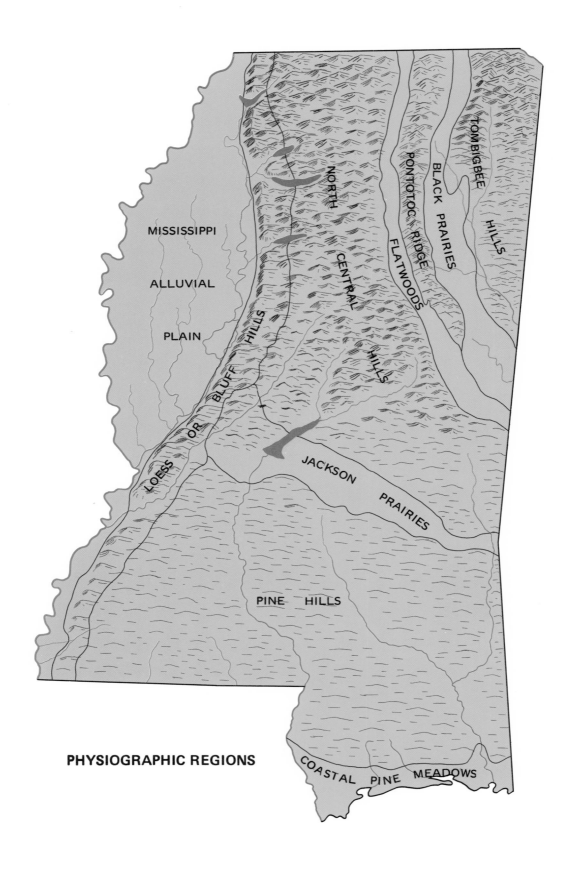

MISSISSIPPI

ALLUVIAL

PLAIN

NORTH

CENTRAL

HILLS

LOESS OR BLUFF HILLS

PONTOTOC RIDGE

FLATWOODS

BLACK PRAIRIES

TOMBIGBEE HILLS

JACKSON PRAIRIES

PINE HILLS

COASTAL PINE MEADOWS

PHYSIOGRAPHIC REGIONS

banks are vertical, and road cuts must be made vertically or erosion is a serious problem. The loess deposits vary from 30 feet to as much as 90 feet in depth in places. Erosion cutting downward has produced an extremely rolling to very hilly landscape.

YAZOO BASIN

In the northwestern part of the state, between the Loess Hills and the Mississippi River and the Walnut Hills at Vicksburg and the Chickasaw Bluffs around Memphis, Tennessee, lies the Yazoo Basin. Locally the Yazoo Basin area is called the Delta, and is almost totally contained between the Mississippi and Yazoo rivers. The region is a floodplain composed of alluvial deposits. The surface of the area appears almost perfectly flat, but close examination reveals slight elevations along the stream banks or along old meander belts of abandoned stream courses. As the streams overflowed, the coarse materials were deposited first along the banks—resulting in a slight building of land higher near the streams than in the surrounding area beyond the stream courses. These uplifted segments of land are known as natural levees. From the natural levees the land tends to slope gently downward into poorly drained topographic depressions known as backswamps. Streams in this region have a very small gradient of less than six inches per mile. They frequently overflow their banks, leaving a thin layer of silt on the natural levees and increasing poor drainage conditions in the backswamp areas. Streams here also tend to shift their courses frequently, often leaving behind a partially water-filled meander loop called an oxbow lake. As a flood control measure artificial levees have been constructed on top of the natural levees. This procedure has resulted in increased deposition of silt on river beds and raised the water level. Reservoirs to regulate stream flow have also been built in the interest of flood control.

JACKSON PRAIRIE

The Jackson Prairie section lies in a narrow belt reaching from Clarke to Madison counties. The region is a flat to undulating area underlain by limestone, marl, and clays of the Vicksburg and Jackson formations. The original vegetation cover consisted of open patches of grasslands, interspersed with woodland areas. The underlying parent materials have resulted in the formation of two distinct major surface regions.

The dark, calcareous surficial area, the product of weathering of limestones and marls, is similar in color and consistency to the surface materials of the Northeast Prairie. The second section is lighter in tone and is a product of weathered clay.

In the Jackson Prairie are not only relatively good agricultural soils, but also sufficient quantities of limestone and clay to support a cement industry. Portland cement plants are located nearby at Vicksburg and Brandon.

PINE WOODS

Extending southward from Jackson Prairie to within twenty miles of the Gulf Coast, and from the Alabama state line to the Brown Loam Belt is the Pine Woods region. The general surface configuration is high and rolling, with moderately high ridges forming divides between streams. Elevations in excess of one hundred feet between the hill tops and stream bottoms are not uncommon. Most of the area is between 300 feet and 500 feet above sea level. The region was at one time covered with a magnificent stand of longleaf pines and was referred to as the Longleaf Pine Belt. The subsurface materials are composed of the Catahoula Sandstone, the Hattiesburg, and the Pascagoula sands and clays; for about eighty miles inland, the hill summits and higher levels are topped with Citronelle deposits. The streams of the area trend southward for the most part, and the region is bisected by the Pearl River near its east–west midpoint. The eastern section is drained largely by tributaries of the Pascagoula River, whereas the western section is drained by a number of streams.

COASTAL MEADOWS

The Coastal Meadows area marks the present shoreline where the Gulf waters meet the land, and extends inland some fifteen to twenty miles. A well defined seaward boundary is not apparent. It is more appropriate to consider this section as being the outer edge of the East Gulf Coastal Plain Province, and as an area continually changing in its character and position. The region's surface is relatively flat with a very slight upslope toward the interior. The surficial materials are largely composed of recently deposited fine sands and silts.

Arthell Kelley

GEOLOGY

Physiographically, Mississippi lies in the East Gulf Coastal Plain Province except for small areas in Tishomingo County which are part of the Interior Low Plateaus region, a subdivision of the Interior Lowlands Province. The Gulf Coastal Plain is formed by gently tilted Mesozoic and Cenozoic deposits which rest on deformed rocks of the Appalachian and Ouachita mountains. These deposits consist of sediments laid down in marine, brackish, and fluvial environments and are tilted toward the Mississippi Embayment in the northern part of the state. The amount of tilting varies between 15 and 35 feet per mile at the surface and increases with depth. The oldest rocks in Mississippi are in the northeastern corner and become progressively younger toward the coast—a result of land building out into the ancestral Gulf of Mexico.

INTERIOR LOW PLATEAUS

The only portion of Mississippi in the Interior Lowlands Province is found along its eastern margin in Tishomingo County where older Paleozoic rocks are exposed at the surface. This area is closely related to the plateau regions of Tennessee and Alabama, and is probably the southernmost extension of the Nashville Dome. The rocks are Devonian and Mississippian in age and consist of limestone, shales, sandstones, and chert.

GULF COASTAL PLAIN

The Mesozoic and Cenozoic surface deposits consist of sediments ranging in age from upper Cretaceous (Gulf Series) to Recent. Rocks representative of the intervals of time from Mississippian to Gulfian, i.e., Pennsylvanian, Permian, Triassic, Jurrassic, Coahuilan (Cretaceous), and Comanchean (Cretaceous) are not present on the surface in Mississippi, but all, except the Permian, have been encountered in drilling for oil and gas.

MESOZOIC ERA

The Cretaceous Period marks the end of the interval of time referred to as the Age of Dinosaurs. Since most of the Cretaceous deposits of Mississippi were laid down under marine conditions, the only dinosaur remains are those of the few marine reptiles living during the time. The oldest Cretaceous deposits at the surface consist of stream sands and gravels, which are overlain by chalk and marls composed primarily

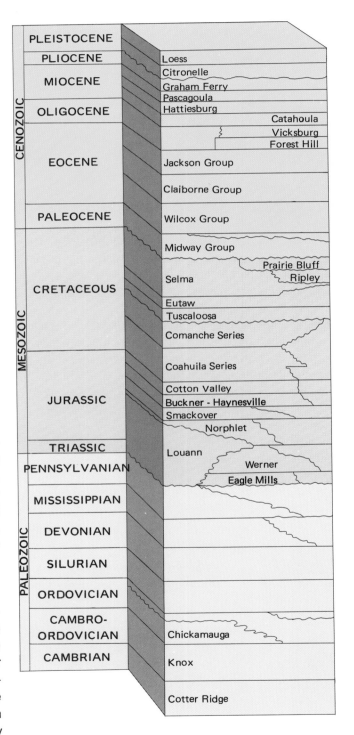

GEOLOGIC COLUMN

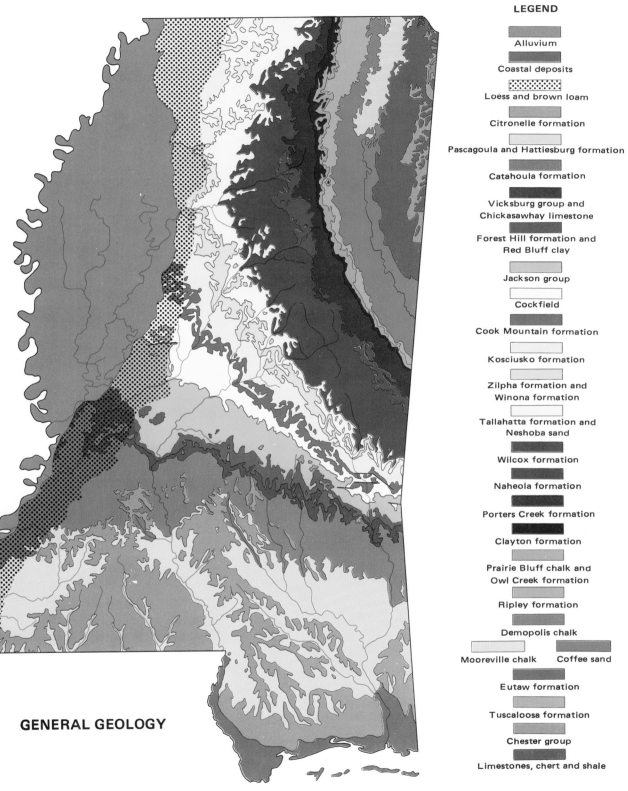

GENERAL GEOLOGY

LEGEND

Alluvium

Coastal deposits

Loess and brown loam

Citronelle formation

Pascagoula and Hattiesburg formation

Catahoula formation

Vicksburg group and
Chickasawhay limestone

Forest Hill formation and
Red Bluff clay

Jackson group

Cockfield

Cook Mountain formation

Kosciusko formation

Zilpha formation and
Winona formation

Tallahatta formation and
Neshoba sand

Wilcox formation

Naheola formation

Porters Creek formation

Clayton formation

Prairie Bluff chalk and
Owl Creek formation

Ripley formation

Demopolis chalk

Mooreville chalk   Coffee sand

Eutaw formation

Tuscaloosa formation

Chester group

Limestones, chert and shale

Source: U.S. Geologic Survey

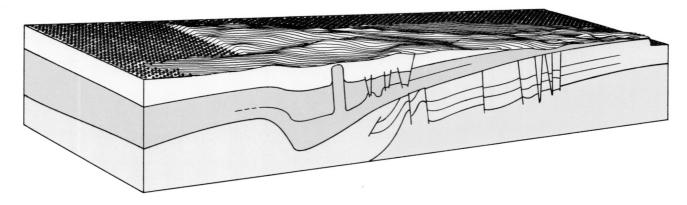

GEOLOGIC CROSS SECTION

Source: Mississippi Geological Survey

of shells of microscopic marine organisms. The chalk and marls support an abundant growth of red cedar. Bentonite clays within these sediments are formed by the alteration of volcanic ash which fell in the northeastern part of the state. Other products of igneous activity include buried intrusions at Jackson and Midnight in Humphreys County which were formed during the same time period as the Bentonite clays.

CENOZOIC ERA

This era marks the advent of forms of life similar to that of today and is often referred to as the Age of Mammals. The Cenozoic deposits of Mississippi cover approximately 85 percent of the state or that portion lying south and west of a line from New Albany to Houston to Starkville to Shuqualak. This era of time is divided from oldest to youngest into the following epochs: Paleocene, Eocene, Oligocene, Miocene, Pliocene, Pleistocene, and Recent.

The Midway Group of the Paleocene Series consists of a basal limestone unit, a middle clay unit, and upper sand and lignitic clay.

The "gas rock" which formerly produced gas in the Jackson field was deposited during the Paleocene Epoch.

The Eocene Series of Mississippi is divided into the Wilcox, Claiborne, and Jackson groups. The Wilcox Group, the oldest of the three, consists of sands, clays, and lignites deposited in brackish marshes and stream valleys. The lignites are intermediate between peat and coal and have heating values ranging from 8,000 to 10,000 BTU. Numerous sharks' teeth have been found in a few thin marine marls in the east-central part of the state. The Wilcox Group is exposed along a ten- to twenty-mile belt extending from Meridian to Louisville and Eupora, stretching into Benton County at the northern end of the state.

The Claiborne Group resembles the Wilcox in the content of brackish clays and fluvial sands, but differs in having a greater percentage of marine green-sands and marls. The marls contain numerous mollusc shells such as those found around Newton. The basal unit of this group is a siliceous siltstone sometimes referred to as buhrstone because it was once used to make grinding wheels for pulverizing grain.

The Jackson Group is best known for its fossil whale bones and large shark teeth as well as for its ability to absorb water and expand. This capability for expansion produces many problems in the construction business, since the force exerted is sufficient to crack foundations and highway surfaces. The Jackson Group is exposed along a belt extending from

Yazoo City to Shubuta with its greatest width lying between Jackson and Canton.

The Oligocene Epoch is represented principally by the Vicksburg Group and also by lignitic sands and clays of the Forest Hill. The latter is interpreted as indicative of deposition under brackish water or deltaic conditions. The Vicksburg Group, overlying the Forest Hill, is marine as indicated by the abundance of marine fossils such as the scallop *Pecten*, the shell which serves as the symbol for the Shell Oil Company. The Vicksburg Group is little more than 100 feet thick and is exposed along a belt only one or two miles wide from Vicksburg to Waynesboro.

The Miocene Series of rocks consists primarily of sediments deposited in fresh water, demonstrated by the presence of fresh water and land plant fossils. This series is difficult to subdivide into formations because of the similarity of rock types, but three units have historically been assigned. These are, from older to younger and north to south, the Catahoula Sandstone, Hattiesburg Formation, and Pascagoula Formation, all of which consist of alternating sands and clays extending to within a few miles of the coast.

The lower part of the Graham Ferry Formation is the only unit that is presently recognized as being Pliocene in age. The Graham Ferry Formation consists of both brackish and marine sands and clays, with mollusc shells being the basis for assigning the lower part of this unit to the Pliocene and the upper part to the Pleistocene.

The Pleistocene sediments of Mississippi were laid down during the Ice Age when glaciers covered North America as far south as southern Illinois. These sediments consist of stream-laid sands and gravels called Citronelle and a windblown silt called loess. The Citronelle Formation overlies formations of a number of epochs of geologic time due to its widespread distribution in the southern part of the state. It also underlies the loess along a narrow belt paralleling the aforementioned bluffs from Louisiana to the Tennessee state line. The loess is a windblown, calcareous silt deposited during the latter part of the Pleistocene Epoch on the eastern side of the Mississippi River floodplain (the Delta area). The loess is approximately 75 feet thick near the bluffs at Vicksburg and Natchez, but thins rapidly to the east. These deposits contain remains of mastodons, tapirs, buffalo, and other Ice Age mammals.

The youngest sedimentary materials in Mississippi are the alluvial deposits of the stream valleys and the shoreline deposits of the coast. The most extensive area of alluvial deposits is found west of the loess bluffs in the Delta, a plain formed by flooding and course changes of the Mississippi River. Ancestral courses of the Mississippi include parts of the present beds of the Sunflower and Yazoo rivers in which the Mississippi River flowed some 4,000 to 5,000 years ago.

Thus far only the near surface sedimentary rocks which are gently tilted toward the Gulf of Mexico have been discussed. In the subsurface, however, the rocks are more strongly tilted, fractured and deformed to produce subsurface basins and ridges. The largest of these features are the Black Warrior basin and the Mississippi salt basin which are separated by the central Mississippi ridge. Recent investigations indicate that the central Mississippi is a deformed area produced when the Ouachita Mountains were sheared from the Appalachian chain. South of the ridge is a fracture zone called the Pickens–Gilbertown fault zone. South of the fault zone is the Mississippi salt basin area, underlain by a thick layer of salt which has flowed upward in many places to form salt domes.

In the southern part of the state are two uplifted areas called the Adams County High and Wiggins Uplift. Oil and gas fields associated with these features are shown in the section on mineral resources. Two small but interesting areas in central Mississippi are designated Midnight Volcano and Jackson Dome. These two features were produced by molten or igneous material pushing its way toward the surface, losing energy, and being subsequently covered by younger sediments.

The preceding summary is an extremely condensed version of the 350 million years represented by the geology of Mississippi. Many details have been eliminated by necessity, but the general reconstruction represents at least a general overview of the geologic formation of the state. Perhaps this overview will create a better understanding of the processes involved in the creation of Mississippi's land configuration and an appreciation for the countless hours contributed by geologists in unraveling the story in the rocks.

Oscar L. Paulson Jr.

CLIMATE

Mississippi has a humid subtropical climate, though microclimatic factors vary from place to place within the state. Mississippi lies outside the principal storm tracts that cross the country; its climatic variations are broadly determined by the large land mass to the north and west and by the Gulf of Mexico to the south. These surface areas produce alternate flows of cold air moving southward and warm, moist air moving northward. Transitions, or fronts, between these flows frequently bring abrupt changes in weather conditions. The climates of Mississippi are the result of such interactions and modifications between the air flows and of the temporal patterns of the weather changes they produce.

MOISTURE

PRECIPITATION—The southern one-third of Mississippi lies within an area characterized by maximum precipitation east of the Rocky Mountains. The mean annual precipitation exceeds 55 inches in the southern one-third of the state and ranges from 60 to 65 inches on and near the coastal region. Elsewhere annual means are 51 or more inches during the year, with the exception of a few scattered locations in central and northern Mississippi where annual precipitation is less than 50 inches. In most years annual precipitation is within 15 inches of the mean. The annual totals of precipitation in Mississippi between 1888 and 1972 have varied from a high of 102.89 inches at Beaumont in 1961 to a low of 25.97 inches at Yazoo City in 1936. In the coastal region, the greatest mean precipitation occurs in summer; in the southeast and southcentral parts of the state, more precipitation falls in spring. Elsewhere rainfall is highest in winter. The season with the lowest mean precipitation is summer in the upper Delta and fall in all other segments of the state. Seasonal precipitation has varied from a high of 36.28 inches in the upper Delta during the winter of 1931–32 to a low of 2.46 inches in the northeastern portion of the state during the fall of 1972, inclusive of the period 1931–1972. Monthly totals at individual stations have varied from 30.75 inches (July, 1916, at Merrill) to zero (reported by various stations ranging from April through November during the period 1888–1972).

EVAPORATION—Evaporation is controlled by heat fluxes at the earth's surface. Some precipitation is returned as water vapor to the atmosphere. Part of the soil moisture is likewise evaporated; some is used in life processes of vegetation and is transpired as water vapor to the atmosphere. The annual mean loss of evapotranspiration is about 54 inches in extreme northeastern Mississippi, and ranges up to about 65 inches in parts of the most southerly Gulf Coast. The rate of evaporation has an important impact on water storage in ponds and reservoirs, and on agricultural crops both irrigated and nonirrigated. The mean evaporation for May through October for northeastern Mississippi is about 39 inches (73 percent of annual) and about 43 inches for the southern Gulf Coast (66 percent of annual). Pan evaporation (estimated evaporation from a NWS class A pan) represents maximum or potential evaporation. Shallow lake evaporation is about 74 percent of pan. The actual soil water loss is usually less since soil moisture is limited.

DROUGHT—Mississippi is vulnerable to short-duration droughts. Normally, the state has abundant rainfall which supplies sufficient soil moisture for crops. Drought is interpreted as a rainfall below normal for several weeks, and is soon detected in deficiencies of soil moisture and other water resources. Mississippi droughts generally occur within the an-

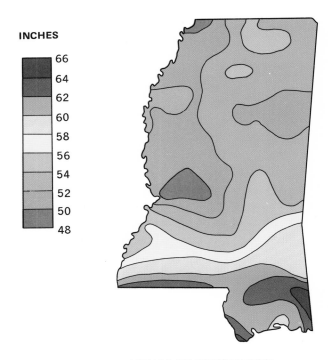

INCHES

66
64
62
60
58
56
54
52
50
48

AVERAGE ANNUAL PRECIPITATION

WINTER PRECIPITATION
December - February
(inches)

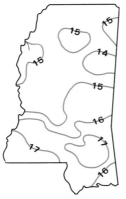

SPRING PRECIPITATION
March - May
(inches)

SUMMER PRECIPITATION
June - August
(inches)

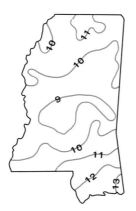

FALL PRECIPITATION
September - November
(inches)

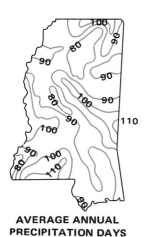

**AVERAGE ANNUAL
PRECIPITATION DAYS**

**GREATEST MONTHLY
PRECIPITATION**
(inches)

Source: National Weather Service, 1891 - 1960

nual growing season. Droughts make irrigation in Mississippi economically feasible at some locations; damaging dry spells often occur during periods when certain crops have critical water requirements for growth. Occasionally during the warmer season, pressure distribution is altered, bringing westerly or northerly winds. If these conditions are prolonged, drought conditions affecting agriculture may develop, and forest fire potential increases. Prolonged droughts are rare in humid Mississippi, but normal ground or surface-water supplies are reduced. However, even during drought periods widely scattered thundershowers usually occur.

THUNDERSTORMS—Thunderstorms occur from 50 to 60 days per year in the northern portions of the state; from 70 to 80 days per year near the Gulf Coast. During the warmer months, the coastal region experiences about 90 percent of these storms between 6 a.m. and 6 p.m. Further inland, 85 percent occur between noon and midnight. The number of thunderstorm days decreases to a minimum in the late fall and early winter as the slow-moving, rain-suppressing high pressure areas increase in frequency. Thunderstorms in the late fall, winter, and early spring are usually associated with passing cyclonic weather systems. These may occur at any hour, and are usually accompanied by higher wind velocities than in summer. In the winter about one-sixth to one-fourth of precipitation days experience lightning and/or thunder. Thunderstorms in Mississippi only occasionally produce hail that reaches the ground. Annually, over half of all hailstorms occur in the spring months; summer thunderstorms seldom produce hail. Most of the hail reported in Mississippi is less than an inch in diameter; hail damage chiefly affects vegetation and is usually confined to small areas of only a few square miles.

SNOW—Measurable snowfalls have occurred in some portions of Mississippi from as early as November to as late as April. The mean annual snowfall is about four inches near the northern border and decreases southward. In the southern third of the state it is usually less than one inch. A record depth of 18 inches on the ground was measured at Mount Pleasant on December 23, 1963. Some years stations may record no snowfall or only trace amounts. A single storm may account for a significant portion of a season's snowfall.

DEGREES
(Fahrenheit)

	69
	68
	67
	66
	65
	64
	63
	62
	61
	60

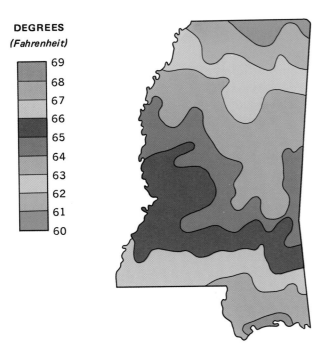

AVERAGE ANNUAL TEMPERATURE

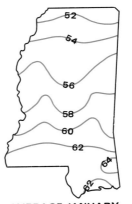

**AVERAGE JANUARY
MAXIMUM TEMPERATURE**
(degrees Fahrenheit)

**AVERAGE JULY
MAXIMUM TEMPERATURE**
(degrees Fahrenheit)

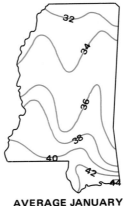

**AVERAGE JANUARY
MINIMUM TEMPERATURE**
(degrees Fahrenheit)

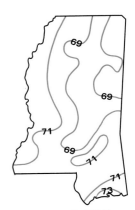

**AVERAGE JULY
MINIMUM TEMPERATURE**
(degrees Fahrenheit)

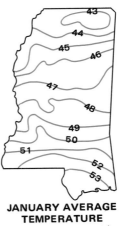

**JANUARY AVERAGE
TEMPERATURE**
(degrees Fahrenheit)

**JULY AVERAGE
TEMPERATURE**
(degrees Fahrenheit)

TEMPERATURE

Mississippi's mean annual temperatures vary with latitude. Northern border counties average 61° F. to 62° F. and increase southward to about 68° F. in the Gulf Coast counties.

MAXIMUM TEMPERATURES—Summer (June, July, and August) is influenced by the position and strength of the Bermuda High pressure system. Moreover, the jet stream is generally weak and located far to the north in summer and cold frontal passages are rare. The mean summer temperature is about 80° F. or 81° F. Except near the Gulf Coast, daytime maximums exceeding 90° F. sometimes occur every day in July or August. Near the immediate Gulf Coast, stations have reported an annual mean of fewer than 65 days when the temperature reaches 90° F. or higher. Inland, the number of days for 90° F. temperatures increases to more than 90 in most of the northern sections of Pearl River, Stone, and George counties. Further inland the number of days increases, exceeding 104 days in some locations. Northward, the mean number of days with temperatures over 90° F. decreases to as few as 80 to 65 days. With the exception of three years (1946, 1958, and 1961) during the period 1888–1972, temperatures rose to 101° F. or higher at one or more Mississippi locations. All of the

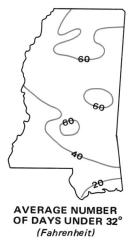

**AVERAGE NUMBER
OF DAYS UNDER 32°**
(Fahrenheit)

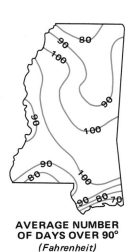

**AVERAGE NUMBER
OF DAYS OVER 90°**
(Fahrenheit)

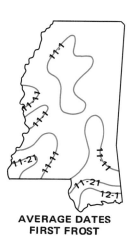

**AVERAGE DATES
FIRST FROST**

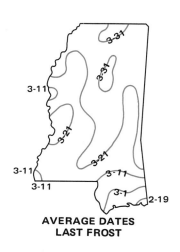

**AVERAGE DATES
LAST FROST**

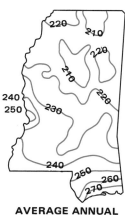

**AVERAGE ANNUAL
FREEZE-FREE DAYS**

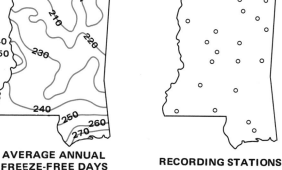

RECORDING STATIONS

Source: National Weather Service

official temperature reporting stations in Mississippi have recorded temperatures exceeding 100° F. Holly Springs reported 20 days with temperatures 100° F. or warmer and reached a temperature maximum of 115° F. on July 29, 1930. Temperatures reached 114° F. at Aberdeen on July 13, 1930, including 24 days 100° F. or warmer.

MINIMUM TEMPERATURES—Minimum temperatures occur during the low sun period or winter season. Mean annual minimum temperatures occur most frequently during the month of January in Mississippi, while December and February rank as the second and third coldest months respectively at most stations within the state.

Stations situated in the northern tier of counties tend to record the lowest January monthly minimums. Here the overall average is about 31.2° F., with reports at individual stations ranging from 29.1° F. to 32.6° F. Proceeding southward, January minimums tend to increase so that stations in the middle of the state experience January minimum temperatures ranging from the middle thirties to the high thirties.

Coastal stations register the highest January minimums. The overall average is approximately 43.2° F. with temperatures occurring at individual stations from 41.2° F. up to 44.2° F.

Absolute minimum temperatures occur most frequently in the month of February in Mississippi. January and December are the only other months in which absolute minimum temperatures have been recorded and rank second and third respectively. The absolute minimum temperature of −16° F. was recorded in February, 1966, at Batesville in Panola County.

SUNSHINE

The mean annual hours of sunshine range from about 2800 in the Upper Delta to about 2600 in other parts of the state. The mean annual percentage of possible sunshine is 60 to 64 percent. On the winter solstice (December 22) the sun is above the horizon for 9 hours and 48 minutes along the extreme northern Mississippi border, and for 10 hours and 13 minutes at the extreme southern tip of the state. After that date, the length of the day increases until the summer solstice (June 21), when the sun is above the horizon for 14 hours and 31 minutes along the state's extreme northern border, and decreases southward to

TEMPERATURE RANGES OF SELECTED CITIES
1951 — 1960

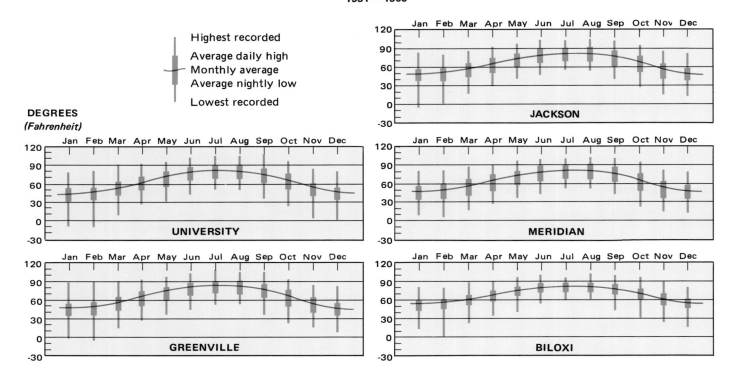

Highest recorded
Average daily high
Monthly average
Average nightly low
Lowest recorded

DEGREES
(Fahrenheit)

JACKSON

UNIVERSITY

MERIDIAN

GREENVILLE

BILOXI

14 hours and 6 minutes at the extreme southern tip. The monthly mean total hours of sunshine reaches a low of 140 hours or less in northern Mississippi in December and January; during these months it is less than 160 hours in the southern part. Maximum period of sunshine occurs in June—time ranges from about 320 hours in the extreme northwest down to about 190 hours in sections of the southeast. In July the number of sunshine hours decreases and ranges from 250 to 260 hours in the southwest and up to 310 to 320 hours in the northwest.

The direct sunshine received is related to cloudiness; annually, cloud cover exists for little more than half of the day. The maximum cloudiness and the minimum sunshine occur in the winter months when rainy and/or overcast days are most frequent. From spring through summer and on to October, the average amount of cloudiness generally decreases in the state except for a July increase along the coast. Usually the least cloudiness occurs in October. The number of clear days is minimum in January and February, generally increasing to a maximum in September and October in most of the state, with the exception of a decrease in June and July near the coast.

HUMIDITY

The annual mean relative humidity is approximately 70 percent near the Tennessee border and increases southward to 76 percent. During a day the relative humidity values vary widely—dropping with rising temperatures and increasing with falling temperatures. Ordinarily the lower relative humidities occur in the warm afternoon hours; later, when temperatures cool, the values increase, reaching high percentages late at night with maximums occurring in the early morning hours. Humidities below 30 percent are most apt to occur in October and November; the number of days with humidities of below 30 percent are fewer in the other months and are at a minimum in the summer. Humidities between 30 and 50 percent occur each month; on an annual basis they total about one-half of the hours in northern Mississippi. Humidities of 90 percent or higher may occur at any hour throughout the year, but are most frequent in the early morning hours and during periods of rain. Heavy fog occurs occasionally near daybreak; it generally dissipates early in the forenoon and rarely lasts through the day. When a combination of high temperature and high dewpoint (high humidity) develops, conditions can

PRECIPITATION RANGES OF SELECTED CITIES
1951 — 1960

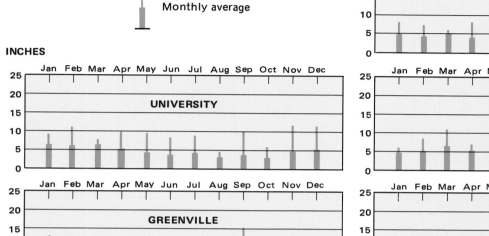

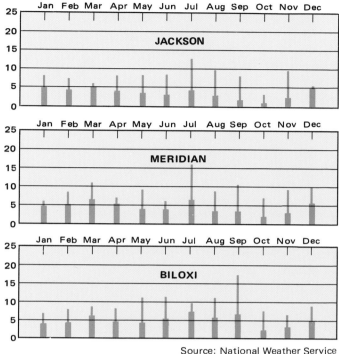

Source: National Weather Service

become uncomfortable. In summer, high humidities may build up progressively for several days, and the nights may become oppressive. Such conditions are most noticeable when wind velocity is very light or calm during the late afternoon or night. The principal means of relief is brought by thundershowers, which are sometimes accompanied by locally destructive and violent winds.

WINDS

Winds in Mississippi occur from the southeast to the southwest quadrants for more hours annually than from other sectors of the compass. The average wind speed is 10 mph or less; wind velocities are higher near and during storm periods. On an annual basis calm conditions are present about one-tenth of the time. Windy weather for a prolonged period accompanies intense, slow-moving pressure disturbances coming from the west, while relatively shorter periods of windy weather are associated with passing fronts, squall lines, or thunderstorms.

Damaging winds may occur any hour during the year. High wind speeds are usually associated with severe local storms which begin as thunderstorms.

Nearly every squall line of moderate to heavy intensity produces damaging winds, damaging lightning strokes, local pockets of hail, and small areas of heavy rain. These areas of damage lie in swaths that extend in the direction of the storm movement. Most of them show direct evidence of being produced by straight-line winds, some of which may have turbulent downdraft gusts of 100 mph or more at the surface.

Tornadoes—Rotary winds in Mississippi appear in the immediate vicinity of a tornado funnel and when these winds touch the ground the ensuing damage shows evidence of the rotary origin. These winds whirl at a rate of 200 mph or more around funnels commonly extending several hundred yards in diameter. These small, severe storms first form several thousand feet above the earth's surface, usually during warm, humid weather, and most frequently in conjunction with a severe thunderstorm. When the weather conditions are right, sometimes a family series of two or more are associated with a parent thunderstorm or with a squall line which may extend for a distance up to several hundred miles. As the storm front moves, tornadoes may form at intervals along its path, travel for a few miles, and dissipate. Heavy hail, downpours of rain, and lightning flashes of high intensity often precede a tornado. Among the random motion of the dark heavy clouds of the parent thunderstorm system, funnel clouds appear below and usually as an extending pendant from the turbulent overcast sky; funnel clouds are wide at the top and taper to a small diameter toward the earth. This funnel is the generally pale, visible condensation around a violently rotating column of air whirling in corkscrew fashion.

Many funnel clouds in Mississippi only exist for a few minutes and never lower to the ground. Others only momentarily touch down, rise, then dissipate and disappear; however, a few stay on the ground for longer periods. The tornado winds have a distinctive roar which can be heard for several miles. The roar of the funnel cloud aloft, a shrill high-pitch shriek, increases as the funnel nears the ground, and is loudest (a deafening roar) when the tornado dips to the ground and churns the earth as it moves across the surface. Spherics measurements show that the tornado is accompanied and preceded by intense electrical activity, resulting in many more lightning discharges than in a typical thunderstorm (more than

five times as many).

Tornadoes in Mississippi are embedded in a wide area of straight-line winds which may be moving at a speed up to 45 mph or more. The tornadoes vary considerably both in intensity and area covered. Funnel clouds range in length from 800 feet to 2,000 feet and most last less than eight minutes. Some touch the ground for less than a minute, or the end that touched down causes damage in an area only a few yards across. Other tornadoes last much longer; the destructive tip at the earth's surface may be as large as 300 yards and at times encompass an area slightly over a mile wide. Inside the spinning funnel a partial vacuum is formed. A tornado-enveloped building explodes outward, while a building at the edge of the funnel blows down. This happens in a matter of seconds, and debris is thrown in all directions.

Tornadoes can occur in any county in Mississippi, but years may go by without a funnel cloud touching down anywhere in the state. Tornadoes may occur at any hour, though their greatest frequency is between 1 p.m. and 7 p.m. Most Mississippi tornadoes occur in sparsely settled areas and without deaths or injuries. The relatively few large, long-lasting, more severe tor-

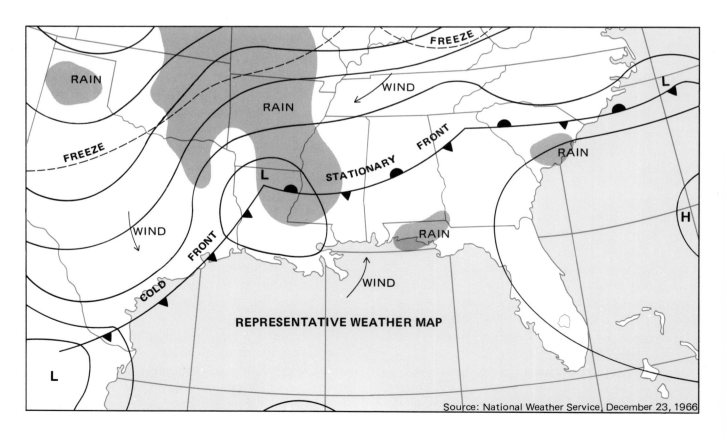

REPRESENTATIVE WEATHER MAP

Source: National Weather Service, December 23, 1966

nadoes can cause considerable damage to life and property, especially if they pass over thickly settled areas. There have been, at rare intervals, days when tornadoes brought death or injury to 500 or more Mississippians. In one-third of the 20-year span 1953–1972 no deaths were recorded due to tornadoes in Mississippi.

Hurricanes—Another hazard to life and property in Mississippi is the tropical cyclone which occurs from June to November. While these storms generally move into the state on the coast, they have on occasion entered Mississippi as far north as Meridian or Greenville after crossing part of Alabama or Louisiana. These latter storms are usually weakened considerably by passage over land. Loss of life and property due to high winds are mostly confined to the coastal areas, with interior losses resulting generally from rain damage to crops and from floods. Hurricanes which move inland over southeast Louisiana may be as damaging on the Mississippi coast as those which cross the coastline. This is especially true of those moving from the southeast, because of the usually more severe winds in the northeast quadrant and because of the high seas which move across the Mississippi

Sound and pile up on the shore. Those which move westward offshore often cause tide and wind damage on the coast. Those which move northeastward across or south of the Louisiana Delta and move inland between Mobile and Panama City are usually less damaging because the winds are offshore and tides are subnormal. Hurricanes which move inland on the Alabama coast may affect Mississippi only slightly because of less intense offshore winds in their western portions.

The chances for hurricane-associated wind damage decreases as one goes inland, away from the Gulf of Mexico. Near the coast, sustained winds of 100 mph or more have a 100-year mean recurrence interval. The eye of Hurricane Camille crossed the Hancock County coast Sunday evening August 17, 1969, over the towns of Clermont Harbor, Waveland, and Bay St. Louis, and moved generally north-northwesterly through the coastal counties. People near the center of the eye reported its passage lasted thirty minutes or so. There were no instrument readings of the top wind velocities near the eye of Camille as she crossed the coastline.

E. J. Saltsman
Ralph D. Cross

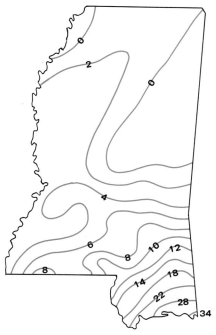

TOTAL NUMBER OF GALE WINDS
1875 – 1959
(over 39 miles per hour)

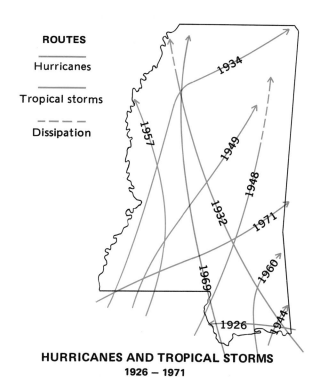

HURRICANES AND TROPICAL STORMS
1926 – 1971

Source: National Weather Service

NATURAL VEGETATION

The pattern of major vegetation zones in Mississippi differs from that of surrounding states in having a predominantly north–south orientation. This pattern, dominated by three zones running essentially the entire length of the state, is due largely to the strong influence of the northward extension of the Gulf Coastal Plain forming the Mississippi Embayment. Even though most of the state lies within the Gulf–Atlantic Coastal Plain Province, Mississippi has an unusually rich and diverse vegetation. The vegetation types and the principal species listed herein refer to potential natural vegetation and do not necessarily reflect the pattern in certain local areas which may be highly modified by agriculture or other land-use practices.

The most prevalent Mississippi vegetation type is the Oak–Hickory–Pine Forest which covers well over half the total area. Interrupted only by two narrow strips of prairie, this zone extends in a broad, almost continuous band more than half the width of the state, from the northeast to the southwest corners. This forest type, found only in the southeastern United States, consists of a complex mixture of hardwoods and pines. With little disturbance the pines tend to be replaced by hardwoods in most areas. However, following such extreme disturbances as fire or cultivation, forests in this area often revert to essentially pure stands of pine. Occasional outbreaks of fire are thought to be a natural part of the ecology of this area, even if man-caused fires are excluded. With the additional extensive disturbance caused by man, the forested portions of this zone now contain considerably more pine than would be true under more natural conditions. The dominant trees of this area include mockernut, bitternut, pignut, shagbark, pale hickories, white oak, post oak, northern and southern red oak, black oak, blackjack oak, loblolly pine, and shortleaf pine. In wet areas yellow poplar, bay magnolia, shumard oak, live oak, willow oak, and sweetgum are common. Understory trees include dogwood, sourwood, and red bay.

Lying west of the Oak–Hickory–Pine Forest is a narrow belt of Oak–Hickory Forest which is discontinuous, but extends for the entire length of the state. This narrow vegetation zone is a southern extension of a forest type that is prevalent on relatively dry sites throughout much of the central Midwest of the United States. It is a complex forest association, and different species appear dominant in various areas throughout the geographical expanse of the forest—black oak, white oak, northern red oak, post oak, shagbark hickory, mockernut hickory, and pignut. Other dominant species that are found in Mississippi include big shellbark black hickory, bitternut, sweetgum, yellow poplar, winged elm, and hackberry. Understory species include dogwood, ironwood, sourwood, serviceberry, and black haw.

The entire length of the western boundary of Mississippi is covered by a rich southern floodplain forest, which extends from the Gulf of Mexico up the Mississippi Valley into Illinois. This forest type is also found in a much narrower band along the valleys of the Pearl and the Pascagoula rivers in southeastern Mississippi. Typical dominant species in this forest include bald cypress, tupelo gum, pecan, willow oak, water oak, shumard oak, overcup oak, and swamp chestnut oak. Understory species in this forest include red bay, rattan vine, cabbage palm, water elm, and red haw.

The Black Prairie consists of two separated bands of dark, heavy soils with associated vegetation. The first is a crescent-shaped area extending northwest to north from the Alabama line at Clarke County. On the deeper soils of this area are found red cedar, overcup oak, shumard oak, green ash, durand oak, laurel oak, and nutmeg hickory. On the thin soils of this zone are glade-like areas which contain species of prairie sunflower, prairie cornflower, prairie rose, cherokee sedge, tuberus milkweed, prairie clover, and big bluestem grass.

The southernmost part of Mississippi gives rise to an extremely rich forest known as the Southern Mixed Forest. Extending from the Gulf of Mexico north for approximately 100 miles, this forest consists of a mixture of pines and both deciduous and evergreen broadleaf trees. The species of pines include longleaf, loblolly, and slash; the broadleaf deciduous species include sweetgum, beech, yellow poplar, white oak, swamp chestnut oak, turkey oak, and cucumber tree; the evergreen broadleaf trees include bay magnolia, southern magnolia, live oak, and laurel oak. Understory species include Florida maple, gallberry, wax myrtle, ironwood, red bay, cabbage palm, dogwood, titi, and holly. On sandy sites near the coast the forest becomes more open, and the pines increase in dominancy.

Joab Thomas

OAK-HICKORY-PINE FOREST
Species include mockernut, pignut, shagbark and pale hickories, white oak, post oak, black oak, northern and southern oak, loblolly and short leaf pine, yellow poplar, bay magnolia, and sweetgum.

OAK-HICKORY FOREST
Species include black oak, white oak, northern red oak, post oak, shagbark hickory, mockernut, pignut, and big shellbark hickory, sweetgum, yellow poplar, winged elm, and hackberry.

SOUTHERN FLOODPLAIN FOREST
Species include bald cypress, tupelo gum, pecan, willow oak, water oak, shumard oak, overcup oak, swamp chestnut oak, cottonwood, red bay, water elm, red haw, and willow.

SOUTHERN MIXED FOREST
Species include sweetgum, beech, yellow poplar, white oak, swamp chestnut oak, turkey oak, cucumber tree, bay magnolia, southern magnolia, live oak, laurel oak, ironwood, red bay, and holly.

PRAIRIE BELT
Species include red cedar, durand oak, overcup oak, shumard oak, laurel oak, green ash, nutmeg hickory, prairie coneflower, prairie rose, prairie sunflower, cherokee sedge, tuberous milkweed, and prairie clover.

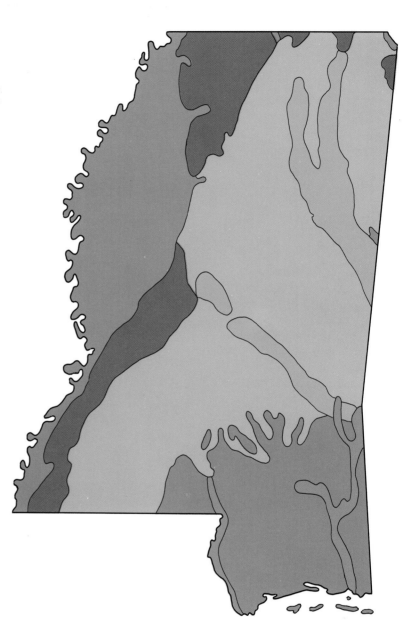

GENERALIZED VEGETATION

Source: A. W. Kuchler, The National Atlas of the United States of America

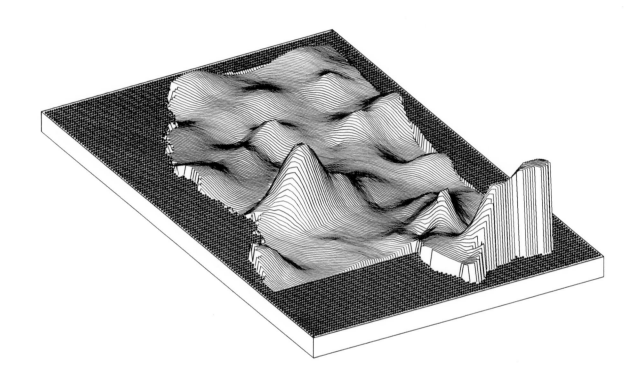

PERCENT CHANGE IN POPULATION
1920—1970

HISTORY

Mississippi is a land of contrasts with a lengthy and interesting history. Mississippi has been a rural state throughout most of its existence, but today the economy is rapidly changing from rural to urban. As cotton agriculture fades from the scene, increasing emphasis is being placed on livestock production. Manufacturing has superseded agriculture in importance. Though the people of Mississippi are basically of Anglo-Saxon origin, since the 1830s Mississippi has had the highest national proportion of Negroes in its population.

The geographical area today known as the state of Mississippi was occupied by the Spanish, the French, the British, and the Spanish again before becoming a part of the United States in 1798. Long before this European occupation, however, it was the home of numerous Indian tribes. In the 1540s Spanish conquistador Hernando de Soto became the first European to explore the region. Shortly thereafter, in 1542, the Spanish abandoned the area. A century and a half later Robert Cavelier, Sieur de LaSalle claimed the Mississippi Valley for the French. In 1699 Pierre LeMoyne, Sieur d'Iberville established the first permanent French settlement in the lower Mississippi Valley at Fort Maurepas, near Ocean Springs. The French began to migrate to this area, part of the Louisiana Territory, settling there from 1699 to 1763.

From 1763 to 1799 most of the settled Mississippi area became part of the royal colony of British West Florida. Then the Spanish military occupied Natchez in 1797, and the second Spanish period in Mississippi history began. The occupation by Spain did not end until 1798 when the Spanish finally carried out their obligations under the Treaty of San Lorenzo of 1795. Thus the original Mississippi Territory, the land between latitudes 31° north and 32° 28' north, extending from the Mississippi River to the Chattahoochee River, came into being. The Georgia and the South Carolina cessions of western land north of latitude 31° 28' north and of the Gulf coastal area below 31° north latitude from the Pearl River to the Perdido River expanded the territory, as did land claimed under the Louisiana Purchase of 1803. Within two decades the Mississippi Territory subsequently was divided into the two states of Mississippi and Alabama with their respective present boundaries.

Mississippi's history as a state can be separated into several well-defined periods. From its admission as a state in 1817 to its adoption of the state constitution of 1832, Mississippi passed through the formative period. The next three decades saw flush times, then depression, the Mexican War, and the growing controversy over slavery.

Mississippi seceded from the United States on January 9, 1861, and shortly thereafter joined the Confederate States of America. For the next four years the state was involved in a destructive civil war that brought deprivation and death to many citizens. The post-war years of 1865–1890 are usually treated as two periods—the Reconstruction Era and the Redeemer Era.

Mississippi's most recent constitution was written and adopted in 1890. It has therefore been customary to treat the last eighty years as one era, but there are certain definable periods within this span of time: the decade of the Nineties; the progressive era; the Bilbo administration; depression and recovery; World War II; and the last quarter-century.

John Edmond Gonzales

INDIGENOUS PROLOGUE

The 35,000 red men living in the forests, along the rivers, and on the coast of Mississippi represented perhaps the most vigorous and impressive aboriginal culture existing in North America at the time of its discovery. These town-dwelling tribes, which migrated mainly from the west to their historical location only a few centuries before Europeans arrived, were members of the Mississippian cultural complex, based on a maize horticulture. Primarily of Muskhogean linguistic stock, they shared basically common material and nonmaterial cultures.

Mississippi's natural resources supported the greatest variety of tribes with the heaviest Indian population of any southeastern state. Of this mélange, three tribes were dominant—the Chickasaws, the Choctaws, and the Natchez. In 1731, the French with their native allies virtually annihilated the Natchez. After that point, the history of Mississippi Indians for over a century prior to their removal becomes the story of the Chickasaw and Choctaw nations. Occupying central and southern Mississippi, the Choctaws were the largest of any southeastern tribe except the Cherokee. Twenty thousand is generally accepted as their population in the early historic period. The northern portion of the state was Chickasaw territory, but their ancient domain included much of western Tennessee as well as the southwestern tip of Kentucky. Though Chickasaws once enjoyed the most extensive territory of the southern Indians, their population certainly never reached more than 5,000, and estimates usually range from 3,500 to 4,500. Almost identical in number, the Natchez before their demise lived in some nine villages along St. Catherine's Creek just above its juncture with the Mississippi.

The small coastal tribes tended to migrate back and forth through the lower Mississippi Valley after the French arrival, disappearing completely from the vicinity shortly after England gained title to the land in 1763. By then disease had depleted their ranks, and amalgamation had obscured tribal identities. In 1699 perhaps as many as 400 Biloxi Indians lived in villages north of Biloxi Bay and along the lower Pascagoula River, but their origin remains unknown. Because they spoke a Siouan dialect, the Biloxi differed somewhat from their Muskhogean-speaking neighbors with whom they shared a common existence. In 1702 or 1703 the Biloxi Indians moved near Lake Pontchartrain, but by 1730, with an intermediate encampment

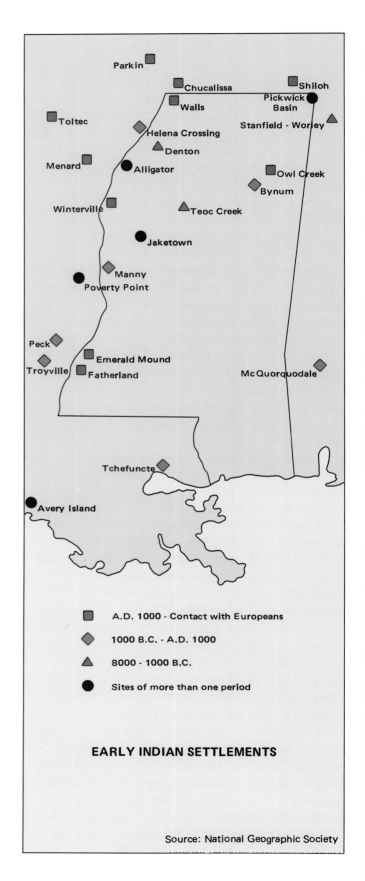

EARLY INDIAN SETTLEMENTS

- ■ A.D. 1000 - Contact with Europeans
- ◆ 1000 B.C. - A.D. 1000
- ▲ 8000 - 1000 B.C.
- ● Sites of more than one period

Source: National Geographic Society

24

on the Pearl River, they had returned to the Pascagoula until the post-1763 exodus to the Red River.

Another sizable coastal tribe, the Pascagoula, occupied towns not far above the mouth of the river bearing their name. In a fate shared with neighboring tribes, their population suffered a steady decrease, and in 1764 the Pascagoula followed the Biloxi to the vicinity of the Red River. Remnants of both tribes eventually sold their holdings in Louisiana, after which they dispersed into Texas and Oklahoma.

Eight tribes were spread along the Yazoo River. The Tunica, Yazoo, Choula, Koroa, and Tiou were of Tunican linguistic stock, but the Ibitoupa, Chakchiuma, and Taposa spoke in the Muskhogean tongue. Though their ancestral home was in northwest Mississippi and neighboring areas of Arkansas, by 1682 the Tunica had settled on the southern bank of the Yazoo River just above its mouth. Weary of Chickasaw aggression, the Tunica in 1706 abandoned their villages on the Yazoo, moving to the east bank of the Mississippi opposite the Red River. Their number had dwindled from a peak of 1,575 to approximately 500. They joined the Houma, who welcomed them hospitably into their town; but shortly afterward, the ungrateful Tunica turned on their hosts. Those who were not slain were driven away. The Tunica occupied the Houma site until the end of the century when they moved up the Red River.

The first Indians to settle on the river which perpetuates their tribal name were the Yazoo, who resided on its south bank some twelve miles above the mouth. Soon after the French constructed Fort St. Peter near them in 1718, an abortive effort was made to establish a plantation, and a missionary came into their midst. During the 1729 Natchez revolt, however, the Yazoo murdered the priest and overran the garrison. The few Yazoo who survived the Natchez War were assimilated by the Chickasaws and Choctaws.

Formerly located on the Mississippi River and in Louisiana, the Koroa constituted another lower Yazoo River tribe. The combined Koroa–Yazoo population in 1698 was probably 600, but after the Indian allies of the French retaliated for the Koroa role in the Natchez uprising, only a small band survived. Though many of the surviving Koroa initially sought refuge among the Chickasaws, most of them eventually became part of the Choctaw Nation.

In Holmes County near the community of Tchula

lived the Choula, a tribe of less than 50 persons according to reports made in 1722. Probably a band of the Ibitoupa, the Choula evidently reunited with them higher up the Yazoo.

Of the three tribes living farthest up the Yazoo, the Chakchiuma were considerably larger than the Ibitouba and Taposa who eventually merged with their more numerous neighbors. According to tradition, the Chakchiuma—who may have numbered as many as 750 in 1850—migrated from the west with the closely related Chickasaws and Choctaws, settling at the head of the Yalobusha. In the eighteenth century, the Chakchiuma moved first to the confluence of the Yazoo and Yalobusha rivers and then down near the Tunica. But their population was so drastically reduced that only 200 remained during the 1720s. When the Chakchiuma were at the mouth of the Yalobusha, the Ibitouba lived below them, and the Taposa homes were a few miles up the Yazoo.

The French presence portended ill for the Chakchiuma. Some members of the tribe killed a missionary, and the French unleased the fury of friendly tribes on the Chakchiuma until they repented and served French interests against both the Natchez and the Chickasaws. That strategy proved to be disastrous. The anti-French Chickasaws punished the Chakchiuma so severely in the late 1730s that the tribe disintegrated, and bands moved into the Chickasaw and Choctaw nations. The Chakchiuma story typifies the fate of the Yazoo Valley Indians. Tribes were generally small and often interrelated, and their complicities in the Natchez War contributed greatly to the extremely rapid reduction in their population, as did incessant raids upon them by the Chickasaw. Most of these Indians lost their tribal identities through absorption into the Chickasaw and Choctaw nations.

The three dominant Mississippi tribes—Chickasaws, Choctaws, and Natchez—were clearly representative of the economic, social, and cultural life of the state's aboriginal population. Though hunting and gathering were certainly important to them as sources of sustenance and shelter, they were primarily agriculturalists. Maize was their chief crop. In addition to their household gardens, the villages generally planted communal farms in meadows or plots laboriously cleared from forests by girdling the trees. Between the hills of corn, they planted beans, pumpkins, peas, melons, sunflowers, and tobacco, and the Natchez grew wild rice on the river banks. Weeding and cultivation were considered work for women and children, but the heavy planting and especially the harvest were communal projects in which men earnestly participated. Much depended on a successful corn harvest. The Choctaws excelled as farmers, consistently producing corn surpluses which were invaluable trade items. After the introduction of cattle, they fed excess grain to sizable herds, another source of trade and income. The sedentary nature of Mississippi tribes, particularly the Choctaws, resulted from the primacy of agriculture in their societies.

Though hunting played a more significant role in the lives of such Mississippi Indians as the Chickasaws, the meat of bison, deer, and bear comprised a basic part of all tribal diets. The Indians also used the byproducts—hides, bones, antlers, entrails, sinews, and claws—in fashioning clothing, implements, weapons, and ceremonial ornaments. The bison, scarce by the late historical period, soon disappeared east of the Mississippi. Some of the meat was eaten fresh, and the balance was dried or smoked. Since the natives felt that attributes of animals might be passed on to the consumer of their flesh, the fleet, elusive deer provided a favorite food. Bear meat was also quite popular. Heavy bearskins made excellent robes, blankets, moccasins, and boots, and bear oil was a highly prized commodity widely used in cooking and in grooming the hair and body.

Depending on the tribe, fish was an important item in some seasons. Fish were trapped, netted, speared, shot, and even caught by hand. Women and children gathered numerous varieties of nuts, wild mulberries, strawberries, blackberries, grapes, plums, persimmons, and onions, as well as edible fungi. Honey was a welcome treat; licks and springs provided salt which some tribes secured through barter. The aboriginal Mississippians concocted numerous potions, teas, poultices, emetics, and other remedies from a host of leaves, barks, roots, herbs, and berries. Just as they sought the flesh of admired animals, the tribesmen avoided eating certain carnivorous creatures and those considered unclean in their habits. Food taboos often were associated with hogs, wolves, panthers, and foxes, and with such rodents as mice, rats, and particularly moles. The avoidance of this possible food supply reflects the abundance of the land and the advanced stages of their cultures.

Ingenious craftsmen, natives of the area made clay pottery for cooking, eating, and storage. They sewed garments of finely tanned deerskins, using thread spun from the inner bark of trees, animal fur, or shredded sinew. After treating scraped skins with cooked brains, they often smoked them to prevent shrinkage in a highly effective process, at times coloring the leather with dyes extracted from roots, berries, and barks. Elaborately constructed houses of log-framed walls covered with woven branches or cane offered protection from the elements. Roofs were generally of thatched grass, and the walls were frequently finished on both sides with clay plaster. Crude beds and stools were common furnishings in homes sometimes lit with pitch torches.

The Mississippi tribes enhanced their economies and life styles through trade. The items exchanged were numerous and depended on their needs and surpluses. Excellent hunters and aggressive people, the Chickasaws exchanged deerskins, bear oil, and Indian slaves to obtain shells, pearls, copper, and materials for implements. The Chickasaws and Choctaws had large numbers of captives, though enslavement of fellow Indians was not limited to these tribes. Slaves were highly prized by women who were anxious for relief from their endless menial tasks at home and in the fields.

The European intrusion intensified the tribes' commercial activities. Certainly the natives did not realize that white traders—the English who came from Charleston in 1698, closely followed by the French on the coast and up the rivers—actually were harbingers of doom. Instead, they plunged into an active trade with the whites, exchanging primarily deerskins and Indian slaves for accouterments of European society. Cloth, guns, powder, shot, beads, knives, and hatchets were exchanged for the pelts, usually measured in pounds, and for slaves destined for Carolina and West Indian plantations. The resulting competition for hunting grounds and the increased demand for slaves intensified warfare and complicated Indian–white diplomacy. The Chickasaws, who incessantly preyed on the Yazoo tribes, were avaricious slavers, raiding such distant points as the Gulf Coast and the Ohio Valley. However, the most devastating impact of the trade was erosion of Indian culture as the tribes became increasingly dependent on European goods.

A matrilineal social order existed in the Mississippi

tribes which were divided into two major moieties. In turn, the moieties were subdivided into clans, and political and religious leaders were selected from the leading clan of the dominant or superior moiety. The exceedingly elaborate class system of the Natchez amounted to a monarchy ruled by the Great Sun and involving deference-regulated behavior. With the exception of the Natchez, tribal government was basically democratic, allowing individuals considerable personal liberty. The basic unit of government, a reflection of the sedentary life style, was the town council above which was a pyramid of councils whose number and location depended on the size of each tribe. Most matters were decided at the town level with only the gravest concerns, usually those of national significance, discussed by the highest council. Meetings on all levels were marked by open debate.

Custom provided the foundation for tribal law which amounted to a common law system. Homicide, theft, blasphemy, and adultery were violations calling for severe punishment. Though local councils sat in judgment of serious offenders, they served more as guardians of custom than as active judges, for relatives of victims generally administered the prescribed retaliation promptly. As a rule, Indians of the region were good citizens who did not abuse their freedoms. The Chickasaws, for example, seriously accepted their civic responsibilities, eagerly revenging encroachments on their national honor. In the legal system of the Mississippi Indians there was no private land ownership. Families might cultivate individual gardens, but the earth was a sacred common trust. Everyone worked in the large communal farms, and hunting grounds belonged to the entire tribe.

Religion permeated all of life in aboriginal Mississippi. Most natural phenomena, especially the mysteries of birth, puberty, maturation, and death were explained in religious terms. Since the sun, the Great Holy Fire Above, had a central place in their hierarchy of deities, sacred fires tended by priests burned in most towns. Even their games, often accompanied by ceremony and pageantry, had spiritual overtones, and festivals celebrated such important natural events as the corn harvest. Though burial customs reflected different attitudes toward the journey after death, the tribesmen believed in life hereafter. The Chickasaws buried the deceased in the floor of their homes in a sitting position facing west toward the land of their

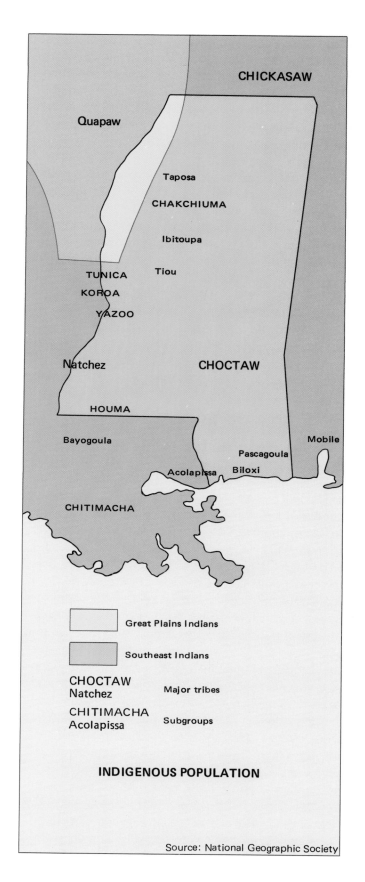

INDIGENOUS POPULATION

Source: National Geographic Society

reward. Choctaw dead were laid to rest on a scaffold until the flesh decomposed. Then a special class known as "bone pickers" cleaned the skeletons which were interred in "bone houses." Funerals of the Natchez, who had by far the most ceremonious religion, often involved the sacrifice of relatives when the deceased was a member of the Sun Caste.

Though monogamous marriages prevailed, polygamy was readily accepted. When a man married sisters, they generally shared a single home; however, separate households were maintained in plural marriages involving unrelated wives. According to European travelers, the women were quite shapely, and their pleasant voices gave the gentle language a musical tone. Since nature influenced every aspect of life, it is not surprising that many taboos related to women who isolated themselves during menstruation, at childbirth, and for a postnatal period.

The greatest dissimilarity among Mississippi tribes related to their attitudes toward war. The more numerous Choctaws, for example, were not aggressive, but they gave a good account of themselves when cornered or harassed. Conversely, the proud Chickasaws, who were never reluctant to shed blood, styled themselves great warriors, preferring the hunt and the warpath to tilling soil. Their self-portrayal was indeed accurate, for they proved to be unconquerable. During the first half of the eighteenth century, the Chickasaws successfully repelled four French invasions despite the technological advantages enjoyed by the Europeans.

The initial Indian–white contact in Mississippi occurred in December, 1540, when Hernando de Soto reached the "Province of Chicaza" on the upper Tombigbee. After experiencing the wrath of the Chickasaws four months later, de Soto's men hastily departed, and for 150 years thereafter the Chickasaws had no direct contact with Europeans. Indians along the Mississippi encountered the Joliet–Marquette and LaSalle parties, but trade was not initiated until Charleston-based Englishmen appeared in 1682. The arrival of the French in 1699 ushered in a period of diplomacy and warfare as whites sought territorial control and the natives spilled blood in quest of pelts and captives—prime trade items. Alignments hardened. A wedge was driven between the English-oriented Chickasaws and the pro-French Choctaws. Coastal tribes, easily dominated by the French, dwin-

dled and dispersed under the impact of disease and cultural disintegration. Natchez resentment culminated in their 1729 rebellion against the French, who annihilated them the following year. The Yazoo tribes were decimated by Chickasaw slave raids or by retaliation for their roles in the Natchez War by French allies. By the end of the French and Indian War of 1763, only two sizable tribes remained in Mississippi —the Choctaws and the Chickasaws.

Rapid deterioration marked the post-1763 period as the English–French–Spanish rivalry took its toll among the Indians. Confusion and disorganization increased among the natives, who were depopulated by disease and war, divided in allegiance, dependent on European goods, and irritated by a swelling tide of British intruders. Ascendance of mixed bloods, descendants of generations of traders who more readily accepted white institutions, further divided the tribes. Another factor complicating the "new" Indian society was the presence of blacks, first introduced by white traders during the 1750s. At the time of their removal, the Chickasaws owned some 1,000 Africans while the Choctaws had twice that number. Black slaves contributed to the improvement of the land and helped Indians bridge the communication gap, but they also heightened the pretensions of their owners who emulated aristocratic white planters.

During the American Revolution, the British armed Mississippi Indians who frustrated American efforts to invade the Old Southwest. Their cause was in vain, however, and after American independence had been won, pressures intensified as the Indians were caught between the Spanish and Americans. Though the Treaty of San Lorenzo reduced the Spanish influence, acculturation continued at an accelerated pace, and the only Indians who prospered were planters, herdsmen, or merchants.

Despite the Indians' active campaigning against the British in the War of 1812 and a string of friendship treaties, encroachment upon tribal lands intensified with each passing year. In four treaties from 1801 through 1816, the tribes abandoned southwestern and southern Mississippi. By 1850 they had forefeited their ancestral domains through a series of "cessions" in exchange for poorer land in the Indian Territory west of the Mississippi.

John D. W. Guice

EUROPEAN PERIOD

A brief interlude in the convulsing wars prompted by the "grand scheme" of King Louis XIV of France was provided through the Treaty of Ryswick of 1697. The agreements hammered out at Ryswick in the fall of 1697 brought peace to Europe, but the accord did not end the rivalry among the contending states of Europe. An important phase of the continuing rivalry was expressed in a new setting.

In 1695 Spain was the major colonial power in the New World. Spanish settlers occupied only a small portion of the New World claim because Spain's principal interest was to discover gold and silver. Spain gave primary attention to those areas rich in gold and silver, and, until the last decade of the seventeenth century, she exerted little influence in attempting to exclude rival nations from settling other areas of North America.

The New World became a battleground in the early 1700s as France and England sought to establish control of land and economic resources in North America. Pursuit of their designs brought them into conflict and it also heightened tensions with Spain. During Ryswick negotiations Spain gave tacit recognition to France's claim to Canada and to the unmapped area south to the Gulf of Mexico.

France took the initiative in establishing an effective claim in the New World by sponsoring an expedition of four vessels under the command of Pierre Le-Moyne, Sieur d' Iberville. The Iberville expedition, with the blessing of Louis XIV, departed Brest, France in October, 1698, with 200 colonists. Iberville's mission was to develop French presence in the Mississippi Valley and therefore preserve LaSalle's claim of 1682. The French feared that Spain and England might attempt to take possession of the area. Iberville intended to accomplish France's colonial objective by developing forts at strategic points in the prized territory of the Mississippi Valley.

Iberville's party arrived at Santo Domingo in December and secured the services of Laurent de Graaf, a former pirate of distinction. De Graaf, "perfectly intrepid in danger," provided valuable assistance to Iberville as a guide. The expedition reached the Gulf of Mexico in early January, 1699, and within a few days discovered that the Spanish had begun erecting fortifications at Pensacola. Pausing only briefly, the adventuring party continued westward until they anchored at Mobile Bay on January 31. Iberville's ex-plorers examined the area, including Dauphin Island, and then proceeded on a western course for a few leagues until they encountered a series of islands which, according to Iberville, provided "good anchorage and refuge against storms." The islands included Petit Bois, Horn, Ship, and Cat. Utilizing the protection afforded by Ship Island, the expedition dropped anchor February 10, 1699. Iberville visited the mainland where he established cordial relations with the Biloxi Indians. The visiting party also made favorable contact with the Bayogoulas who provided Iberville with information about the Mississippi River.

Iberville embarked on his journey to discover the Mississippi on February 28, 1699. His party of 54 men used two longboats and several bark canoes as they moved cautiously from Ship Island to the branch of the river known as the North Pass. Iberville wanted to advance up the river until he had positive proof he had located the Mississippi. After twelve days the expedition reached the village of the Bayogoulas whose chief assisted them. The party advanced two days' journey north of Istrouma, which the French translated as Baton Rouge, and then began to make a careful retreat to Ship Island. For the return Iberville divided the party into two units and instructed his brother, Jean Bienville, to retreat down the river on the course which they had followed. Iberville wanted to gather additional information about the river and its environment so he returned along a route that carried him through Bayou Manchac and Lakes Maurepas and Pontchartrain.

The adventure was a profitable one, for Iberville became convinced that he had located the Mississippi River. Supporting his contention was the fact that he had contacted the Houmas who gave him a letter that had been written by Henri de Tonty to LaSalle fourteen years earlier.

In his explorations of the river and the Gulf shoreline, Iberville discovered several suitable locations for building a fort and for establishing a small settlement. The site selected for the first French fort in the region was on the eastern shore of Biloxi Bay. The location was chosen because the bay provided good protection and allowed small vessels good access at all times.

Iberville described Fort Maurepas as a "wooden fort with four bastions; two are made of hewn timber . . . one foot and a half thick, nine feet high; the other two of double pallisades. It was mounted with 54 pieces of cannon." The fort was completed in May, and Iberville promptly prepared to return to France. Before departing, he entrusted the command to Sauvolle de la Villantry, assisted by Bienville.

During Iberville's absence Sauvolle directed several explorations along the coast and up the Mississippi River. Bienville was responsible for most of this activity in the summer and fall of 1699. A very significant development occurred in September while Bienville was exploring the river. He encountered an English ship, the "Carolina Galley," under the command of Captain Barr. Possibly unaware that he was on the Mississippi, Captain Barr told the Frenchman who had boldly boarded the ship that he was searching for the Mississippi where he intended to establish an English settlement. Bienville promptly advised Barr that the French had already developed a settlement on the river. Barr submitted without a confrontation and returned to the Gulf. In their elation over the English retreat the French named the site of the encounter Detour des Anglais.

The "English Turn" incident convinced French officials that it was necessary to establish a fort on the river as a symbol of French control over the territory. Upon Iberville's return to Biloxi in 1700, plans were made for the construction of Fort Boulage. The fort, consisting of about a dozen pieces of cannon and five or six cabins, was hardly a bastion of defense but it was evidence of an actual claim posted by France.

In 1701 the French decided to locate a new settlement at Mobile Bay, and Bienville was charged with supervising the construction of Fort Louis. The French erected a much more secure fort at Mobile in 1702 than they had built at Biloxi three years earlier. Completion of Fort Louis diminished the importance of the settlement at Biloxi, and, except for a detachment of twenty soldiers, everyone moved to Mobile. Iberville, responsible for establishing cordial relations among the Indians at Biloxi and Mobile and for confirming France's claim to the Mississippi Valley, died four years after Fort Louis was established.

France was more successful in constructing forts at several strategic sites along the river and on the coast than in developing the settlements—the colony never attracted a large influx of settlers. France's interest in Louisiana did not seriously encourage emigrants to brave the dangers of a youthful, distant colony. France wanted only to extract quick economic gains and prevent rival nations from claiming the potentials of the vast unmapped region. There were twenty-seven families with ten children in the colony in 1704, while the military garrison assigned to the three forts numbered about two hundred.

Frequent changes in leadership and dissension among officials hampered the smooth, orderly growth of the colony. These conflicts diverted attention from more important issues and sapped valuable energy which could have been applied in developing the settlement. Bienville's authority was challenged in the first years of the eighteenth century, and he was charged with misconduct in office. This perplexing situation prompted Louis XIV to allow a private company to assume control of the colony.

In 1712, wealthy merchant Antoine Crozat received a fifteen-year contract to control and develop Louisiana. The charter gave Crozat a monopoly on trade and manufacturing. Crozat's primary interest was to develop trade with Spain, but he became discouraged and, in 1717, asked to be released from the contract. Although Crozat did not realize the desired economic gains from his venture, he did succeed in constructing two additional forts in the Mississippi Valley. Fort Toulouse, located on the upper Alabama River, was erected in 1714, and Fort Rosalie was built at Natchez in 1716.

Following the sudden collapse of Crozat's experiment, the king extended a new charter to the Mississippi Company, a division of the Company of the Indies. The Mississippi Company agreed to settle 6000 colonists and 3000 slaves in Louisiana before the expiration of its charter. In return the company received broad privileges and attractive benefits. It enjoyed a monopoly on trade in Louisiana as well as a monopoly on the beaver trade with Canada. The company was given the power to appoint the governing officials for the colony, but had to assume all responsibility for its development. John Law was a leading figure in the Mississippi Company's efforts to promote prosperity. Law's speculative scheme failed, but the Company of the Indies continued its supervision over Louisiana until 1732, at which time Louisiana again became a crown colony.

The colony showed signs of growth and development between 1717 and Bienville's final departure

EARLY TOWNS AND VILLAGES

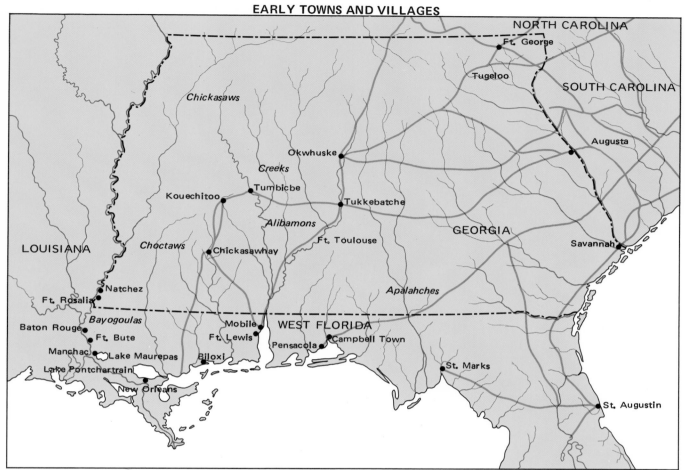

Source: Adapted from B. Romans, A General Map of the Southern British Colonies, 1776.

from Louisiana in 1740. The population of the colony had increased significantly. The settlement around Fort Rosalie included more than 700 persons by 1792. Sixteen hundred people populated New Orleans, which became the colony's capital in 1722. Many German, Swiss, and French settlers arrived in Louisiana during this period. Tobacco, rice, indigo, pitch, tar, and lumber were the leading products exported during the 1720s.

The rate of Louisiana's development declined with the advent of the Indian wars in the mid 1730s. Battle with the Chickasaws and Choctaws after 1740 retarded France's development of Louisiana. The French and Indian War of 1756–63, known as the Seven Years War in Europe, proved to be the final encounter between France and England for many years. The war proved disastrous to the French, who were forced to cede a vast territory in North America to

England. This transfer to England of all Louisiana east of the Mississippi, excluding the Isle of Orleans, ended French control of the colony. Spain gained the Isle of Orleans and territory west of the Mississippi.

England's acquisition of the eastern portion of Louisiana was confirmed in the 1763 Treaty of Paris. The great empire builder then proceeded with the organization of a new colony, British West Florida. The boundaries of British West Florida were established in February, 1764. The frontier colony extended from the Gulf of Mexico to a northern border of 32° 28′ north latitude. It was bounded on the west by the Mississippi and Iberville rivers and Lakes Maurepas and Pontchartrain; the eastern boundary was the Appalachicola and Chattahoochee rivers.

During 1763 and 1764 the Board of Trade, meeting in London, formulated plans for governing and developing British West Florida. Virtually all decisions relating to the administration of the colony were made by the home government. Policies were implemented by crown-appointed resident officials and by military officers in West Florida.

The colony was under military rule from 1763 until the fall of 1764. Military officials handled the transfer proceedings as the French and Spanish authorities evacuated their posts. Lieutenant Colonel Augustine Prevost, commander of the Third Royal American Battalion, worked with the resident Spanish governor at Pensacola, Don Diego Oritz Parrilla, in preparing for British control of what had been Spanish Florida. Parrilla and Prevost had a cordial, friendly relationship. Governor Parrilla completed Spain's evacuation of the post on September 2, 1763.

Prevost and other English officers were apparently surprised about the condition of the Pensacola settlement, because their correspondence is filled with references to its poor condition. Prevost believed the "insuperable laziness" of the Spanish was the major reason for the deplorable condition of the settlement. British officials took immediate steps to repair and strengthen the fort at Pensacola which Major Forbes described as "so defenseless that anyone can step in at pleasure."

Captain John Farmar, who relieved the French of their control of Mobile in October, also discovered a post that had been poorly maintained. Farmar's report of the fort's condition noted that "all the barracks and guard rooms in the fort are in a ruinous condition." He also indicated the need for repairs to many of the buildings.

Relations between British and French officials at Mobile were strained as they quarrelled about many aspects of the transfer proceedings. The discouraging conditions at Mobile and Pensacola impressed upon British officials the need to organize the colony more effectively.

Civilian rule replaced military rule when George Johnstone, first provincial governor, arrived in Pensacola in October, 1764. Johnstone inherited several problems, including revitalization of the forts at Pensacola and Mobile. It would be his responsibility to organize a government, develop a sound economic base, and establish friendly relations with the Indians. Soon after his arrival Johnstone appointed a council which assisted him in governing the colony. Each councilor had a primary area of responsibility, such as

John Stuart, who served as superintendent of Indian affairs. The governor also selected twenty-eight people to act as justices of the peace, a most important responsibility in a frontier colony. A complete judicial structure, including a court of pleas and a vice-admiralty court, was created in 1765. The attorney general and chief justice of West Florida had power to convene a supreme court of judicature.

From 1764 until the organization of West Florida's first assembly in the fall of 1766, the responsibility for enacting ordinances and laws for the colony rested with the governor and his council. The council passed many provisions in an attempt to provide a stable, effective government, such as the measures limiting the sale of liquor in the colony. Persons were prohibited from selling or giving liquor to the Indians. The regulations further declared that only three retailers would be licensed to sell liquor in Pensacola, while four retailers were alloted for Mobile. The council also commissioned Elias Durnford, surveyor for the colony, to draft a plan for a town at Pensacola. Durnford's proposal provided space for building lots, military, naval, and governmental functions. Building lots were a standard size of 80 by 160 feet.

Governor Johnstone's years as governor were distinguished by serious disputes and problems with the military officials. He was anxious for the military to recognize his position as captain-general and governor-in-chief. The military commanders at Pensacola and Mobile, however, refused to acquiesce to Johnstone's insistent claim of superior authority over the colony. The controversy gave rise to petty quarrels and dissension between the executive office and the military. The question of disputed authority came to the attention of officials of the home government. Early in 1765 Lord Halifax communicated the crown's decision by announcing that the governor had responsibility over civil matters, and the commanding officer had jurisdiction over military affairs. This ruling, however, was not decisive and therefore did little to resolve the dilemma. Disputes, sometimes quite serious, continued until Governor Johnstone was recalled from his position in 1767.

England intended to capture the economic potential of West Florida by providing favorable conditions that would encourage colonists to make their homes there. In order to make the frontier colony safe for settlement, officials recognized the necessity of maintaining good relations with the Indians. Governor Johnstone, who received wise counsel from John Stuart, recognized the importance of a peaceful Indian policy. In 1765 Johnstone, Stuart, and several council members hosted two important Indian congresses. The meetings were designed to insure friendly relations with the Indians and to reach a mutual understanding about certain boundary lines and trade. The British also hoped to secure additional cessions of land.

The first conference, held in Mobile in March, was attended by leaders of the Chickasaw and Choctaw nations. The ten-day meeting, characterized by a cordial spirit, produced a treaty which included a declaration of friendship and a land cession to the British. The treaty also established regulations involving trade, the work of the Indian commissioner, and procedures for dealing with law violators.

The Creeks met with West Florida's officials at Pensacola later in the year. This conference produced a treaty similar to that of the Mobile conference. Both treaties were good, but the British were ever aware of a need to improve relations with the various Indian nations. This need was recognized by every West Florida governor in the colonial period, from Johnstone to Peter Chester. Although particular attention was given to the Indian matter, officials never satisfactorily resolved the perplexing problem.

After Johnstone's recall, Lieutenant Governor Montford Browne assumed the duties of leadership until the second governor of the province arrived in 1769. Browne was interested in developing the western section of West Florida. He was particularly interested in the potential of the area around Natchez and Fort Bute. An exploratory visit there in 1766 confirmed Browne's assessment of the region and supported the recommendation which he had made to officials in London. Browne described the area as "one of the finest counties in the British American Dominion." There was an "abundance of buffaloes, venison, geese, turkeys, ducks, and . . . fish" and the soil seemed "exceedingly" fertile.

Browne suggested that towns should be established at Natchez and Fort Bute. In spite of the untapped resources offered in the western section of the province, British officials could not take advantage of the opportunities at this time. Browne's disappointment over colonial affairs deepened when he was re-

called from his duties in 1769.

West Florida's second governor, John Eliot, arrived in 1769. Eliot's tenure was brief, however; he took his life in April, the same year of his arrival. Lieutenant Governor Elias Durnford, formerly surveyor general, served in the absence of a governor for twelve months. Durnford's major work involved supporting a new law to improve regulation of trade with Indians and encouraging the further development of West Florida.

Durnford believed that reestablishing a post at Fort Bute and developing a settlement there would stimulate the growth of West Florida. He contended that such measures conformed to England's colonial philosophy. Durnford's objectives for expansion were not achieved during his brief service as chief executive of the colony, but his support of the proposal helped keep the idea before the home government. Durnford's perspective was valuable to Governor Peter Chester, who arrived in August, 1770.

Governor Chester, with Durnford's support, continued to urge the crown to approve greater development of West Florida. He reminded his superiors that the colony had progressed very slowly since 1763. The major expense for England, if the crown approved, would be in providing protection of new settlements. Colonial officials finally acquiesced, and they witnessed a large influx of settlers in the Mississippi region around Natchez in the 1770s. By 1774 over 3000 persons lived in the area, and Chester described it in 1777 as a "flourishing" settlement. Representatives to the 1778 meeting of the assembly included delegates from new election districts in Natchez and Manchac. The population of West Florida tripled from 1765 to 1775.

The colony's principal towns in the late 1770s, Pensacola, Mobile, Manchac, and Natchez, were small villages. The sparseness of the population helps explain the meager institutional accommodations in the colony. No adequate church facility was erected at any of the settlements during the period of British control of West Florida. In 1770 Nathaniel Cotton, a minister in Pensacola, reported that his congregation was "destitute of cloths and napkins for the communion tables." After Cotton's death the following year, Pensacola did not have another resident Anglican minister before Spain took control of the colony in 1778.

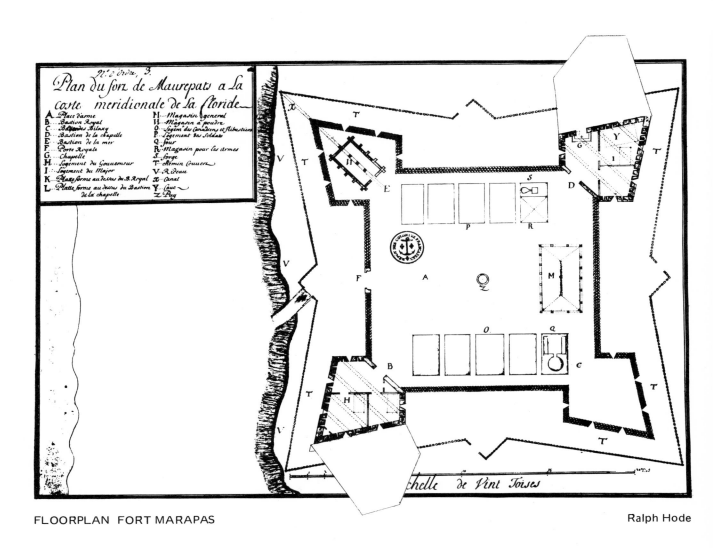

FLOORPLAN FORT MARAPAS

Ralph Hode

British West Florida also had a disappointing record in providing educational opportunities. John Firby, Pensacola's schoolmaster, advised Governor Chester in 1772 that the province had not assumed responsibility for erecting a school building and appropriating funds for its support. Chester favored Firby's request for support, but other problems commanded higher priority.

A thorny issue which Chester encountered involved the colony's assembly. The governor called a meeting of the assembly and issued election writs in 1771. These writs, unlike those of the three previous elections, did not detail the length of service for the three assemblymen. Chester declared that to do otherwise would infringe on the king's prerogative. The decision, however, provoked a storm of protest. In defiance of the governor, the electors of Mobile refused to select representatives. The governor refused to yield to their position and he prorogued the assembly. Chester did not call another assembly until 1778.

West Florida, generally undisturbed by the events of the American Revolution, was shocked by the plundering raid of James Willing in 1778. Willing's army, numbering approximately 100 men, suddenly attacked settlements at Natchez and Manchac. After gathering spoils, the raiders descended the river to New Orleans where they were received by Governor Bernardo de Gálvez of Louisiana.

Since the intruders left as quickly as they appeared, Chester did not have time to dispatch a force to intercept them. He did protest Gálvez's actions and he demanded restitution for all property losses. Within a few months the rebel band dissolved, but Willing was later captured by the British. The Willing raid was but a prelude to a more serious attack against West Florida in 1779.

Authorities at Pensacola received the disturbing news in September, 1779, that Spain had joined France in declaring war against England. British officials, fearing overt actions from the Spanish, immediately alerted the military commanders at several forts. The precautions, however, were not adequate to repulse the Spanish offensive assault at Fort Bute and Baton Rouge. Spain's victory at Baton Rouge enabled her to take control of the Natchez area. Within two years Mobile and Pensacola fell, and Spain controlled all of West Florida.

The first Spanish rulers over the Spanish province were military commandants. In addition to their military duties, commandants served as justices of the peace, sheriffs, judges, police captains, and counselors. Treasury officials, secretaries, royal quartermasters, and a post adjutant assisted the commandants.

Manuel Gayoso de Lemos was appointed first governor of Spanish Natchez in 1798. Gayoso was selected because he had outstanding experience as a diplomat, was a gifted military tactician, and spoke English fluently. These qualities were particularly important in view of the preponderant English population in Natchez. Gayoso often consulted prominent settlers of the province before he initiated any laws.

One of Gayoso's principal concerns was strengthening the colony's defense by repairing old forts and building new ones. In 1791 Fort Nogales was erected to symbolize Spain's control on the Mississippi River. Officials in the province also spent $37 thousand in revitalizing the old French fort at Natchez. Gayoso also sought to utilize various established military groups and militia organizations. In addition to the Louisiana Infantry Regiment, the governor could request help from the Cuban and Mexican infantry regiments. A well-organized militia unit was maintained in Natchez.

Spain's power was never seriously challenged by rival nations, although there were numerous rumors about impending danger to the colony. Perhaps the colony was more vulnerable to Indian attack than to overt attack by other rivals. That governing officials recognized the importance of maintaining friendly relations with the Indians is evidenced by two treaties of the 1790s. The Treaty of Natchez of 1792 with the Chickasaws, Choctaws, Creeks, Talapuches, Alibamons, and the Cherokees helped ameliorate Choctaw discontent about the construction of Fort Nogales. The Treaty of Nogales created a reciprocal offensive-defensive pact between the parties.

A peaceful colony was an impetus to settlement in the Spanish province. The census of 1792 reveals that the population of the Natchez District alone exceeded four thousand. Gayoso provided effective leadership in developing the colony until 1795, when the Treaty of San Lorenzo yielded Spain's control over the Natchez District to the United States.

Byrle Kynerd

TERRITORIAL AND EARLY STATEHOOD

Following the pattern established in the Northwest Ordinance of 1778, the United States Congress passed an act in 1798 creating the Mississippi Territory. Accordingly, the President held responsibility for appointing a governor, a secretary, and three judges to administer the territory. The land composing the original Mississippi Territory was carved out of the area acquired in 1798 by the Pinckney Treaty of 1795. As previously noted, the lands included in the original territory were bordered on the north by the parallel of 32° 28′ north latitude, on the south by the 31° parallel, and from the Mississippi River on the west to the Chattahoochie on the east. Additional lands were acquired north and south of these lines between 1804 and 1813 from Spain, and from the states of Georgia and South Carolina. With these acquisitions the territory contained all the area found today within the present states of Alabama and Mississippi. Thus, the territorial period encompasses the history of two states.

Four men actually served as governors during the territorial period and guided the territory to statehood. The first appointee never really held office. George Matthews, a Georgia land speculator, had

so much opposition to his appointment that another governor had to be appointed almost immediately. Hence, Winthrop Sargent of Massachusetts was the first territorial governor to actually serve in office. Sargent, a Federalist, followed party policies and sided with the Natchez merchants and bankers. He was somewhat autocratic and soon gained the disfavor of the people. During his term in office he set up three counties—Adams, Pickering, and Washington.

The second territorial governor, W. C. C. Claiborne, took office in November of 1801. Claiborne, an Antifederalist, immediately began to make changes. The second stage of territorial government was given to the area. This meant the election of a territorial assembly and a territorial delegate to Congress. During Claiborne's term Pickering County was redesignated Jefferson County. Adams County was split; its southern part became Wilkinson County, and the new county of Claiborne was created north of Jefferson County. To further reduce the power of the Natchez Federalist, the territorial capital was moved to the small town of Washington, about six miles from Natchez. In 1804 Claiborne became the governor of the Territory of Orleans and in 1812 the first governor of

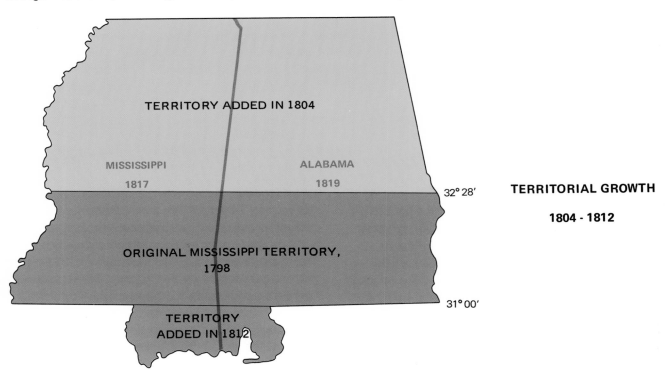

TERRITORY ADDED IN 1804

MISSISSIPPI
1817

ALABAMA
1819

32° 28′

ORIGINAL MISSISSIPPI TERRITORY, 1798

TERRITORY ADDED IN 1812

31° 00′

TERRITORIAL GROWTH

1804 - 1812

Source: John K. Bettersworth, Mississippi: A History

the state of Louisiana.

Cato West, the territorial secretary, served as a temporary interim governor after Claiborne moved to Orleans until Robert Williams was appointed in 1805. Williams, technically only the third of the main four governors to serve the territory, was confronted with many problems owing to internal growth. During his administration the first Choctaw cession occurred. Williams also had to deal with the "backwoods" people of the Tombigbee area who felt neglected by the western capital. The controversy with Spanish West Florida bloomed but was not resolved. Then Aaron Burr led an expedition into the territory and was suspected of treason. He was arrested, tried, and subsequently acquitted.

The last of the territorial governors was David Holmes. Holmes was considered the most able administrator of the four. Holmes came from Virginia where he had served that state as a representative to the United States Congress. The first crisis to confront Holmes was the West Florida Revolution which subsequently led to the annexation of most of West Florida by Mississippi. The second crisis Holmes had to face during his tenure was the War of 1812, which included the Creek wars. The war began in the territory with the Battle of Burnt Corn in 1813 which the Creeks won. This battle was closely followed by the massacre at Fort Mims from which only 36 persons escaped. The massacre terrified the people of the territory and prepared them for ensuing battles. The fighting ended in 1815 with the Battle of New Orleans, when Andrew Jackson, aided by territorial volunteers under Thomas Hinds, defeated the British. David Holmes, who had managed the affairs of the territory from 1809 to 1817, was elected without opposition to be the first governor of the state of Mississippi in 1817.

Throughout the territorial period the population was scattered. The first five counties organized were along the Mississippi River—Wilkinson, Adams, Jefferson, Claiborne, and Warren. They dominated territorial affairs at the time of statehood. The other major pockets of settlement were in the areas around Mobile and in the bend of the Tennessee River.

In March of 1817, Congress passed an enabling act dividing the territory with a north–south surveyor's line. The western part of the territory, taking the territorial name Mississippi, was admitted into the

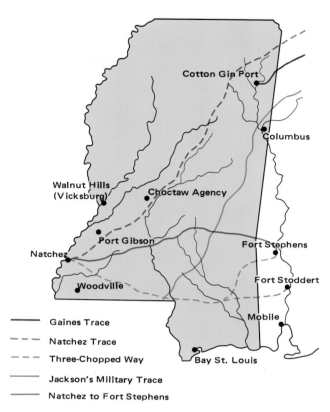

EARLY TERRITORIAL ROADS

Source: John K. Bettersworth, Mississippi: A History

Union as the twentieth state on December 10, 1817. Alabama, the eastern part of the territory, became a state two years later. This division of the territory gave each state lands bordering on the Gulf of Mexico rather than dividing the territory with an east–west line thereby creating one land-locked state and one Gulf Coast state.

The four decades of statehood prior to secession in 1861 were periods of tremendous growth for Mississippi. In 1830 the state's population was 132,631; in 1850 it was 696,526. These were the two decades of greatest population growth in the history of the state of Mississippi. By 1840 blacks were more numerous than whites in Mississippi for the first time. In 1860, slaves constituted 55.2 percent of the total state population. As evidence of this population growth, it should be noted that sixty of the present eighty-two counties had been organized in Mississippi by 1852.

The location of the state capital in Jackson in 1822, along with the Indian treaties of Doak's Stand (1820) and Dancing Rabbit Creek (1830) with the Choctaws and of Pontotoc (1832) with the Chickasaw, opened

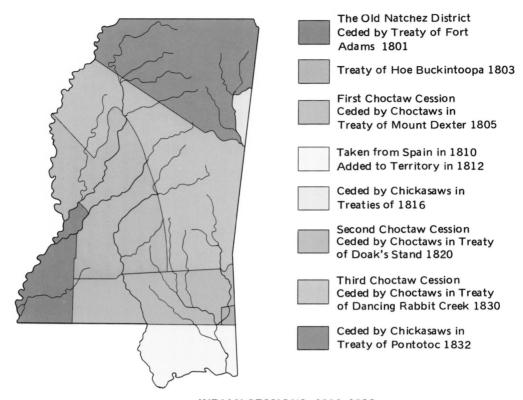

The Old Natchez District Ceded by Treaty of Fort Adams 1801

Treaty of Hoe Buckintoopa 1803

First Choctaw Cession Ceded by Choctaws in Treaty of Mount Dexter 1805

Taken from Spain in 1810 Added to Territory in 1812

Ceded by Chickasaws in Treaties of 1816

Second Choctaw Cession Ceded by Choctaws in Treaty of Doak's Stand 1820

Third Choctaw Cession Ceded by Choctaws in Treaty of Dancing Rabbit Creek 1830

Ceded by Chickasaws in Treaty of Pontotoc 1832

INDIAN CESSIONS: 1801-1832

Source: John K. Bettersworth, Mississippi: A History

two-thirds of the lands of the state to white settlers and resulted in a dimunition of the power of the Old Natchez District. By the time of the Civil War the most densely settled and most politically powerful part of the state was the northern counties created from these Choctaw and Chickasaw lands. As evidence of this shift of power, the legislature in 1841 selected Oxford in northern Lafayette County as the site of the first state-supported university in Mississippi.

Mississippi rewrote its constitution only once in the antebellum period. Mississippians became dissatisfied with the undemocratic and obsolete features of the 1817 constitution and wrote a new document in 1832 which served their purposes well. This constitution was the most democratic in the South and, for whites, in the entire nation. It called for a completely elective judiciary.

Cotton, slavery, and the plantation system dominated the agricultural economy. The mansions in Natchez today are reminders of the great wealth created in the state during these years. But the largest white element in the socio-economic structure of antebel-

lum Mississippi was the yeoman farmer group. Unfortunately, the activities of this group are not as well known as those of the planters. Mississippi witnessed considerable diversification of agriculture in the 1840s and 1850s. The production of corn, wheat, oats, rye, barley, millet, cowpeas, sweet potatoes, orchards, rice, and livestock increased tremendously. Mississippi's biggest economic problems during early statehood were transportation and finance.

During the 1830s and 1840s, Mississippi was a two-party state. Both the Whigs and Democrats vied for political control. Mississippi lapsed back into one-party politics only with the approach of the Civil War.

In the 1830s Mississippi experienced a prosperity followed by a severe economic depression. In the 1840s came the involvement in the Mexican War and the growing sectional controversy over slavery. By 1854 the fire-eaters were in control of the state, and events moved swiftly to the act of secession on January 9, 1861.

John Edmond Gonzales

CHICKASAW INDIAN LANDS

Monroe

CHOCTAW INDIAN LANDS

Washington

Madison

Warren

Hinds

Rankin

Claiborne

Copiah

Simpson

Jefferson

Franklin

Lawrence

Covington

Jones

Wayne

Adams

Amite

Pike

Marion

Perry

Greene

Wilkinson

Hancock

Jackson

COUNTIES OF MISSISSIPPI

1832

Source: John K. Bettersworth, Mississippi: A History

COUNTIES OF MISSISSIPPI

1839

Source: John K. Bettersworth, Mississippi: A History

WAR, RECONSTRUCTION, AND CIVILIAN RULE

When the secession convention voted to sever the state's relation with the Union, few Mississippians anticipated the devastating war which followed. In the initial stages of popular support for the war, the number of volunteers exceeded the state's financial capacity and logistical apparatus for enrolling and arming the men. Two Mississippi generals, James L. Alcorn and Reuben Davis, were considered alarmists when they pressed the governor to inaugurate military training for the recruits. Illusions of peaceful separation were dispelled when the sounds of war echoed throughout Mississippi in early 1862. Following the battle of Shiloh, Mississippi became the focal point of the war in the west as General U. S. Grant and Admiral David Farragut deployed their forces in the effort to capture Vicksburg. The Battle of Vicksburg proved to be the most significant battle of the war in Mississippi. In 1862 the only major Confederate stronghold denying the Union free use of the Mississippi River was Vicksburg. The first attempt to take Vicksburg came in the spring of that year. Two squadrons, under the commands of Farragut to the south and Admiral David Porter to the north, bombarded the city for two months without success. Next Grant attempted to divert Confederate troops from Vicksburg by attacking General Pemberton at Grenada while dispatching General Sherman to invade Vicksburg. After Sherman's defeat at the hands of Stephen D. Lee, Grant tried to reach Vicksburg via the Yazoo River Valley and other Delta streams. Once again the Confederates foiled Grant. Grant then attempted to bypass Vicksburg by trying to divert the Mississippi into the Red River, first through a bayou and then by digging a canal. Grant failed at both endeavors to open the river for the Union. Finally, Colonel Benjamin Grierson conducted a daring cavalry raid through Mississippi. Grierson's diversionary tactics disrupted the Confederacy's strategy to maintain Vicksburg. After Grierson's raid the final siege of Vicksburg began; on July 4, 1863, the city fell and was occupied by Union troops. After the fall of Vicksburg, General Nathan B. Forrest prevented Mississippi from being completely occupied by Union forces for a considerable time. But eventually, despite Forrest's daring tactics, the state's remaining units were forced to surrender on May 4, 1865, and the military phase of the war was over. Of the 78,000 Mississippians mustered into service, only 50,000 survived the war. Those who

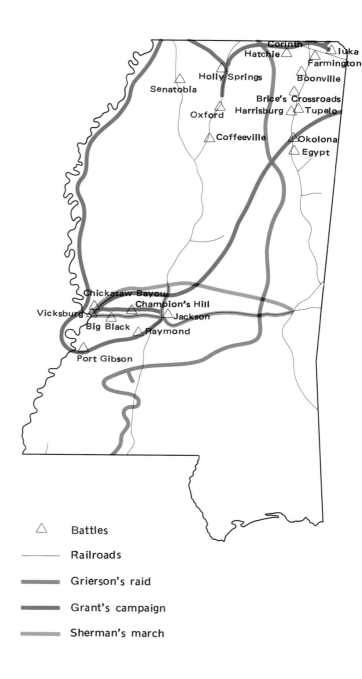

Battles

Railroads

Grierson's raid

Grant's campaign

Sherman's march

FEDERAL RAIDS

did return found the state reduced to economic shambles and gripped in social changes that staggered their collective imaginations. The numerous battles and skirmishes and the emancipation of 436,631 slaves created such disorder that complete chaos was averted only by the presence of Union troops.

In 1865 political leadership was exercised by recently pardoned ex-Confederates and a handful of Unionists who failed to comprehend the social and political changes attending military defeat. When the legislature in 1865 practically reestablished slavery in the form of "Black Code," northern sentiment shifted to the other extreme by demanding political and civil equality for blacks. The enfranchisement of Mississippi Negroes resulted in the reapportionment of the legislature, which before the war had been based on white population only. The Delta and Mississippi River counties with their high concentrations of black populations received the major benefit from this reapportionment. But the new political order, based on black participation, was aborted when the color line was drawn in Mississippi politics during the election of 1875.

After Democrats regained control of the state, a white minority in the predominantly black counties monopolized political power through continued control over the legislature. These new leaders, called "Bourbons," were preoccupied with industrial development. After years of neglect by the Bourbon rulers, white farmers in the northeast hill section and the Piney Woods began to raise demands for regulation of railroads and banks. Other reform groups cooperated in support for a convention to draft a new constitution. It was intended that the constitution would eliminate blacks from politics and that a more equitable apportionment for whites would be made.

The Mississippi constitution of 1890 did virtually eliminate blacks from politics and allowed the state to draw more realistic congressional districts. But the reapportionment plan did not remove the power from the black counties. White counties were duped into thinking that an increase of thirteen new seats would enable them to control the legislature and the Democratic convention. The black counties, however, continued to control both; thus the "revolt of the rednecks" was temporarily averted. Moreover, the Bourbon oligarchy diverted power from the governor to the speaker of the state house of representatives.

U.S.S. CAIRO

State A & I Board

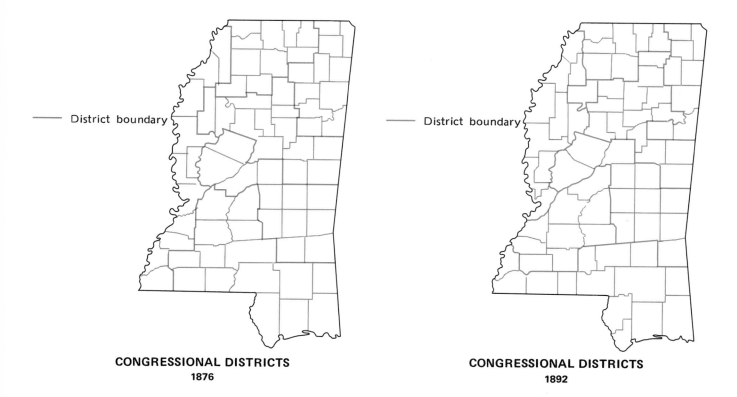

CONGRESSIONAL DISTRICTS
1876

— District boundary

CONGRESSIONAL DISTRICTS
1892

— District boundary

Not only the monopolistic political practices of the Bourbons, but their economic policies as well, stirred widespread unrest among white farmers and laborers. That railroad, banking, and corporate interests were being promoted to the neglect of agricultural interests was graphically illustrated by the deteriorating conditions among Mississippi farmers. Forced to pay freight charges imposed by unregulated railroads, high interest rates, and exorbitant markups by county merchants, farmers soon found themselves hopelessly indebted and reduced to tenancy. In 1890, 62.7 percent of Mississippi farmers were tenants, and in several counties the tenancy rate was over 90 percent. Since two-thirds of Mississippi families were farm families, the figures indicate that a substantial majority of Mississippians were trapped in the rural isolation and despondency of tenancy. Home tenancy was even higher at 77.3 percent. Additional evidence of agriculture problems is reflected in the comparative statistics of agricultural and industrial production increases from 1870 to 1890. The total value of farm products rose only fractionally, notwithstanding the fact that there were 2,500,000 more acres in cultivation in 1890 than in 1870. Mississippi farmers were caught in the cycle of declining prices and increased

production. Cotton prices dropped from 15.1 cents per pound in the early 1870s to 7.8 cents per pound in the early 1890s. Yet the crop lien system, under which a farmer mortgaged his crop against credit advances, dictated the steady increase in cotton production. The only encouraging aspect of Mississippi agriculture was truck farming, which by 1890 was becoming an important source of revenue in the areas less suited to cotton production.

On the other hand, the total value of manufactured goods increased over 100 percent from 1870 to 1890. This gain resulted chiefly from timber, cotton, and woolens production. Timber values increased from $2,160,667 in 1870 to $5,670,774 in 1890. Cotton manufacturing expanded from four mills to nine mills, and products valued at $234,445 increased to $1,333,398 over the same period. Woolens production showed a similar increase from four mills and a value of $147,323 in 1879 to seven mills and a value of $924,185 in 1890. In cotton and woolens manufacturing the number of workers rose from 450 in 1870 to 2,226 in 1890 and their annual income averaged $263. The average income for all laborers and farmers was $311 as compared with the national average of $484.

The most spectacular industrial growth in the three decades following the war occurred in railroad construction. Track mileage increased from 872.30 miles of track in 1860 to 2,332.03 miles of track in 1890. During 1883, Mississippi laid more track than any other state in the nation. For the decade 1880–90 the state's percentage increase of 108.4 percent miles of track laid was much higher than the national rate of 86.29 percent. Few farmers benefited from this railroad development, however, and continued to condemn the practice of "flat rates" charged for shipping goods weighing less than 100 pounds.

During the last three decades of the nineteenth century, Mississippi's population growth kept pace with national trends. From 1870 to 1900 the state's population rose from 827,922 to 1,551,270. From 1880 to 1890 the percentage population increase was 36.7 percent, significantly higher than the national rate of 30.1 percent. The following decade the state's population increase of 20.3 percent also compared favorably with the national rate of 20.7 percent.

Towns and cities, especially those along major railroad lines, reflected Mississippi's growth trends in the late nineteenth century. Among those cities showing the most significant growth were Vicksburg, the state's largest city, which increased from 3,158 in 1860 to 13,373 in 1890, and Meridian, the next largest city, which rose from a small hamlet in 1860 to a population of 10,624 by 1890. Jackson, although the state capital, showed only a modest growth by 1890. The population of Jackson in 1860 was 2,107 and in 1890 it was 5,290. Among the towns that grew in response to railroad increases were Greenville and Hattiesburg. Greenville's population increased over 300 percent from 1880 to 1890; and the population of Hattiesburg, incorporated in 1888, numbered 4,175 only twelve years later.

During the three decades following the Civil War, the Mississippi economy was characterized by industrial development on the one hand and agriculture decline on the other. This imbalance stirred political unrest among the masses of white farmers and laborers. An emerging leadership both responded to and exploited that unrest. After first eliminating blacks from political activity, the "redneck" politicians then wrested power from the Bourbons and inaugurated their own brand of "southern progressivism."

David Sansing

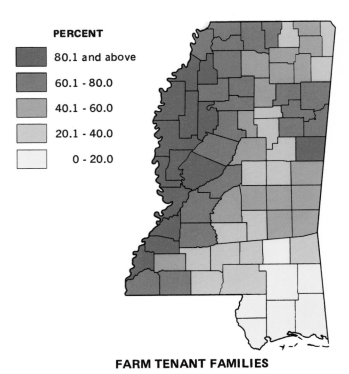

PERCENT

- 80.1 and above
- 60.1 - 80.0
- 40.1 - 60.0
- 20.1 - 40.0
- 0 - 20.0

FARM TENANT FAMILIES
1890
Source: U.S. Census of Agriculture

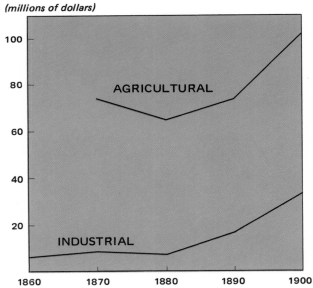

PRODUCTION
(millions of dollars)

AGRICULTURAL AND INDUSTRIAL PRODUCTION
1860-1900

Source: U.S. Census of Manufactures
Source: U.S. Census of Agriculture

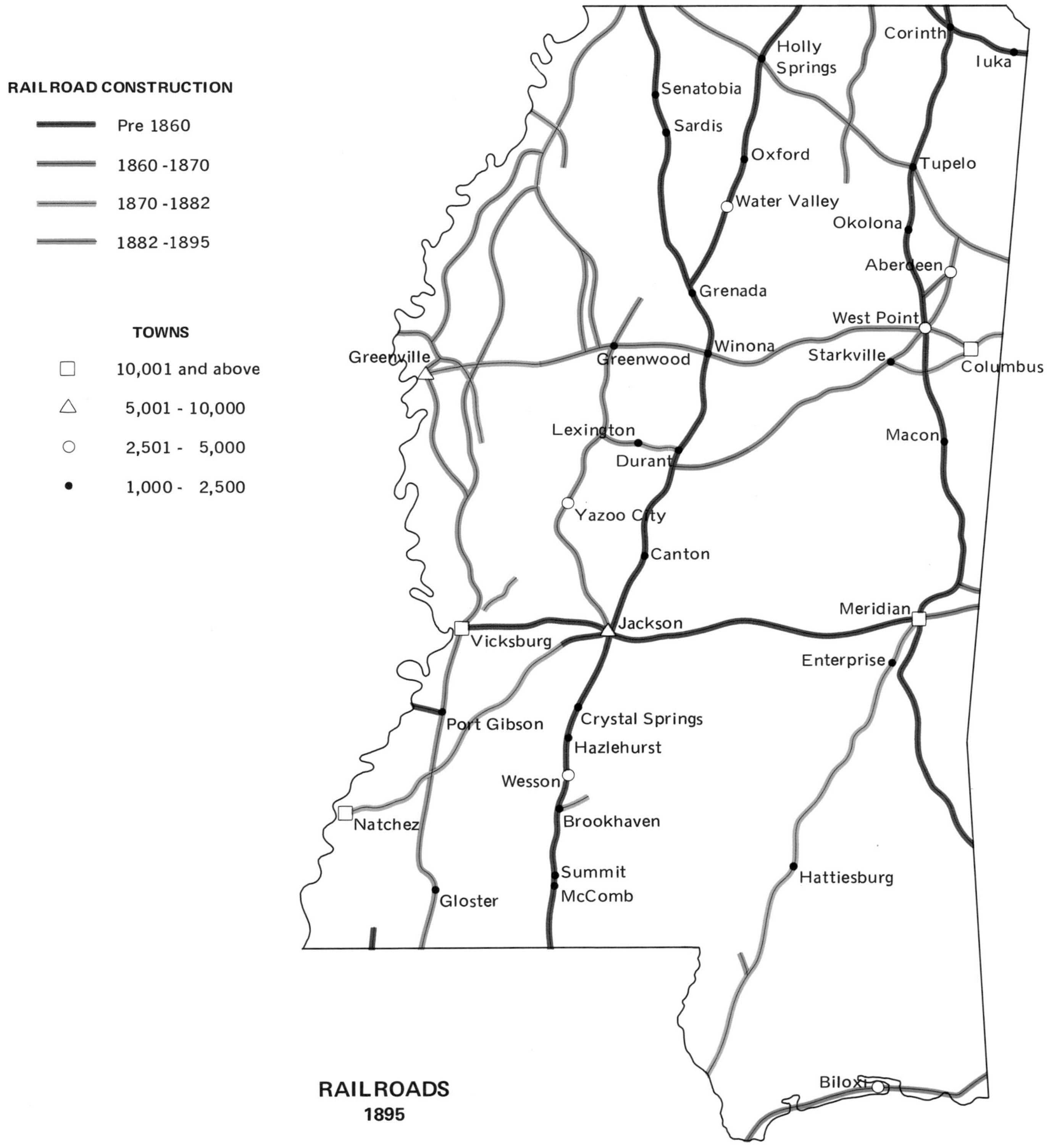

RAILROAD CONSTRUCTION

▬▬▬▬	Pre 1860
▬▬▬▬	1860 -1870
▬▬▬▬	1870 -1882
▬▬▬▬	1882 -1895

TOWNS

□	10,001 and above
△	5,001 - 10,000
○	2,501 - 5,000
●	1,000 - 2,500

Corinth
Iuka
Holly Springs
Senatobia
Sardis
Oxford
Tupelo
Water Valley
Okolona
Aberdeen
Grenada
West Point
Greenville
Greenwood
Winona
Starkville
Columbus
Lexington
Macon
Durant
Yazoo City
Canton
Meridian
Vicksburg
Jackson
Enterprise
Port Gibson
Crystal Springs
Hazlehurst
Wesson
Natchez
Brookhaven
Summit
McComb
Hattiesburg
Gloster
Biloxi

RAILROADS
1895

MODERN PERIOD

Since the end of the Civil War, Mississippi political leaders and newspapermen had glorified the new age which, according to the leaders of the day, the people of the state were already in or were about to enter. In fact, the institutions and ideas dominating the Mississippi scene in 1890 were hardly different from those characterizing the state two generations earlier in 1830. Mississippians earned the same livelihood, farmed the same crops, and lived in the same places that they had sixty years earlier. The slavery system had been destroyed by the Civil War, but the status of Mississippi's blacks had changed little. Economically, politically, and socially, the Negro in 1890 enjoyed only those rights which the minority chose to give him.

In 1890, Mississippi's economy was still overwhelmingly agricultural and based on only one chief money crop—cotton. The state's economic fortunes rose and fell with the price of cotton, as they had since 1830. The long-awaited trend toward crop diversification was still nearly two generations away. In addition, more and more of Mississippi's farms were tilled by sharecroppers, a system which had been developed after the Civil War as a means of

dealing with the newly freed slaves. Yet by 1890 more and more sharecroppers were whites, the former small independent farmers who were losing their lands because of the combined pressures of debt, low cotton prices, and one-crop farming.

Demographic patterns in Mississippi also were essentially the same in 1890 as in 1830. In 1830 the population of the state was overwhelmingly rural and agrarian. It was the same in 1890. In the 1830s the bulk of Mississippi's people lived in the southwestern, central, and northwestern counties. Although by 1890 some population growth had occurred in the Piney Woods and the coastal counties, central and northern Mississippi still dominated the politics and had the highest density population of the state.

Slavery became an institution in Mississippi in the 1830s when the Indian lands in northern Mississippi were opened and cotton agriculture subsequently boomed. In that decade alone Mississippi's slave population soared nearly 200 percent. By 1890 there were about six blacks for every four whites in Mississippi's population. Although slavery had disappeared by 1890, it only gave way to political emasculation, segregation, and the economic oppression of share-

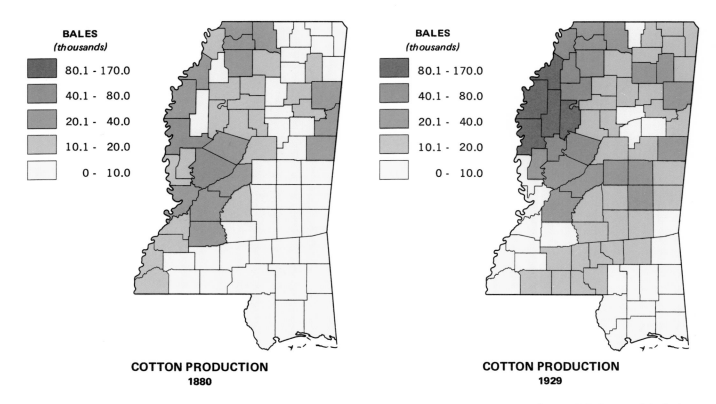

BALES
(thousands)

80.1 - 170.0
40.1 - 80.0
20.1 - 40.0
10.1 - 20.0
0 - 10.0

COTTON PRODUCTION
1880

BALES
(thousands)

80.1 - 170.0
40.1 - 80.0
20.1 - 40.0
10.1 - 20.0
0 - 10.0

COTTON PRODUCTION
1929

Source: U.S. Census of Agriculture

46

cropping for Mississippi's blacks. Hence the racial situation had changed only in name.

Populism, a movement which grew out of the small farmer's grievance toward low prices, unresponsive state government, and the exploitative characteristics of sharecropping, produced some demands for reform. Among these were the regulation of big business, inflation of the currency by the coinage of silver, a graduated income tax, federal credit for the farmers, and direct election of United States senators. Although they failed in achieving any deep change in the basic institutions of the state, the Populists voiced their discontent and showed that things need not always remain the same.

The Populists' third-party labors did have some effect. In the first two decades of the twentieth century their efforts invaded the dominant Democractic party, and produced some significant social and political reform. Personified by such reform leaders as Governor James K. Vardaman and Theodore G. Bilbo, Mississippians entered into the Progressive era. It was, however, "Progressivism for whites only." Beginning with Vardaman's administration (1904–08) and ending with the first Bilbo administration (1916–

20), a spate of legislation altered significantly the economic, political, and social face of the state. The direct primary election law replaced the old convention method of nominating party candidates. Tax equalization and greater support for public education pleased the small hill farmers. Governor Vardaman ended the inhumane and corrupt system of leasing state convicts to private individuals and established state penal farms.

Despite the reforms advocated by the Populists and those accomplished by the Progressives, Mississippians entered the 1920s solidified into the rigid social controls of segregation. Blacks still outnumbered whites. Mississippi remained predominantly rural, agrarian, and unindustrialized.

If the 1920s produced little progress, the 1930s were years of unrelenting disaster for Mississippians. By 1932 cotton sold for five cents a pound and almost one of every ten Mississippi farms went under the auctioneer's hammer in that year alone. The Depression proved a great affliction for Mississippians. The national relief programs of the New Deal had limited effect in what remained a nineteenth-century state with a nineteenth-century economy, but some impact

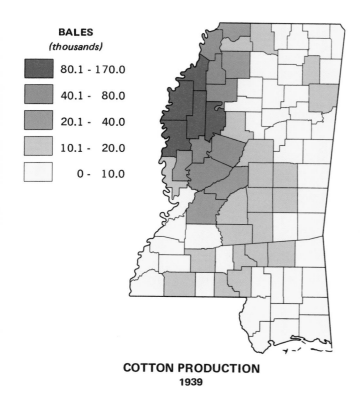

BALES
(thousands)

- 80.1 - 170.0
- 40.1 - 80.0
- 20.1 - 40.0
- 10.1 - 20.0
- 0 - 10.0

COTTON PRODUCTION
1939

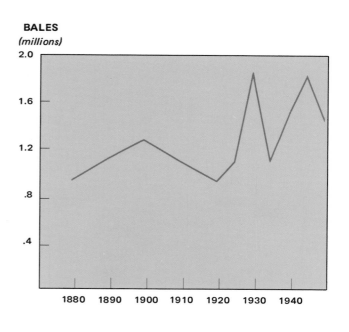

BALES
(millions)

COTTON PRODUCTION
1879-1949

Source: U.S. Census of Agriculture

was felt. Many rural farmers obtained their first electric lights because of the REA (Rural Electrification Authority), and some were able to buy their first farm machinery with federal benefit payments under the AAA (Agricultural Adjustment Act).

Yet perhaps the most lasting effect of the Depression was to point up dramatically and irrefutably the grinding effects of one-crop agriculture based on sharecropping and the necessity of "balancing agriculture with industry," as Governor Hugh L. White phrased it. It was out of that realization and the efforts of Governor White in 1936 that the first serious, planned attempt to industrialize Mississippi's economy grew.

The BAWI plan (Balance Agriculture with Industry) provided the mechanics which the state and local governments could use to attract industry. Under its provisions local governments could issue bonds to build plants, which in turn were leased to industries. Such benefits coupled with tax exemptions began to pay immediate dividends. Among the first to take advantage of this innovative program was the Ingalls Shipbuilding Corporation, established in Pascagoula in 1938.

But the changes wrought between 1890 and 1940 were largely superficial. "King Cotton" still sat on his throne. The mule and the sharecropper were still ubiquitous, and segregation still kept Mississippi blacks in the social and economic backseat.

World War II was the catalyst for change in the state of Mississippi. The four years of war opened Mississippi to the outside world, and for the first time introduced the people of the state to the fruits of prosperity. The war inevitably set in motion forces which over the last generation have altered fundamentally the institutions under which Mississippians live. The long-sought dream of agricultural diversification was finally achieved. The years since 1945 marked the transition of Mississippi from an agrarian society to an industrial and commercial economy.

The agricultural revolution after World War II was sudden and complete. King Cotton was deposed by a host of new crops or old ones which had been revitalized. Soybeans, beef cattle, poultry, and rice supplanted cotton in much of the state. Only in the Delta is cotton grown in abundance today. The drive toward agricultural mechanization was an equally fundamental change, and it produced radical changes in

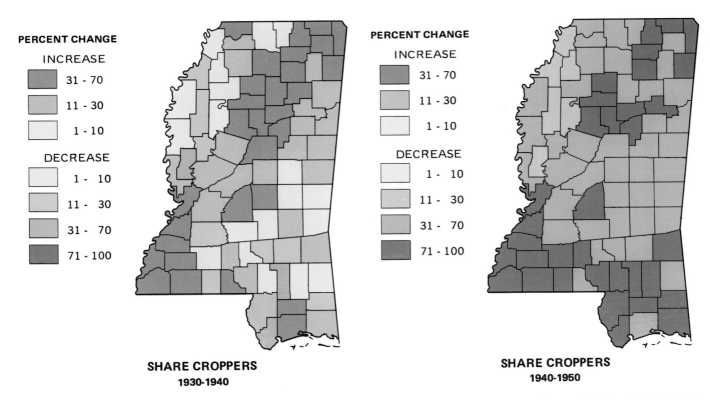

PERCENT CHANGE

INCREASE

31 - 70

11 - 30

1 - 10

DECREASE

1 - 10

11 - 30

31 - 70

71 - 100

SHARE CROPPERS
1930-1940

PERCENT CHANGE

INCREASE

31 - 70

11 - 30

1 - 10

DECREASE

1 - 10

11 - 30

31 - 70

71 - 100

SHARE CROPPERS
1940-1950

Source: U.S. Census of Agriculture

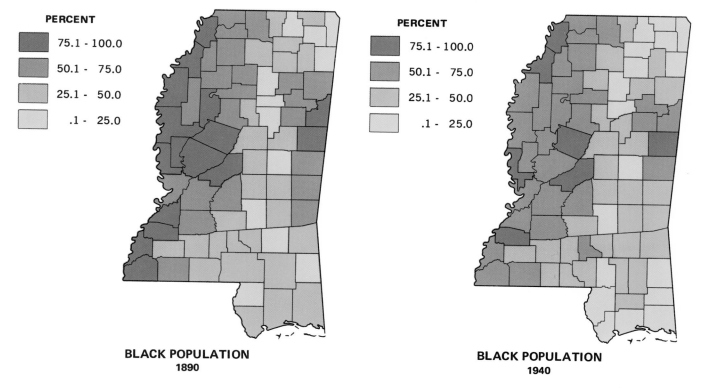

Source: U.S. Census of Population

PERCENT

75.1 - 100.0
50.1 - 75.0
25.1 - 50.0
 .1 - 25.0

BLACK POPULATION
1890

PERCENT

75.1 - 100.0
50.1 - 75.0
25.1 - 50.0
 .1 - 25.0

BLACK POPULATION
1940

the way farming was conducted. Mechanized agriculture made inevitable ever greater centralization and, hence, spelled the end of sharecropping. No longer could farming be considered a way of life; it had become a commercial enterprise. Thousands of agricultural jobs disappeared. In 1940 more than one of every two jobs was in the agricultural sector. Twenty years later fewer than one in each five was in agriculture. Not only did cotton lose its throne to other products, but agriculture lost its primacy in Mississippi's economy.

After the second world war Mississippians saw industrialization finally became a reality. In 1965, for the first time in the state's history, manufacturing employment was greater than agricultural employment. In 1947, slightly more than 75,000 Mississippians were employed in 1,982 manufacturing plants. In 1967, more than 160,000 Mississippians worked in nearly 3,000 manufacturing establishments. Although the state is still not heavily industrialized by comparison with some other states, Mississippi's industrial growth over the last two decades represents a dramatic and irreversible break with her agrarian past.

It was not without great emotion and some violence

that the last of Mississippi's ties with its own past were broken. Segregation was substituted in the late nineteenth century for the social controls over blacks which slavery had afforded. Strengthened and crystallized into law through the first four decades of the twentieth century, segregation came under attack in the 1950s and 1970s from the black-led civil rights movement and the federal government. Mississippians did not easily relinquish their last institutional tie with the past. Yet Mississippi's blacks enjoyed by 1970 more freedom, economic prosperity, and opportunity than ever before.

One cannot conclude that the past is altogether dead in Mississippi. Yet one by one in the last three decades all of the basic themes of the previous hundred years have been altered—King Cotton and agrarianism, sharecropping and segregation, a feeling of alienation and insulation from the world outside. In their places by 1970 have come modern transportation and communication, industrialization, recession of the race question, agricultural diversification —institutions not unlike those in other states.

John R. Skates, Jr.

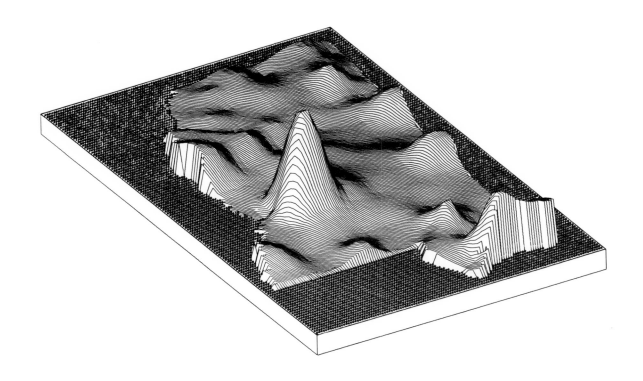

TOTAL POPULATION

POPULATION AND SOCIAL INSTITUTIONS

Life in Mississippi is an interweaving of many complementing factors. Mississippi is its people, and their varied lifestyles are reflected in the social institutions of the state.

Since statehood in 1817, Mississippi has experienced periods of population gain and population loss. Though traditionally a black state, Mississippi in the 1960s and 1970s has noted an ever decreasing percentage of blacks in its population. Other recent population trends include a decreasing birth rate, large out-migration, and an increasing number of urban residents.

The rise of manufacturing in Mississippi has corresponded with an increase in per capita personal income. Although mean personal income still ranks below the national average, the gap is closing rapidly, with the two projected to converge by 1992.

Government at the state level has a bicameral legislature, an executive branch, and a judicial branch. The executive arm of government is composed of a number of agencies and departments; the judicial division has a hierarchy of courts ranging from state to local levels. Municipal and county governments operate typical subordinate divisions. Mississippi supports numerous planning and development agencies, both public and private, which deal with economic programs and are often concerned with some aspect of land or water use.

Education at all levels in Mississippi continues to improve. The Civil Rights Act of 1964 forged a new direction for statewide education, but the long-range effects of that abrupt alteration of the traditional educational system are yet to be seen.

Another area of progressive development in Mississippi is that of physical and mental health. Regional and local hospitals are easily accessible to the citizenry, and public health clinics are ubiquitous. The ratio of doctors, dentists, and nurses to population is good and improving. In many areas of health care the state ranks above the national average.

Ralph D. Cross
Jesse O. McKee

POPULATION CHARACTERISTICS

POPULATION GROWTH

Mississippi became a territory in 1798 and attained statehood in 1817. In 1820, the first state census recorded a population of 75,448; by 1830, it had increased to 136,621. During the 1830s, often considered "flush times" in Mississippi history, the state's population increased rapidly; by 1840 it totaled 375,651 persons, an increase of 175 percent over the preceding decade. Population continued to grow, and by 1860, on the eve of the Civil War, the state's residents totaled 791,305. The 1860s was a period of small population gain. During the 1870s, however, Mississippi had its last large absolute increase, when the population rose from 827,922 to 1,131,597 persons, a growth of 36.7 percent. After 1880, the state's number of residents rose slowly, leveled off, then began to decline.

By the time of the 1920 census, statistics showed that Mississippi had experienced its first absolute loss in population. Many scholars attribute the loss in part to the influx of the boll weevil, a decline in cotton prices, and increased farm mechanization—variables which provided a "push" for persons to migrate out of the state. Job opportunities in the North, resulting from a growth in industrial production and a decline in the flow of immigrants from Europe during World War I, provided the "pull" for these southern migrants. By 1930, state population figures showed a slight gain; a decrease was not evident again until 1950 when the census indicated a two-tenths of one percent (.2%) loss. Population continued to decline through the 1950s, including the year 1960. During the 1960s the downward trend reversed itself, and population rose from 2,178,141 persons recorded in the 1960 census to a total of 2,216,912 in 1970. If present indicators are accurate, the 1970s will be another growth decade for the state.

Historically, the geographical centers of state population have changed during the course of economic development. In 1820, the state's population core was located in the southwestern portion of the state near Natchez. Forty years later, the population was still concentrated around Natchez, but other clusters of people had arisen—in the northeast around Columbus, in areas along the Big Black and Yazoo rivers centered mainly on Vicksburg and Jackson, and in the northern tier of counties along the Tennessee border. Natchez continued to be the largest urban center, and in 1860 had a population of 6,612. By 1870 Vicksburg had replaced Natchez as the largest urban center in the state. It was not until after 1880 that the Delta region and the southeastern

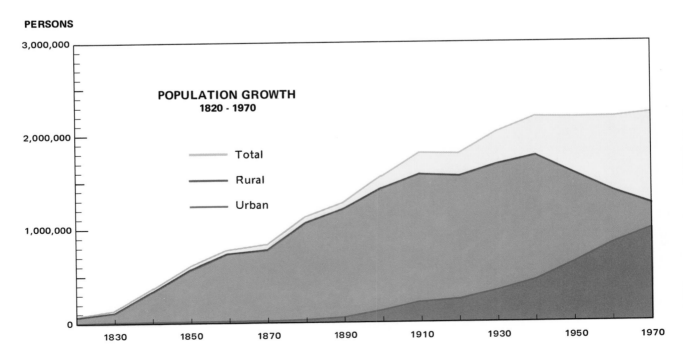

PERSONS

POPULATION GROWTH
1820 - 1970

Total
Rural
Urban

Source: U.S. Census of Population, 1960

52

portion of the state started to attract and develop a large amount of settlement.

POPULATION DISTRIBUTION

Hinds and Harrison counties rank first and second as the two most populated counties in Mississippi with 214,973 and 134,582 persons respectively. No other county in the state exceeds a population of 100,000. Jackson County on the coast, Lauderdale County in the eastern part of the state, and Washington County in the Delta region comprise the next most populated set of counties. The remaining counties with significant populations are located in the Delta, in northeastern Mississippi, and scattered throughout the southern parts of the state. The city of Jackson within Hinds County, Warren County, and Rankin County form the central core of the state's inhabitants. The two least populated counties are Issaquena (2,737 persons) and Benton (7,505).

POPULATION DENSITY

Crude population density refers to the number of people occupying a specific areal unit of land. To some extent, it is a measurement used to assess overpopulation or underpopulation in a given geographic region. The density is obtained by dividing an area's total population by its total acres or square miles. The average density for Mississippi is 46.9 persons per square mile, which is lower than the national average of 54 people per square mile.

In Mississippi, the most densely populated counties are Hinds (245.4 persons per square mile) and Harrison (203.4 persons per square mile). Forrest, Jackson, and Lee counties follow with 123.6, 119.5, and 101.4 inhabitants per square mile respectively. The counties with smallest population densities are Issaquena and Greene with 6.6 and 11.7 persons per square mile respectively.

POPULATION CHANGE

The term "population change," as used in this section, refers to change in the number of persons living in Mississippi between the census of 1960 and 1970. The change is determined by calculating the difference between the crude birth rate and crude death rate of the state, and the variance between the number of out-migrants and the number of in-migrants. In 1960 the population of Mississippi was

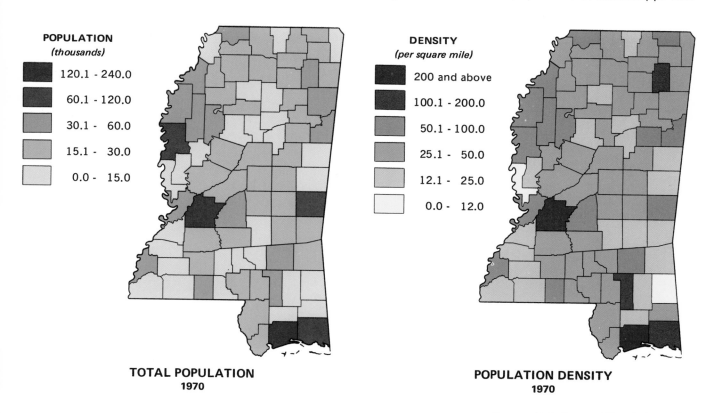

POPULATION
(thousands)

120.1 - 240.0
60.1 - 120.0
30.1 - 60.0
15.1 - 30.0
0.0 - 15.0

TOTAL POPULATION
1970

DENSITY
(per square mile)

200 and above
100.1 - 200.0
50.1 - 100.0
25.1 - 50.0
12.1 - 25.0
0.0 - 12.0

POPULATION DENSITY
1970

Source: U. S. Census of Population, 1970

2,178,141 persons; by 1970 the population had increased to 2,216,912 persons, showing a statewide gain of 1.8 percent.

Of the state's eighty-two counties, thirty-four gained population during the decade of 1960–70. The two counties with the largest percentage increase were Jackson (58.5 percent) and De Soto (50.2 percent). Gains in industrial employment have contributed substantially to the increase in Jackson County population. De Soto County's close proximity to Memphis, Tennessee, a rapidly growing city, influenced its population expansion. In the same decade, the counties of Rankin, Pearl River, and Hancock experienced 20–30 percent gains.

Not only did Jackson County have the largest percentage increase in population, but it also had the largest absolute gain—from 55,522 people in 1960 to 87,975 in 1970, an increment of 32,453 persons. Hinds County ranked second with an increase of 27,928 inhabitants (from 287,045 to 214,973).

Most of the population losses occurred in the Delta region of the state. Tunica County showed the largest percent decrease in population (−29.5 percent),

followed by Quitman (−24.4 percent), Humphreys (−23.5 percent), and Issaquena (−23.5 percent). Much of the decrease in this region of Mississippi can be attributed to out-migration of black residents.

NET MIGRATION

Net migration is the difference between the number of out-migrants and in-migrants. The Delta region, together with the counties of Wilkinson, Kemper, and Noxubee, had the highest amount of out-migration. Washington and Bolivar counties in the Delta sustained the largest losses with 21,023 and 15,799 persons respectively. On a percentage basis, Tunica County had the greatest rate of net-migration loss— 48.9 percent.

Only seven counties gained in net-migration. Jackson County led with a gain of 19,000 in-migrants; De Soto County was second with an increase of 6,735. Although the majority of Mississippi counties experienced a loss in population through out-migration, particularly Delta counties and other counties with large numbers of blacks, the downward trend ought to lessen in the 1970s.

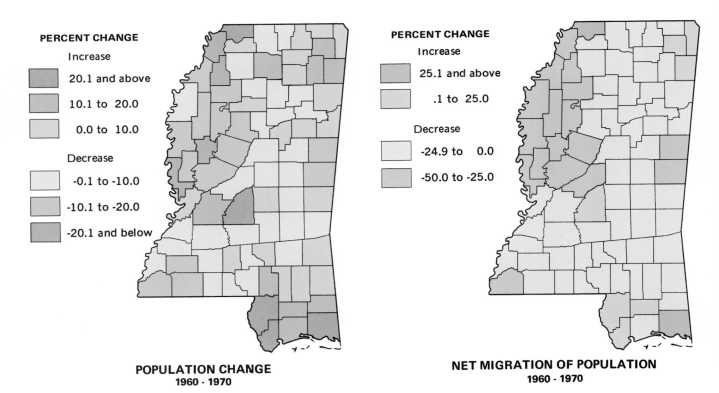

PERCENT CHANGE

Increase

20.1 and above

10.1 to 20.0

0.0 to 10.0

Decrease

-0.1 to -10.0

-10.1 to -20.0

-20.1 and below

POPULATION CHANGE
1960 - 1970

Source: U.S. Census of Population, 1970

PERCENT CHANGE

Increase

25.1 and above

.1 to 25.0

Decrease

-24.9 to 0.0

-50.0 to -25.0

NET MIGRATION OF POPULATION
1960 - 1970

Source: Rand McNally, Atlas and Marketing Guide, 1973

POPULATION AND LAND AREA

County	Area (Sq. Miles)	Total Number (1970)	Percent change 1960–70	Percent of Population Urban (1970)	County	Area (Sq. Miles)	Total Number (1970)	Percent change 1960–70	Percent of Population Urban (1970)
State	47,296	2,216,912	1.8	44.5	Leflore	592	42,111	−10.7	53.2
Adams	449	37,293	−1.2	52.8	Lincoln	586	26,198	−2.1	40.8
Alcorn	405	27,179	7.5	42.6	Lowndes	508	49,700	6.6	60.1
Amite	729	13,763	−11.6	—	Madison	727	29,737	−9.6	35.3
Attala	724	19,570	−8.3	37.1	Marion	550	22,871	−1.8	33.2
Benton	412	7,505	−2.8	—	Marshall	710	24,027	−1.9	23.8
Bolivar	923	49,409	−9.3	42.6	Monroe	769	34,043	0.3	39.3
Calhoun	575	14,623	−8.3	—	Montgomery	403	12,918	−3.0	42.7
Carrol	637	9,397	−15.9	—	Neshoba	568	20,802	−0.6	30.2
Chickasaw	506	15,805	−0.5	34.0	Newton	580	18,983	−2.7	18.7
Choctaw	417	8,440	0.2	—	Noxubee	695	14,288	−15.1	18.3
Claiborne	489	10,086	−7.0	25.7	Oktibbeha	454	28,752	9.8	55.5
Clarke	697	15,049	−8.8	18.0	Panola	693	26,829	−6.8	14.1
Clay	414	18,840	−0.5	46.3	Pearl River	828	27,802	24.1	37.6
Coahoma	569	40,447	−12.5	53.6	Perry	653	9,065	3.7	—
Copiah	780	24,749	−8.5	35.4	Pike	409	31,756	−9.4	37.7
Covington	416	14,002	2.7	—	Pontotoc	501	17,363	0.8	19.9
De Soto	476	35,885	50.2	24.9	Prentiss	418	20,133	12.2	29.3
Forrest	468	37,849	9.7	77.8	Quitman	412	15,888	−24.4	16.4
Franklin	568	8,011	−13.7	—	Rankin	775	43,933	28.0	28.1
George	481	12,459	12.3	—	Scott	615	21,369	0.9	31.6
Greene	728	8,545	2.1	—	Sharkey	436	8,937	−16.8	—
Grenada	431	19,854	7.8	50.1	Simpson	587	19,947	−3.5	14.9
Hancock	482	17,387	23.8	56.7	Smith	642	13,561	−3.2	—
Harrison	585	134,582	12.6	83.0	Stone	448	8,101	13.5	37.0
Hinds	876	214,973	14.9	83.9	Sunflower	694	37,047	−19.0	31.2
Holmes	769	23,120	−14.7	23.8	Tallahatchie	644	19,338	−19.7	14.6
Humphreys	421	14,601	−23.5	21.5	Tate	405	18,544	3.2	22.9
Issaquena	414	2,737	−23.5	—	Tippah	464	15,852	5.0	22.0
Itawamba	541	16,847	11.7	17.2	Tishomingo	443	14,940	7.6	—
Jackson	736	87,975	58.5	71.2	Tunica	458	11,854	−29.5	—
Jasper	683	15,994	−5.4	—	Union	422	19,096	1.0	33.7
Jefferson	521	9,295	−8.4	—	Walthall	403	12,500	−7.5	—
Jefferson Davis	414	12,936	−4.5	—	Warren	581	44,981	6.6	56.6
Jones	702	56,357	−5.3	51.1	Washington	734	70,581	−10.2	69.3
Kemper	757	10,233	−16.6	—	Wayne	827	16,650	2.4	26.2
Lafayette	668	24,181	13.2	57.3	Webster	416	10,047	−3.0	—
Lamar	500	15,209	11.2	1.9	Wilkinson	674	11,099	−16.1	—
Lauderdale	708	67,087	—	67.2	Winston	606	18,406	−4.4	36.0
Lawrence	433	11,137	9.0	—	Yalobusha	488	11,915	−4.7	27.6
Leake	586	17,085	−8.4	17.7	Yazoo	938	27,304	−13.7	39.5
Lee	455	46,148	13.7	44.4					

AGE STRUCTURE

The age pyramid is utilized to graphically represent age structure of a population by sex and number. Under ideal conditions the number of persons in each designated age group will be fewer than the preceding age group; therefore, the ideal model of an age structure for a population tends to take the shape of a pyramid when represented graphically. However, a high degree of symmetry is usually not present, because such events as wars, famines, baby booms, economic depressions, and out- or in-migration can affect the pyramid profile. Moreover, since females tend to live longer than males, females are inclined to predominate in the elderly age group.

The age pyramid for Mississippi reflects several interesting facts. First, the number of live births has decreased during the last few years in conjunction with national trends; consequently, the number of persons in the 0–4 and 5–9 age groups are smaller than in the 10–14 age groups. Secondly, the sharp decline in Mississippians aged 20–39 is indicative of the relatively large amount of out-migration the state has experienced in the last twenty to forty years; and, finally, the 40–75 age group is symmetrical in shape.

According to the 1970 census, the sex ratio in Mississippi was 94 males per 100 females. This figure probably results from the fact that basically Mississippi has had a larger out-migration of males than females, and that females tend to live longer than males —thus, females dominate the elderly age group and distort the sex ratio. Sex ratios below 90 and over 110 are usually considered unbalanced.

A large proportion of Mississippians aged 18 and under reside in the Delta region. Not surprisingly this geographical area of the state also has a high fertility rate. A high fertility rate, to be sure, is often influenced by such social and economic indicators as low educational attainment, a high percentage of rural population, a large percent of persons with incomes less than poverty level, and a small number of persons engaged in manufacturing. All of these factors are prevalent in the Delta.

The extreme northeastern section of Mississippi has the lowest percentage of population in the under-18 category. However, many of these counties have a high percentage of people in the non-reproductive years of 65 and over. Counties with a high proportion of persons over 65 years of age show a direct positive

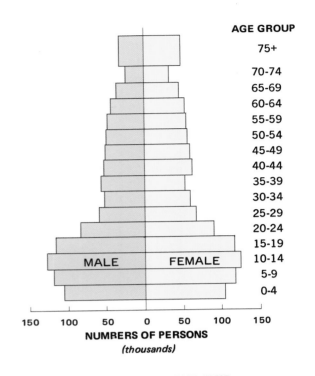

POPULATION AGE PYRAMID

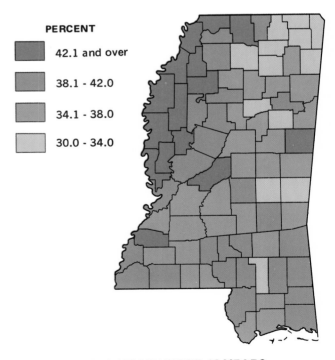

PERCENT

42.1 and over

38.1 - 42.0

34.1 - 38.0

30.0 - 34.0

POPULATION UNDER 18 YEARS

Source: U.S. Census of Population, 1970

correlation with rural areas of the state. Basically, the more economically progressive counties—Jackson, Harrison, Hinds, De Soto, Lowndes, and Lee—have a lower percentage of persons over 65.

BLACK POPULATION

In the first Mississippi census of 1820, the state had a total population of 75,448, composed of 33,272 blacks and 42,176 whites. Following the Indian Removal Act of 1832, Mississippi's population increased rapidly due to the arrival of white immigrants and importation of black slaves; by 1840, blacks outnumbered whites 196,577 to 179,074.

Following the Civil War some blacks moved to the North, but the first large migration of blacks from Mississippi did not occur until the period between 1915 and 1925. The black northward migration has been rather continuous since that time, although there is some evidence that it is ebbing. This high out-migration of blacks in the past has been reflected in the changing ratio of white to non-white population composition of the state. For example, 52.3 percent of the population in Mississippi in 1920 was non-white. By 1940, the non-white population fell to 49.3 percent. In 1970, the non-white population was approximately 39 percent, and blacks accounted for 36.8 percent.

In the early days of Mississippi four factors were inseparable—good soil, planters, cotton production, and Negro slaves. Most blacks were therefore located in the better farming areas of the state. These areas were around Natchez, the river valleys and bluff hills to the north of Natchez, the Black Prairie extension of the Alabama Black Belt, and later the Delta region. A similar pattern is reflected in 1974, as indicated by the large number of blacks in Adams County, the Delta region, and the Black Prairie centered in Lowndes County. With increased urbanization and job opportunities available in Hinds, De Soto, and the Gulf Coast counties, a recent significant in-migration of blacks into these areas has occurred. The poorer soils and hillier topographic areas of Mississippi traditionally have not supported agriculture and have had a lower number of blacks.

The counties with the largest number of blacks are Hinds (84,064), Washington (38,460), and Bolivar (30,338). The counties of Coahoma (26,013), Leflore (24,374), Harrison (22,743), and Lauderdale (20,-

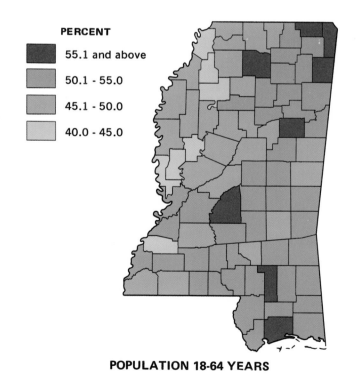

PERCENT

- 55.1 and above
- 50.1 - 55.0
- 45.1 - 50.0
- 40.0 - 45.0

POPULATION 18-64 YEARS

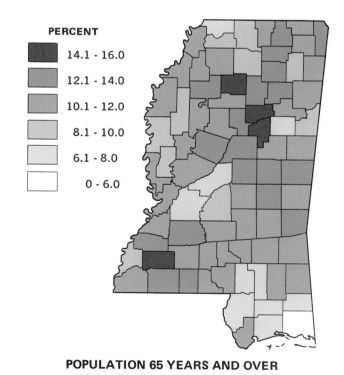

PERCENT

- 14.1 - 16.0
- 12.1 - 14.0
- 10.1 - 12.0
- 8.1 - 10.0
- 6.1 - 8.0
- 0 - 6.0

POPULATION 65 YEARS AND OVER

Source: U.S. Census of Population, 1970

630) all have black populations exceeding 20,000. The highest percentages of black in relation to total county populations are found in Jefferson (75.3 percent), Claiborne (74.6 percent), and Tunica (72.7 percent) counties. Bolivar, Coahoma, Holmes, Humphreys, Issaquena, Madison, Marshall, Noxubee, Sharkey, Sunflower, Tallahatchie, and Wilkinson counties all have black populations exceeding 60 percent.

SELECTED MINORITIES

Minority groups, other than blacks, have not been prevalent in Mississippi for various social, economic, and political reasons. The Choctaw Indians are the second largest minority group in Mississippi today.

In 1970, seventy-nine of the eighty-two counties of the state reported Indian residents. The exceptions were Greene, Prentiss, and Webster coutnies. The largest tribe—the Choctaws—numbered over 3,000 inhabitants in the state. The majority of the Choctaws resided in seven communities, in three counties. The largest concentration was recorded in the community of Pearl River outside of Philadelphia in Neshoba County. The three counties with largest Choctaw con-

centrations, in rank order, include Neshoba (1,603), Leake (535), and Newton (432).

A few Chinese migrated to Mississippi and settled in the Delta region about 1870. Some of these Orientals came to Mississippi as farm laborers; but many others, upon entering Mississippi, quickly turned to the grocery business, selling to urban and plantation blacks. The Chinese appear to have adjusted to life in the Delta and have maintained a strong cultural identification.

RURAL FARM AND NON-FARM POPULATIONS

According to the Bureau of Census, persons living in centers with less than 2,500 inhabitants are considered rural residents and are classified as either farm or non-farm. Those classified as rural farm dwellers are defined either as persons living on farms of ten or more acres with sales from farm products amounting to $50 or more, or as persons living on farms of less than ten acres with sales of $250 and above.

The counties with the highest percentage of rural farm populations in 1970 were located in the Delta

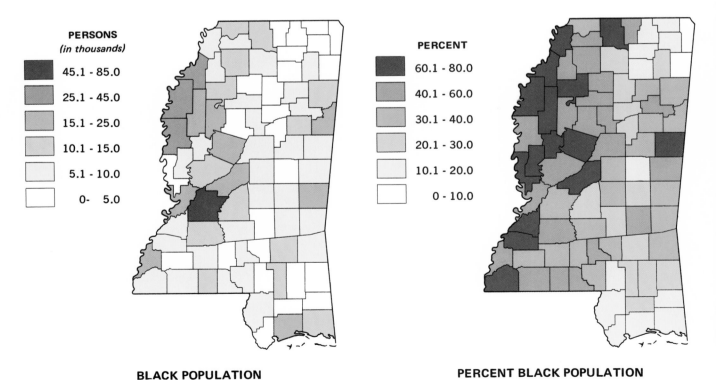

BLACK POPULATION

PERSONS
(in thousands)

45.1 - 85.0
25.1 - 45.0
15.1 - 25.0
10.1 - 15.0
5.1 - 10.0
0- 5.0

PERCENT BLACK POPULATION

PERCENT

60.1 - 80.0
40.1 - 60.0
30.1 - 40.0
20.1 - 30.0
10.1 - 20.0
0 - 10.0

Source: U.S. Census of Population, 1970

region and included Tunica (51.6 percent), Tallahatchie (45.5 percent), and Sharkey (40.1 percent).
Other counties with large rural populations are scattered throughout the state, although some dominantly
rural counties do occur in eastcentral Mississippi.
Some 55.5 percent of the state's population was considered rural in 1970; rural non-farm inhabitants accounted for 43.7 percent and rural farm dwellers for
11.8 percent of that total. Only 5.2 percent of the rural
non-farm population live in communities having between 1,000 and 2,499 residents, and 2.7 percent in
places of less than 1,000 population.

URBANIZATION

In 1970, 44.5 percent of Mississippi's population
was classified as urban. This was a substantial increase since 1960, when only 37.7 percent was classified urban.

The two most urbanized counties are Hinds and
Harrison with 83.9 percent and 83.0 percent of their
respective residents classified as urban. These two
are followed by Forrest (77.8 percent) and Jackson
(71.2 percent) counties. Twelve additional counties
are listed as having more than 50 percent urban pop-

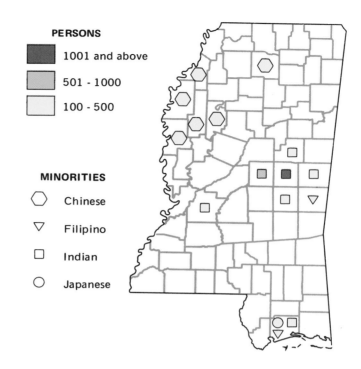

SELECTED MINORITIES

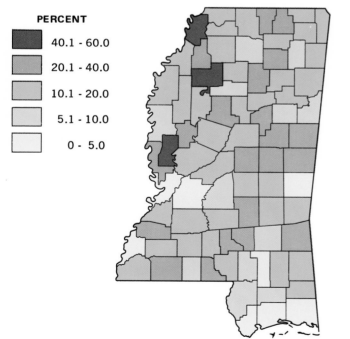

RURAL FARM POPULATION

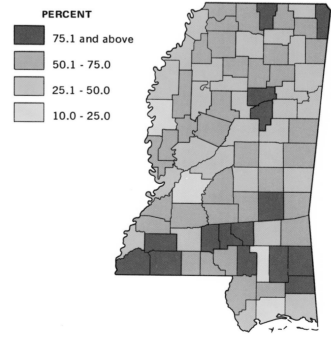

RURAL NON-FARM POPULATION

Source: U.S. Census of Population, 1970

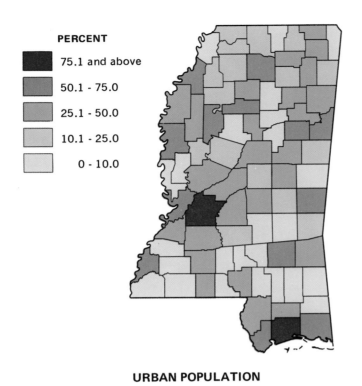

PERCENT

■ 75.1 and above

50.1 - 75.0

25.1 - 50.0

10.1 - 25.0

0 - 10.0

URBAN POPULATION

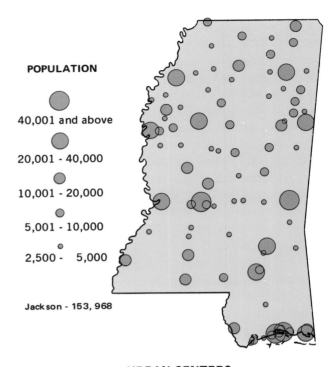

POPULATION

40,001 and above

20,001 - 40,000

10,001 - 20,000

5,001 - 10,000

2,500 - 5,000

Jackson - 153,968

URBAN CENTERS

Source: U.S. Census of Population, 1970

ulations; in contrast, a total of twenty-three Mississippi counties are classed as 100 percent rural.

Mississippi has two SMSAs (Standard Metropolitan Statistical Areas). SMSAs are bounded by county lines and are centered upon metropolitan areas having a population in excess of 50,000. The Jackson SMSA, including Hinds and Rankin counties, is the state's largest. The other SMSA includes only Harrison County and is centered upon Gulfport–Biloxi.

There are eighty-three urban centers in Mississippi with populations exceeding 2,500 persons. The breakdown of these centers is as follows:

Number of Urban Centers	Population per Center
36	2,500–4,999
23	5,000–9,999
15	10,000–24,999
8	25,000–49,999
1	over 50,000

Jackson serves as the state's capital and is also the largest city, with 153,968 inhabitants in 1970. Three of the eight cities having populations between 25,000 and 49,999 are located on the coast; two are situated along the Mississippi River; and the remain-

ing three are in the eastern and southern sections of the state.

Of the nine largest cities in Mississippi, three lost population during the decade 1960–70—Vicksburg (−12.6 percent), Meridian (−8.7 percent), and Greenville (−4.5 percent). Three other cities experienced gains of more than 10 percent—Pascagoula (58.9 percent), Gulfport (35.1 percent), and Biloxi (10.1 percent).

The fastest growing city in the state, percentagewise, during the 1960–70 decade was Moss Point, which increased from 6,631 in 1960 to 19,321 inhabitants in 1970, an increase of 191.4 percent. Other urban centers experiencing growths of more than 100 percent since 1960 included Waveland (181 percent), Oxford (162.1 percent), D'Iberville (142.5 percent), Clinton (110.8 percent), and West Gulfport (110.5 percent). In contrast, the urban centers with the greatest percentage of population loss were Belzoni (−24.0 percent), Pass Christian (−23.2 percent), and Natchez (−17.2 percent).

Jesse O. McKee

PERSONAL INCOME

Of the several means of measuring economic growth, personal income (income of residents from all sources) is about as significant an indicator of overall economic activity as is available. Personal income series consists of private and government wage, salary payments in cash and in kind, farm and non-farm proprietors' incomes, interest, net rents, dividends, and transfer payments, less personal contributions before social insurance. Personal income is measured before the deduction of personal income tax or other personal taxes. In Mississippi, this income rose approximately 7 percent in 1970, about equal to the national increase of 7.5 percent.

Notwithstanding the recent surge of activity, Mississippi does have economic problems. In per capita income (total personal income divided by total population), Mississippi ranks lowest among the six states of the southeastern region—Alabama, Florida, Georgia, Louisiana, Tennessee, and Mississippi. Mississippi's average income of $2,575 per person in 1970 was substantially below the nation's $3,921 and the southeastern region's $3,204.

Since the 1940s, per capita personal income has uniformly increased in the United States, in the southeastern region, and in Mississippi. In 1950, per capita personal income was $755 in Mississippi; by 1960, it had increased to $1,206, and in 1970 it was $2,575— a total increase of $1,820 over the twenty years. (Since total and per capita personal income are here measured in current dollars, "corrections" for changes in the real dollar value would lower the increase considerably.) The figures for the southeastern region between 1950 and 1970 show a gain from $1,019 to $3,204, an increase of $2,185. The nation's per capita income in the same period rose from $1,496 to $3,921, or by exactly $2,425. Therefore, impressive as the sustained growth of per capita income has been in Mississippi throughout this twenty-year period, many more years will pass before the state's per capita income approximates the national average. Nevertheless, in view of the fact that per capita personal income has risen from 50 percent of the national figure in 1950 to over 65 percent in 1970, it can be anticipated that a convergence of the state per capita income with the national average will occur.

The mean (average) income of families by counties in 1969 indicated a considerable degree of variance among areas of the state. The largest mean incomes, ranging from $9,451 to $9,837, were in

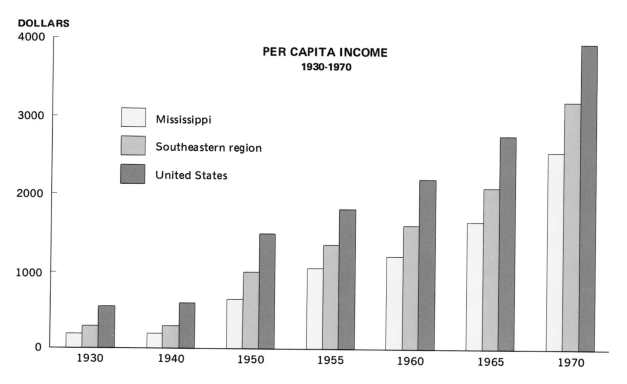

DOLLARS

PER CAPITA INCOME
1930-1970

- Mississippi
- Southeastern region
- United States

Source: U. S. Department of Commerce, 1972

Jefferson and Hinds counties respectively. Six Mississippi counties—Adams, De Soto, Harrison, Lee, Rankin, and Warren—had a mean family income of $8,000–9,000. Sixteen counties had a mean family income between $7,000 and $8,000; thirty counties were classified in the $6,000 to $7,000 class interval, and twenty-eight had a mean family income of $4,000 to $6,000. The mean income of families in the United States in 1969 was $10,577. The mean income of families in Mississippi, $7,292, was decidedly lower. No county in Mississippi equaled the national average family income.

Data concerning the mean income of all families and unrelated individuals who are members of households present figures that are lower than mean family income, since this information is obtained by dividing an aggregate personal income by the total number of persons (or families). In 1969 this average income figure was $6,116 for Mississippi. Jackson County was the only area in the state with a mean income ($8,597) for households in excess of $8,000. Six counties fell within the $7,000 to $8,000 range, and thirteen counties were classified in the $6,000 to

$7,000 category. Forty-three, or slightly more than 50 percent of Mississippi counties, had a mean income for families and for unrelated individuals of between $5,000 and $6,000. Nineteen counties registered in the $3,000 to $4,000 class interval.

Despite this growth, in the early 1970s a sizable minority of Mississippi's population remained poor. In 1969, over 35 percent of the state's population was below the poverty level, almost three times the national average. Poverty level is based on a definition formulated by the Social Security Administration. Annual cost-of-living adjustments are made in the poverty threshold based on changes in the Consumer Price Index. Other adjustments are made for family size, sex of family head, and age of individuals. The farm poverty index is 85 percent of the non-farm level to compensate for possible "nonmoney" forms of income, such as products grown and consumed on the farm. The average poverty level in 1969 for a non-farm family of four headed by a male was $3,745. Within Mississippi, 65 percent of the black population lived below the poverty level, whereas only 18 percent of the white persons were similarly classified in

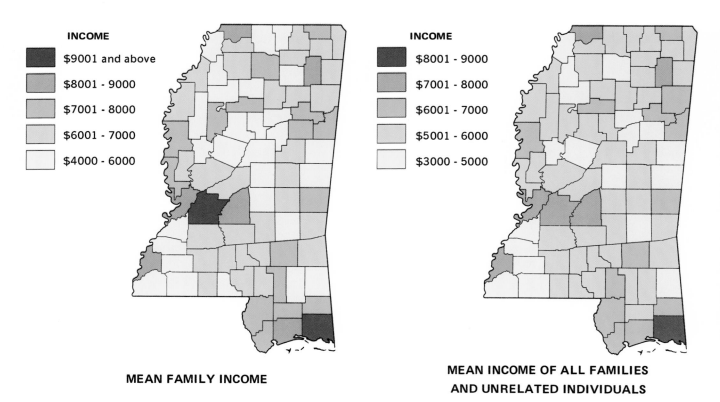

INCOME

$9001 and above

$8001 - 9000

$7001 - 8000

$6001 - 7000

$4000 - 6000

MEAN FAMILY INCOME

INCOME

$8001 - 9000

$7001 - 8000

$6001 - 7000

$5001 - 6000

$3000 - 5000

**MEAN INCOME OF ALL FAMILIES
AND UNRELATED INDIVIDUALS**

Source: U.S. Census of Population, 1970

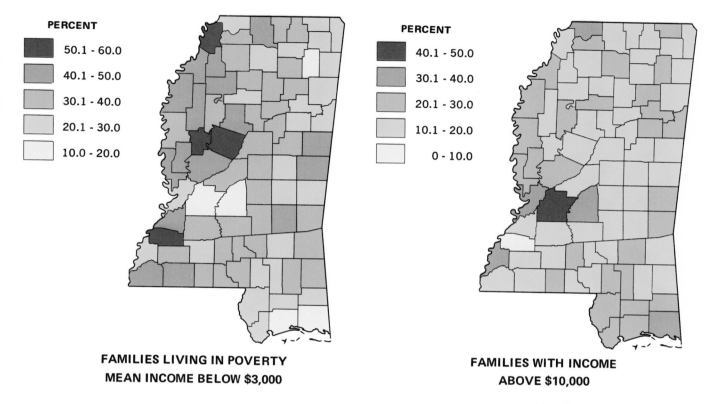

Source: U. S. Census of Population, 1970

PERCENT

50.1 - 60.0
40.1 - 50.0
30.1 - 40.0
20.1 - 30.0
10.0 - 20.0

FAMILIES LIVING IN POVERTY
MEAN INCOME BELOW $3,000

PERCENT

40.1 - 50.0
30.1 - 40.0
20.1 - 30.0
10.1 - 20.0
0 - 10.0

FAMILIES WITH INCOME
ABOVE $10,000

1969. Of the persons 65 years of age and older, 55 percent had incomes below poverty level.

In 1969, four counties—Holmes, Humphreys, Jefferson, and Tunica—showed 50 percent or more of their families living on a mean income of less than $3,000. In fifty-two counties 30 percent of the families lived below the poverty threshold, and thirty counties had 20 percent or less similarly classified. The Mississippi Delta, with a high density of black residents, had a high poverty index. In contrast, there was less poverty in the northeastern and southeastern sections of the state.

A noteworthy item about 1970 family incomes in the United States is the extraordinary increase of those in the $10,000-and-over category. Their numbers have been increasing much faster than the total number of family units. The bulk of this growth in Mississippi has occurred in the $10,000 to $25,000 subgroup. The 1969 census data indicated that 27 percent of all Mississippi families had incomes over $10,000, including 36 percent of the families inside central cities and 18 percent of the farm families. Hinds County ranked highest with 40 percent of its families having incomes above $10,000. Adams, De

Soto, Jackson, Rankin, and Warren counties had 30–40 percent of families with incomes above $10,000; twenty-eight other counties were in the 20–30 percent range, and forty-eight Mississippi counties, or 58 percent, were in the 10–20 percent class. One county, Jefferson, had but 9.2 percent of its families with incomes of $10,000 or greater.

Some indication of income and employment trends for particular segments of the state's economy is provided by the Mississippi Employment Security Commission. In 1969, covered employment (employment covered by the Unemployment Compensation Law) in Mississippi totaled 385,086 persons. Wages paid to this group came to $2 billion, for an average annual per capita wage of $5,326. This was a substantial increase over the 1967 and 1968 figures of $4,689 and $5,049 respectively. The largest employment gains were experienced in manufacturing industries, particularly in electrical machinery–equipment–supplies and in furniture. Lumber, textiles, and transportation equipment industries also recorded sizable gains.

Joseph H. Clements

POLITICAL STRUCTURE

Mississippi has a typical state government. It was designed by a convention in 1890, and contains the Jacksonian ideas that were popular at the time.

STATE GOVERNMENT

LEGISLATIVE BRANCH—The Legislature is bi-cameral, with a house of representatives numbering 122 members, and a senate with 52 members. A powerful speaker presides over the house and appoints all house committees. He is a member of the rules committee which can adjust the calendar or the schedule for debating bills. The lieutenant governor presides over the senate and is almost as influential as the speaker. He appoints most, but not all senate committees.

When the legislature was recently authorized by constitutional amendment to meet annually, it made a major effort at reform to speed legislative work and increase efficiency. The number of committees was reduced to twenty-five in each house (the number is not constant). Timetables were established for completion of different types of work, such as committee action on bills, and action of the house on bills reported by committees. A plan was adopted whereby legislators may "prefile" bills when the legislature is not in session, and may get legal assistance for drafting bills between sessions as well as during session.

The legislature is equitably apportioned, but a Federal three-man district court was responsible. The legislature passed a reapportionment plan after the 1970 census, but the court did not accept it and prepared its own plan. County lines serve as boundaries, and both single–member and multi–member districts are used. The district court is under orders of the United States Supreme Court to divide Hinds County, the location of the capital, into single–member districts to give blacks a better chance to elect representatives. The redistricting is not yet completed.

EXECUTIVE BRANCH—The work of administration is divided among ninety different departments or agencies. The governor and the heads of the ten most important departments are elected directly by the people. Fifty boards and commissions and five individual department or agency heads are appointed by the governor, but terms of the members of boards and commissions are longer than that of the governor, and he cannot remove them. The governor himself is a member, usually chairman, of about twenty-five

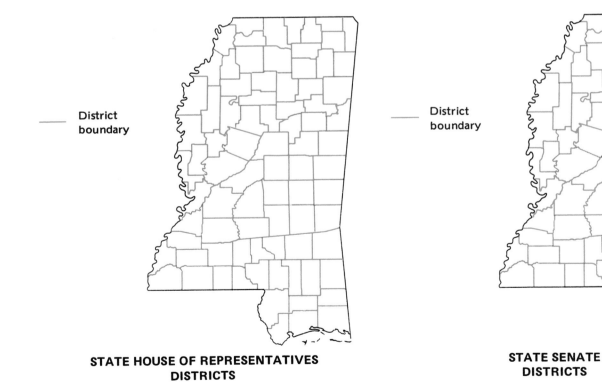

District boundary

STATE HOUSE OF REPRESENTATIVES DISTRICTS

District boundary

STATE SENATE DISTRICTS

Source: Mississippi Economic Council

boards and commissions.

The governor has the usual legislative powers, and tries to build a reputation from his legislative program. He sends messages to the legislature. He may even call special legislative sessions and designate the only business that can be considered (except investigations). He has a veto, including power to veto individual items in appropriation bills while approving the rest. His veto can be overridden by a two–thirds vote of the legislature. If he vetoes a bill after the legislature has recessed, he must so report when that group meets again, at which time the legislature may override the veto.

The governor may not hold two terms in succession. Since the 1890 constitution was written, only two Mississippi governors have held office two full but separated terms.

The governor has important emergency powers in two situations. If there are civil disorders, he may, for limited periods, use the state highway safety patrol to restore order, and may issue temporary regulations, such as curfews and orders to close liquor stores. (The jurisdiction of the highway patrol is normally restricted to the highways.) In case of foreign attack, the governor may assume direct control of the civil defense organization.

The state constitution provides for a secretary of state, an attorney general, a treasurer, and an auditor. All are elected for four–year terms, as are all elected officials except supreme court justices.

As noted, the work of the executive branch is scattered among over ninety largely independent agencies. A few of the more important are described below.

Department of Education—Although the public schools are administered by local districts, either consolidated or municipal, there is a state department of Education to supervise and assist them. This department is headed by an elective state superintendent, who is supplemented by an exofficio Board of Education consisting of the superintendent, the secretary of state, and the attorney general. The department licenses teachers, distributes large state appropriations for public schools, and supervises local budgets, bus transportation, and the design of many local school buildings.

Tax Collecting Agencies—There are two major state tax collecting agencies: the state Tax Commis-

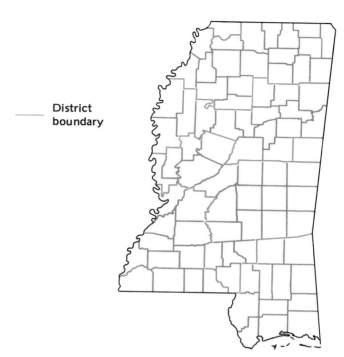

District boundary

NATIONAL CONGRESSIONAL DISTRICTS

Source: Mississippi Laws, 1972

sion, which collects most taxes, and the Motor Vehicle Comptroller, who collects the gasoline tax, inspects gasoline for quality, and checks equipment using liquefied compressed gas for safety.

Agencies Dealing with the Land—State services related to agriculture and natural resources are scattered among several agencies. These include the Department of Agriculture, the Board of Animal Health, a central market board, and the State Forestry Commission.

Board of Health—Health work in Mississippi is directed by the thirteen-member Board of Health. The board licenses physicians, recommends (and can remove) county health officers, and manages a state laboratory and the state tuberculosis sanatorium.

State Highway Commission—State highways are constructed and maintained by the Highway Commission composed of three members who are elected by districts. Although each commissioner is primarily concerned with his own district, the legislature requires the commission to operate the department as a unit, with a central director and a central chief engineer in charge.

Department of Public Welfare—Welfare work is centralized in the Department of Public Welfare. There is an appointed director and a board at Jackson, as well as an appointed local director in each county, advised by a county board of welfare.

Boards for State Institutions—All state-supported four-year universities are under one board of 12 members, appointed by the governor and state senate. (A thirteenth member represents a special endowment fund and votes only on matters which concern the University at Oxford). All members serve 12 years with staggered terms. There are now eight universities in Mississippi, three of which have about 8,000 on-campus students. All institutions are open to students of all races, but three remain predominantly black.

A state board coordinates a system of junior colleges, but each college is managed by a board from its own district. Separate boards also have charge of two schools for the blind and deaf, three mental institutions, four charity hospitals, a penitentiary, and two training schools for juvenile delinquents.

Regulatory and Promotional Agencies— Mississippi has fourteen additional agencies regulating or promoting other activities. Among these are the Agricultural and Industrial Board, the Game and Fish Commission, the Oil and Gas Board, and the Public Service Commission, all of which serve the state's citizens.

JUDICIAL BRANCH—Mississippi has a dual system of main trial courts. There is a complete set of circuit courts, and a complete set of chancery courts. Circuit courts handle law suits and serious criminal cases. Chancery courts handle chancery, divorce, probate, and, in most counties, juvenile cases. Below the circuit courts are the usual justices of the peace. In small towns, mayors may act as police judges, although this is currently being challenged in federal court. In cities of 10,000 or more population, trained lawyers are appointed by the governing bodies as police judges. At the top of the system is a supreme court of nine justices.

In about fifteen of the more populated counties a county court has been inserted in the hierarchy between the justice of the peace and the circuit and chancery courts. The county court handles law and chancery suits that do not involve over $10,000, juvenile cases, and criminal cases that do not carry death penalties. Felony cases must be started by indictment by the grand jury in circuit court and referred down to the county court. This is rarely done.

All judges except police judges in the larger cities

____ District boundary

CHANCERY COURT DISTRICTS

____ District boundary

CIRCUIT COURT DISTRICTS

Source: Mississippi Laws, 1972

are elected. Supreme court justices are elected for eight-year terms, others for four. All judges from county courts upward must be licensed attorneys with at least five years' experience.

STATE BUDGET AND FINANCES

BUDGET-MAKING—The initial draft of the budget is prepared by the Commission of Budget and Accounting. The governor is chairman, but ten members are legislators. The commission not only prepares the draft budget submitted to the legislature at the beginning of a session, but after appropriations are made it also doles out the money to many state agencies on a semi-annual basis. In addition the commission supervises and assists the agencies in making purchases, employing a director to manage details. The governor may submit a separate budget if he wishes, but he rarely does so.

STATE FINANCES—Mississippi had a budget for the fiscal year ending June 30, 1970, of slightly more than $1 billion (including both general and special funds). Of this, 23 percent or $244 million came from the United States government. (All figures are given in round numbers.)

The largest appropriations were for education—public schools, colleges, and universities. Mississippi devoted 26.3 percent of its budget to education, a total of $271 million including federal funds channeled through the state. The second largest cost was for highways, 14.7 percent of the total budget, or $141 million. (This was before the major rebuilding program was begun.) Public welfare came third, being allotted 8.5 percent of the budget or about $87 million.

Revenues, other than those from federal sources, came from many different state taxes, but the largest amount came from the retail sales tax of 4 percent. Mississippi was the first state to develop the general retail sales tax, which yielded $157 million in fiscal 1970. In that year the gasoline tax of seven cents per gallon raised $64 million. No other tax has yielded support sums as large as the foregoing. Social Security and retirement taxes are for special purposes and not support.

Mississippi leaves the general property tax to local government except for a very small amount used largely to cover unexpected shortages in the treasury.

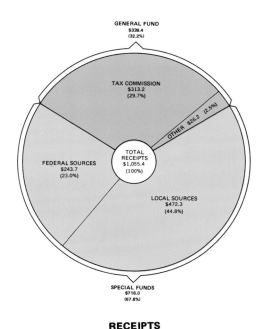

RECEIPTS

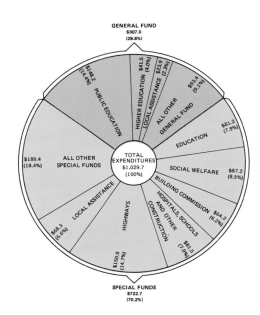

EXPENDITURES

**COMBINED GENERAL AND SPECIAL FUNDS
FISCAL YEAR ENDING JUNE 30, 1970**

Source: Mississippi Tax Commission, 1970

LOCAL GOVERNMENT

COUNTY GOVERNMENT—A county government in Mississippi consists of numerous elected officials, largely independent of each other. The county board is composed of five supervisors elected from five districts. At–large elections are permitted but not common. The board levies all rural taxes, including those of smaller districts and school districts, and maintains county roads. An elected sheriff and constables provide most rural police protection. Taxes are assessed and collected by elected clerks. There may be a county prosecuting attorney, but most criminal prosecution is done by a district attorney elected in an area covering several counties.

MUNICIPAL GOVERNMENT—Mississippi municipalities have three common forms of government; most have a mayor–council type of government, composed of an elected mayor and an elected board of five or seven aldermen depending on whether municipal population is under or over 10,000; some have adopted the commission form of government, where three elected commissioners are in charge of both legislative and executive functions. Recently, a few cities have adopted the council–manager form of

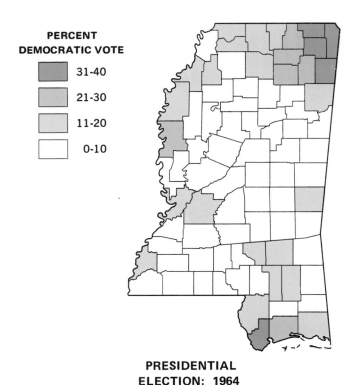

PERCENT DEMOCRATIC VOTE

- 31-40
- 21-30
- 11-20
- 0-10

PRESIDENTIAL ELECTION: 1964

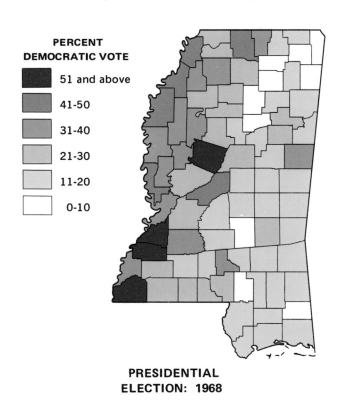

PERCENT DEMOCRATIC VOTE

- 51 and above
- 41-50
- 31-40
- 21-30
- 11-20
- 0-10

PRESIDENTIAL ELECTION: 1968

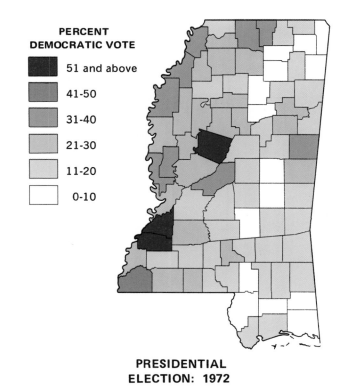

PERCENT DEMOCRATIC VOTE

- 51 and above
- 41-50
- 31-40
- 21-30
- 11-20
- 0-10

PRESIDENTIAL ELECTION: 1972

Source: Mississippi Secretary of State

government in which an appointed, professional manager serves with an elected council.

SCHOOL DISTRICTS—Mississippi has eliminated small rural school districts so common in the early history of the country. Now only municipal and consolidated districts are permitted, and most rural districts are county–wide. (In 1967–68 there was one remaining small district.) Boards of trustees in municipalities are appointed by the governing bodies; those in rural districts are elected.

POLITICAL PARTIES

In the 1963 race for governor, Paul B. Johnson, Jr. became the first Mississippi gubernatorial candidate to face a serious challenge from a Republican. Governor Johnson received 62 percent of the votes. Four years later, John Bell Williams defeated a Republican for the governorship by obtaining 70 percent of the votes cast. In the 1971 gubernatorial election there was no Republican challenger. However, victor Governor Bill Waller, a state Democrat, faced a black challenger, Charles Evers, a member of the national Democratic party who ran as an independent. Evers received 22 percent of the vote.

VOTING RIGHTS ACT

Since the passage of the Federal Voting Rights Act of 1965, voting participation has increased greatly. Although the population has remained fairly static, voting participation has more than doubled. In 1960, before the act was passed, the vote cast for President was just under 300,000. In 1968 it was 654,000. In 1972, after enfranchisement of eighteen-year-olds, the total vote was 646,000. The same voting pattern has occurred in gubernatorial races. In the first Democratic primary of 1959, there were 441,000 votes for governor; in 1971, there were 763,000. Before 1963, few voters turned out for the November elections for governor, since the Democrat always won. In 1963 there was a Republican challenger, and in that election the total vote for governor was 364,000. In 1971, after the Voting Rights Act had been operating for six years, the vote for governor was 780,000 in a year in which the challenger was a black independent rather than a Republican.

Leon A. Wilber
Anne Tatalovich

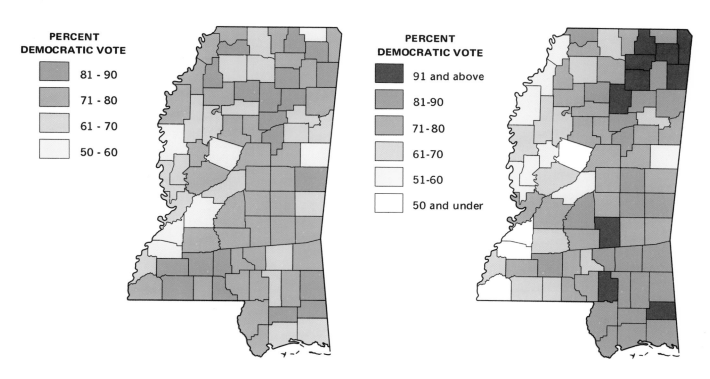

PERCENT DEMOCRATIC VOTE

- 81 - 90
- 71 - 80
- 61 - 70
- 50 - 60

GUBERNATORIAL ELECTION: 1967

PERCENT DEMOCRATIC VOTE

- 91 and above
- 81-90
- 71-80
- 61-70
- 51-60
- 50 and under

GUBERNATORIAL ELECTION: 1971

Source: Mississippi Secretary of State

PLANNING AND DEVELOPMENT AGENCIES

A listing of all agencies either directly or indirectly involved with planning and development in Mississippi is too long to be included here. The following are among those agencies whose impacts on the state's future are perhaps most profound.

STATE PLANNING AND DEVELOPMENT AGENCIES

The Agricultural and Industrial Board was created as an economic development agency for Mississippi. Although its primary responsibility lies in industrial development through its Industrial Development Department, the A&I Board is also involved in the promotion of tourism through its Travel Department, in domestic and international marketing through its Marketing Council, in technical and financial assistance to small business through its Small Business Assistance Department, in youth involvement and guidance through its Youth Affairs Department, and in general aid to Mississippi industry for the promotion of growth and expansion.

The Research and Development Center was formed to develop jobs for Mississippians, either through new industry or expansion of old industry, and to aid communities through planning and community development. The R&D Center's mission focuses on the production of more and better jobs, payrolls, and tax revenues, on helping communities become more competitive to realize job potentials, and on developing a total program for expediting Mississippi's economic progress. The overall goal of the R&D Center is to increase Mississippi's average per capita income to equal that of the United States as a whole by 1992. The R&D Center provides management, engineering, and planning assistance, conducts information services through a data center, library, and computer facilities, and carries out manpower research programs.

PLANNING AND DEVELOPMENT DISTRICTS AND COUNCILS

In 1965 the United States Congress enacted the Public Works and Economic Development Act providing for the establishment of the Economic Development Administration under the authority of the secretary of commerce. This legislation offered technical and financial assistance to encourage geographically and economically linked counties to join together in economic and local development districts. It was under this act that seven of Mississippi's Planning and

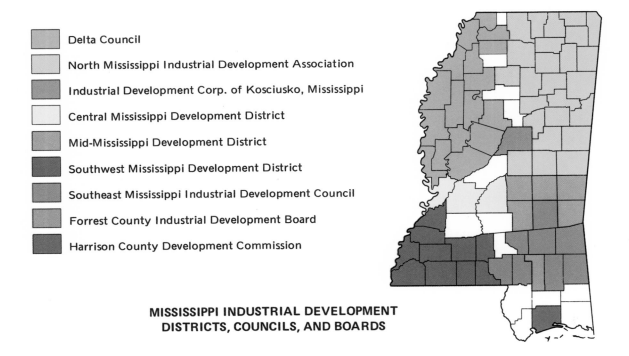

Delta Council

North Mississippi Industrial Development Association

Industrial Development Corp. of Kosciusko, Mississippi

Central Mississippi Development District

Mid-Mississippi Development District

Southwest Mississippi Development District

Southeast Mississippi Industrial Development Council

Forrest County Industrial Development Board

Harrison County Development Commission

MISSISSIPPI INDUSTRIAL DEVELOPMENT DISTRICTS, COUNCILS, AND BOARDS

Source: Mississippi Research and Development Center, 1972

Development Districts were formed. Three additional districts were organized under the Appalachian Regional Development Act of 1965.

Each planning and development group has as its primary goal the improvement of the local economy. These groups, therefore, involve themselves with comprehensive planning for the district as a whole, as well as with county and local planning. Mississippi's Planning and Development Districts were formed with nine general goals and responsibilities:

(1) To carry on a comprehensive planning program that supplements and coordinates, but does not duplicate, the planning program of the member units;

(2) To serve as a clearinghouse, for the benefit of member units, of information concerning both common problems and the state and federal services available to assist in the solution of these problems;

(3) To coordinate public and private planning;

(4) To help local governments and other groups within each district's jurisdiction obtain federal assistance;

(5) To provide technical assistance to local units of government undertaking planning programs;

(6) To avoid duplication and overlap of federal, state, and local programs;

(7) To keep the public informed about the district's programs;

(8) To improve regional and community recreation, housing, educational, and transportation facilities;

(9) To provide programs for the aging, aid in health planning, and develop environmental controls.

The Gulf Regional Planning Commission was formed in 1964 under the statutes of the state and is the oldest state-organized planning agency in Mississippi. Although it is without the implementation power of the planning and development districts, it does have much wider ranging duties and responsibilities than do the public industrial development districts and councils. The Gulf Regional Planning Commission therefore occupies a unique position among planning organizations. It has jurisdiction over Pearl River County and the Gulf Coast counties of Hancock, Harrison, and Jackson.

Other planning agencies include the Mississippi–Arkansas–Tennessee Council of Government (MATCOG), which plans for the Memphis metropolitan area (in Mississippi this includes the northwestern portion of De Soto County), and the Hinds–Madison–Rankin–Capital City Council of Government which plans for the Jackson metropolitan area.

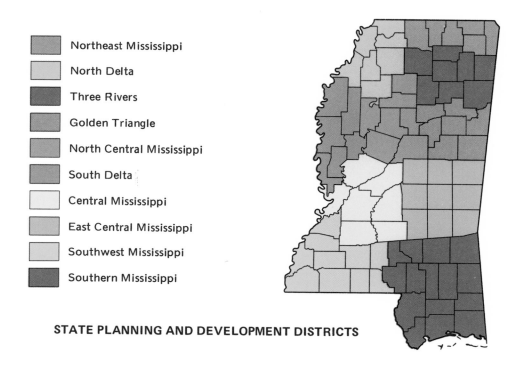

Northeast Mississippi

North Delta

Three Rivers

Golden Triangle

North Central Mississippi

South Delta

Central Mississippi

East Central Mississippi

Southwest Mississippi

Southern Mississippi

STATE PLANNING AND DEVELOPMENT DISTRICTS

Source: Mississippi Research and Development Center, 1972

STATE WATERWAY DISTRICTS

Waterway Districts (see map on page 129) were formed by the Mississippi legislature to act as agents of the state in the development of water resources within each district's jurisdiction. The major goals and objectives of the waterway groups are:

(1) To provide a sufficient supply of water for industrial development and urban expansion;

(2) To minimize flooding and erosion;

(3) To provide drainage and irrigation for agricultural improvement;

(4) Improvement of the navigability of streams for mineral, agricultural, and industrial development;

(5) Conservation of fish, vegetation, and wildlife resources;

(6) Maintenance of water quality through pollution control;

(7) Development of recreation facilities related to water.

Each Waterway District plans, coordinates, and implements a comprehensive development program. It has the authority to impound water, divert streams from their natural courses, inundate public lands and property, and to exercise eminent domain. The districts can also construct works, plants, and related facilities for municipal, domestic, commercial, industrial, agricultural, and manufacturing purposes. Each district group interprets needs within its jurisdiction, provides the administrative and financial base to meet the need, identifies specific program capabilities, researches these capabilities, develops and constructs facilities, and manages the completed improvements.

PUBLIC INDUSTRIAL DEVELOPMENT DISTRICTS AND COUNCILS

The Public Industrial Development Districts and Councils are usually the industrial development arms of local or county governments, although several are multi-county organizations. The primary goal of these public agencies is to further the economic growth of their community or area by encouraging prospective industrialists to locate in the community. They accomplish this task by:

(1) Advertising, market surveys, and hosting visiting prospects;

(2) Assisting out-of-state industry to locate in the community;

(3) Assisting existing industry to expand and create additional employment opportunities;

(4) Serving as a source of information to potential industry.

PRIVATE INDUSTRIAL DEVELOPMENT GROUPS

Of all the private industrial development groups, the electric power companies of Mississippi have been most instrumental in developing the state. Their major goal is to assist the economic development of the areas they serve through the stimulation of industrial growth. The electric power companies assist new industries interested in locating in the area and serve present industries with their expansion plans. Each company prepares and maintains information and statistics on the communities which it serves, confers with prospective industrialists throughout the nation, assists prospects visiting the community, helps in site selection, and gives advice to the communities it serves in order to make them more attractive to prospective industries.

The major railroads of Mississippi also have industrial development departments offering essentially the same services as the electric power companies. Many of the natural gas, petroleum, and pipeline companies are similarly active in encouraging industries to locate within the state.

THE PORT AUTHORITIES AND CHAMBERS OF COMMERCE

The port authorities of Mississippi have long been involved in planning and industrial development. The Mississippi State Port Authority at Gulfport, the Warren County Port Commission, the Greenville Port Commission, the Natchez Port Authority, the Jackson County Port Authority, the Biloxi Port Commission, and the Hancock County Port and Harbor Commission all maintain industrial parks with direct access to major shipping or barge channels.

Although the state's chambers of commerce are primarily interested in attracting tourists to the community, they are also involved in industrial development. The chambers provide information, host visiting prospective industrialists, and attempt to obtain favorable publicity for their community.

Gary W. Matthews
James A. Head

EDUCATION: HISTORY AND DEVELOPMENT

The following narrative and accompanying maps are an attempt to portray an overview of education in Mississippi—current data are shown by maps and historical perspective is portrayed through textual material. The narrative for this section depends heavily on the 1972 publication *History of Mississippi*, edited by Richard A. McLemore, and the script from the dramatic presentation "A Mind to Shape: An Educational History of Mississippi" as featured at the First Annual Governor's Conference on Education, September 13–17, 1973.

The story of education in Mississippi begins with the frontiersmen in the Mississippi Territory. The social class struggle started early, the "compulsory guests" arrived from Africa, and a third group of settlers migrated from the Carolinas and Georgia to join the earlier colonists. The education of the time consisted primarily of tutoring at home. However, the wealthy landowners of the Natchez area sent their sons and daughters to the eastern states for schooling.

As early as 1799, Governor Winthrop Sargent called for selection of a suitable site on which to construct an academy. On May 13, 1802, the territorial legislature created Jefferson College in Washington, Mississippi. Early academies included Franklin Academy, founded in Jefferson County in 1807, and Madison Academy, opened in Claiborne County in 1809. By the time of statehood in 1817, nine academies had received a state charter.

The state's first constitution strongly supported education, and the academy movement continued to develop. Elizabeth Female Academy, the first state academy exclusively for women, and Franklin Academy of Columbus, the first free public school in Mississippi, were chartered after 1817. Hampstead Academy, later to become Mississippi College, was established in Clinton in 1826. Oakland College was founded by the Presbyterians in 1830 and subsequently became Alcorn A&M. During the period 1817–60, approximately 200 academies were incorporated and at least 84 others operated without charters.

The early education of the Choctaws and Chickasaws came from the missionary efforts of religious groups endeavoring to "civilize" the Indians. To qualify for government financial support, missions were required to teach the Indian children useful courses—

mechanical arts for the boys and domestic arts for the girls. Mississippi cut off state funds to the missions in 1830 due to controversy between the missionaries and the United States War Department, and the missions had no choice but to close.

Revenue to support early education came from such sources as sixteenth-section lands. In 1803, 661,000 acres of these lands were deeded to the state by the federal government. To this day these lands remain a somewhat controversial issue. Another early source of revenue was the Literary Fund, originated by Governor Poindexter for the education of poor and orphaned white children of the state. By 1833, the fund had an endowment of $50,000.

The decade of the 1840s was a landmark in Mississippi educational history. On February 20, 1840, the first state university, the University of Mississippi at Oxford, was established. "Ole Miss" was chartered with a staff of five professors, one of which, the president, taught Mental and Moral Philosophy, Logic and Rhetoric, and lectured on the evidence of Christianity. The president received $2,000 and the other faculty members $1,500 in annual wages. Eighty students were enrolled the first year.

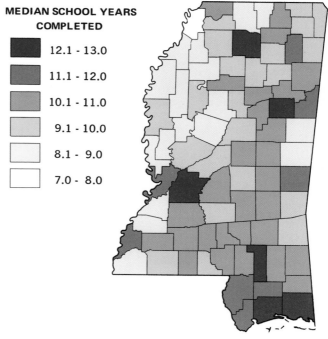

MEDIAN SCHOOL YEARS COMPLETED

- 12.1 - 13.0
- 11.1 - 12.0
- 10.1 - 11.0
- 9.1 - 10.0
- 8.1 - 9.0
- 7.0 - 8.0

EDUCATIONAL ATTAINMENT
1970 - 1971 ·

Source: Mississippi State Department of Education

In 1840, an estimated 382 public schools in Mississippi had enrolled approximately 8,000 pupils. The ungraded schools emphasized the basic skills of reading, writing, and arithmetic and operated for approximately three months during the year. Albert Galletin Brown, the leading advocate from 1832 to 1860 of a public education system, was elected governor in 1843. In 1846 he succeeded in securing passage of the first statewide school law. Unfortunately, the law conformed to the philosophy of local control, requiring consent in writing of a majority of heads of township families prior to levying taxes. This consent clause proved to be its undoing. Between 1848 and 1860, 125 different school laws were produced. Nonetheless, by 1860 there were 40,000 white students in 1,116 schools funded with $375,677.

After the war, Negro schooling was largely controlled by the Freedman's Bureau and a number of church and charitable organizations from the North. Soon black schools appeared in all parts of Mississippi, but no state efforts were made to cope with the problem of Negro education.

In 1870 one of the most important school laws in Mississippi history was passed. The law included free public schools in each district with each county constituting a district. Incorporated cities with 5,000 or more population were exceptions to the law, and organized separate school districts. All children from five to twenty-one years of age were to have equal advantage. The law did not provide for separate schools for the races. The new system of public education provided for an elected state superintendent of education to be assisted by a state board which, in turn, would appoint county superintendents. In 1873, a four mill state tax was established to be parceled among the counties on the basis of school population.

Article VIII of the 1890 constitution saw one major change in public education. Attempting to deal with one of the fears of the people, Section 207 provided for separate schools for white and black children. The 1869 constitution had made no such provision.

In 1890, teacher salaries averaged $33 a month for whites and $23.40 for blacks. To upgrade teacher qualifications, the legislature created a State Board of Examiners in 1896. In the board's first biennium, it passed four of the eighteen applications for professional licenses and issued 496 state licenses.

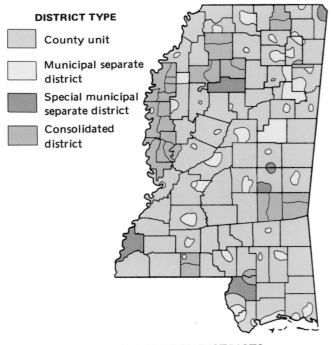

DISTRICT TYPE

County unit

Municipal separate district

Special municipal separate district

Consolidated district

PUBLIC SCHOOL DISTRICTS
1971 - 1972

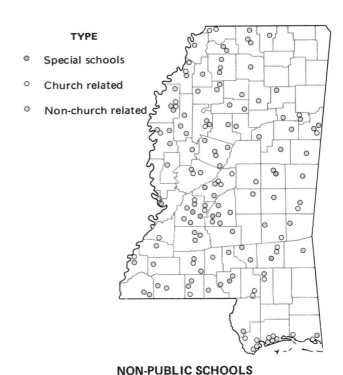

TYPE

○ Special schools

○ Church related

○ Non-church related

NON-PUBLIC SCHOOLS
1971 - 1972

Source: Mississippi State Department of Education

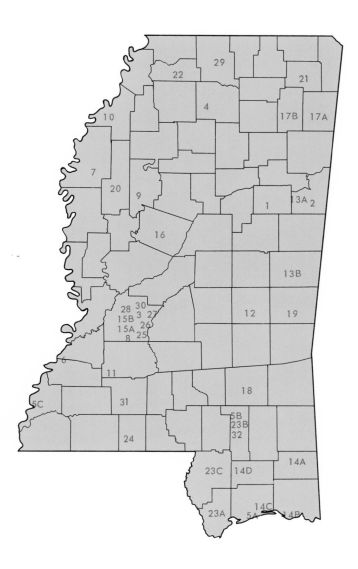

1. Mississippi State University
2. Mississippi State College for Women
3. University Medical Center
4. University of Mississippi
5. Univeristy of Southern Mississippi:
    5A. Gulf Park
    5B. Hattiesburg
    5C. Natchez
6. Alcorn College
7. Delta State College
8. Jackson State College
9. Mississippi Valley State
10. Coahoma Junior College
11. Copiah - Lincoln Junior College
12. East Central Junior College
13. East Mississippi Junior College:
    13A. Golden Triangle Center
    13B. Scooba Center
14. Gulf Coast Junior College:
    14A. George County Center
    14B. Jackson County Center
    14C. Jeff-Davis Center
    14D. Perkinston Center
15. Hinds Junior College:
    15A. Jackson Center
    15B. Raymond Center
16. Holmes Junior College
17. Itawamba Junior College:
    17A. Fulton Center
    17B. Tupelo Center
18. Jones Junior College
19. Meridian and Harris Junior Colleges
20. Mississippi Delta Junior College
21. Northeast Mississippi Junior College
22. Northwest Mississippi Junior College
23. Pearl River Junior College:
    23A. Hancock Center
    23B. Hattiesburg Center
    23C. Poplarville Center
24. Southwest Mississippi Junior College
25. Utica Junior College
26. Belhaven College
27. Millsaps College
28. Mississippi College
29. Rust College
30. Tougaloo College
31. Whitworth College
32. William Carey College

INSTITUTIONS OF HIGHER LEARNING

Source: State Department of Education, Mississippi.

In 1878, the Agricultural and Mechanical College (now Mississippi State University) in Starkville became a land grant college for whites. In 1871, the only state-supported Negro college was Alcorn University, which changed to Alcorn A&M College when endowment was provided under the Morrill Act. Tougaloo University, a private school, was established in the post-war era by the American Missionary Association in 1869, and Millsaps College opened in Jackson in 1892 through a $100,000 endowment provided by Reuben W. Millsaps. Rust University, originally known as Shaw University, was taken under the supervision of the Methodist Episcopal Church in 1890. Efforts to provide educational opportunities for women were implemented by the opening of the Industrial Institute and College in Columbus in 1885, later to become Mississippi State College for Women (MSCW). MSCW was the first state-supported college for women in the United States.

Legislative measures established agricultural high schools in 1908, and, in 1910, consolidation of schools became a major goal. Some fifty county boarding schools were developed within eleven years. As the consolidated schools grew, the agri-

cultural high schools began to disappear or were converted into junior colleges. During the period 1928–53 most of the state's junior colleges were founded and located according to the zones established in the basic law.

Previous to the adoption of the 1890 constitution the state had founded schools for the blind (1847) and for the deaf and dumb (1854). It was not until the second and third decades of the twentieth century, however, that Mississippi Industrial and Training School, to be located at Columbia, was established by legislative act, approved March 28, 1916. The legislature of April 3, 1920, established the Mississippi School and Colony for the Feeble Minded at Ellisville.

Several colleges had their beginning in the early twentieth century. Mississippi Normal College, now the University of Southern Mississippi, was authorized by the 1910 legislature and opened in 1912. Belhaven College was founded by the Presbyterians in 1911 as a college for women; it later became co-educational. Mississippi Women's College, a Baptist institution, was opened by 1911; it is now the coeducational William Carey College. Blue Mountain College, originally for girls, was formed under Baptist

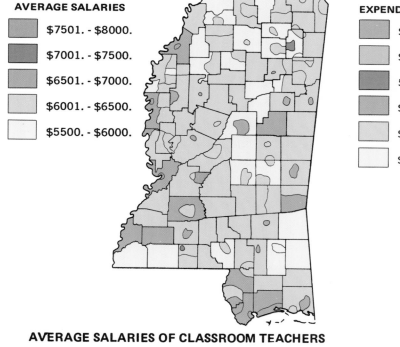

AVERAGE SALARIES

- $7501. - $8000.
- $7001. - $7500.
- $6501. - $7000.
- $6001. - $6500.
- $5500. - $6000.

AVERAGE SALARIES OF CLASSROOM TEACHERS
1971 - 1972

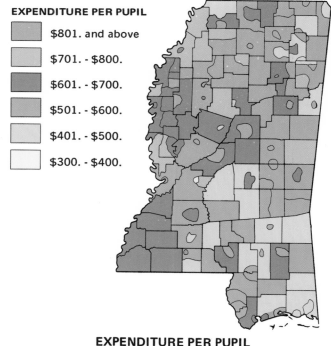

EXPENDITURE PER PUPIL

- $801. and above
- $701. - $800.
- $601. - $700.
- $501. - $600.
- $401. - $500.
- $300. - $400.

EXPENDITURE PER PUPIL
1971 - 1972

Source: Mississippi State Department of Education

control; it now admits male students to certain curricula. Delta State University was established in 1924 as a teacher's college. Jackson State University, started in Natchez in 1877, was moved to Jackson in 1882, where it became a part of the state system in 1940 as a teacher training college for blacks. In 1910 Professor Lawrence Clifton Jones, an outstanding educator and a pioneer of education for poor Mississippi Negroes, founded Piney Woods School. Valley State University began as Mississippi Vocational College for Negroes in 1946.

Mississippi enacted a compulsory school attendance law in 1918, and late in 1956 repealed it in the midst of the classroom integration controversy. The Smith–Hughes Act of 1917 greatly improved education in the state. This measure provided federal funds for the salaries of vocational teachers. By 1931 a total of 22,957 students were enrolled in vocational courses—15,068 in vocational agriculture, 1,644 in trade courses, and 6,245 in vocational home economics. In 1943, 57,163 students were enrolled in vocational courses, then a part of the regular educational program in public high schools.

The curriculum revision program of 1934 attracted the favorable attention of the educational leaders of the nation. In 1935 Mississippi had a larger percentage of consolidated high schools and teachers' homes than any other state in the country. The Southern Association of Colleges and Secondary Schools, in a 1935 report, ranked Mississippi first among southern states in percentage of white high school graduates entering colleges. Under Governor Paul B. Johnson, Sr. the legislature of 1940 passed a free textbook law for grades one through eight and the next year included all grades.

In 1952, House Bill Number 51 (amended in 1956 and 1960) became the first comprehensive educational law for exceptional children. This act provided for the education of any of "educable and trainable mind under twenty-one years of age." The law provided for administration of the program by the state Department of Education. In 1960, House Bill Number 404 was enacted, providing that one-half of the teacher units for special classes be allocated by the state to school systems.

The Civil Rights Act of 1964 and the guidelines prepared by the United States Office of Education resulted in the desegregation of the public school system in Mississippi. Soon after Congress approved the act and the guidelines were published, the Mississippi Board of Education drew up its proposed plan of compliance, submitted it to the United States Commissioner of Education in February, 1965, and received approval. Under these adverse conditions and at variance with the customs and traditions of the past, four districts were brought under court order for the 1964–65 session; the following year, 107 districts complied voluntarily and 24 were ordered to do so by the court. During the 1966–67 session, 93 of 149 districts in the state complied voluntarily and 42 were ordered to do so by the court.

Continuation and maintenance of public education in Mississippi appeared to be in doubt at times. As court-ordered plans of school integration were implemented during the early months of 1970, many white children withdrew from public schools and enrolled in hastily established private schools. At the end of the first month in the 1970–71 session, the state education superintendent requested an enrollment and average daily attendance report from every district. The results indicated that 92 percent of all students who had been enrolled in September of 1969 were still enrolled in 1970–71.

State teachers' associations have played a major role in the development of educational curricula for the children and youth of Mississippi. As early as 1838 a state teachers' association existed; it survived for four or five years, but was dissolved due to travel difficulties. The Mississippi Teachers' Association was organized in 1877 and held regular annual meetings beginning in 1885. In 1922, the group changed its name to the Mississippi Education Association. This organization accepted only white teachers as members; the Mississippi Association for Teachers in Colored Schools was established for black teachers. In 1947 the name was changed to the Mississippi Teachers Association.

Public schools continue to improve in Mississippi under the auspices of the state Department of Education with its statewide needs assessment and goals for education projects.

Walter E. Cooper
Eric M. Gunn
Richard Kazelskis

HOSPITALS AND RELATED FACILITIES

In recent years Mississippi has made significant headway toward making available to its people medical and public health facilities and personnel. Several measures of both the quality and the quantity of these facilities and their staffs can be noted—by the number, size, and kind of hospitals and public health centers, and the number of physicians, dentists, and nurses.

In late 1973, Mississippi had 131 non-federal hospitals, five federal hospitals (VA or military base facilities), and 89 local public health centers or departments. Of the 131 non-federal hospitals, 115 were short-term general hospitals with a bed complement of 10,605; the remaining 16 were classed as either special or limited service, providing some 6,386 beds. Collectively the state had 7.7 hospital beds per 1,000 population. With the exception of the federally owned hospitals, the remainder were owned and maintained by a variety of such organizations and institutions as the state, churches, counties, and associations.

Most short-term general hospitals offer a diversity of services ranging from major and minor surgery to orthopedics and coronary care. Among the 16 special or limited service hospitals are institutions for surgery and medicine (2), chronic disease, obstetrics, and medicine (1), mental and nervous disease (4), eye, ear, nose, and throat (1), tuberculosis (1), and obstetrics, minor surgery, and medicine (7).

Only seven of Mississippi's eighty-two counties are without hospital facilities; however, facilities are readily available in adjacent counties. The location of hospitals tends to follow the general pattern set by population distribution. The highest concentration of facilities is to be found in Hinds County (Jackson) with seven hospitals, five having more than 200 beds each. Jackson is the medical center of the state, not only because of the number of hospitals, but also because of a concentration of physician specialists and the presence of the University of Mississippi School of Medicine. The only remaining significant concentrations of hospitals are in Lauderdale County (Meridian) and Harrison County (Gulfport–Biloxi urban area).

In addition to the hospitals, there are also 89 public health centers or departments distributed throughout the state. These centers provide a variety of services to local residents. The general plan for the construction of hospitals and related medical facilities within

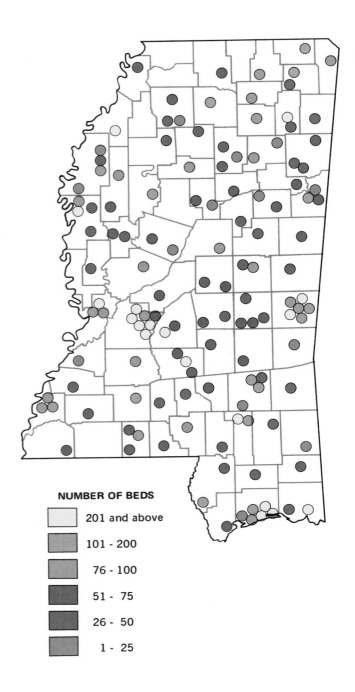

NUMBER OF BEDS

201 and above

101 - 200

76 - 100

51 - 75

26 - 50

1 - 25

HOSPITALS

Source: Miss. Commission on Hospital Care, 1973

the state calls for the existence of some form of emergency medical service within 15 miles of the place of residence of all Mississippians. Such emergency service is quite often provided by public health centers, particularly in rural areas.

As of July, 1973, there were 2,047 licensed physicians living in Mississippi. This number represents a gain of 115 over the previous year. All counties of the state, with the exception of Issaquena, and all incorporated towns (2,500 or more population) have at least one physician. As with hospitals, the distribution pattern of physicians is closely tied to total population densities and distribution. Hinds County has the largest number of resident physicians, 658; 622 of these live in Jackson. Harrison County follows Hinds with 180 doctors, and Lauderdale is third with 103 physicians. In the state as a whole, 85 percent of the doctors are located in urban areas. Of the 305 rural physicians almost 20 percent are over 60 years of age. Only 3 percent, or 60 of the state's doctors, are nonwhite. Overall, there are 1,083 persons per physician within Mississippi.

At the beginning of 1973 there were 598 licensed dentists either in private practice (577), in federal and state government work (17), or who divided their time between government service and private practice. Benton, Issaquena, and Kemper counties have no dentists; fourteen counties have only one dentist; the remaining counties have more than one. The largest concentrations of dentists are found in the more populated areas of the state. Hinds County is in the forefront with 109 resident dentists, of which 104 are located in the city of Jackson. The Gulf Coast county of Jackson is second with 29, while Jackson, Harrison, and Hancock counties together have a total of 83 dentists. As with doctors, the majority of dentists (515) have residence in towns with 2,500 or more persons. In the state overall there are approximately 3,698 persons per dentist.

The ratio of nurses to total population is, as might be expected, better than for either doctors or dentists. In October, 1973, there were 6,748 registered nurses (RN) and 5,780 licensed practical nurses (LPN). Counting both groups, there is a ratio of one nurse per 176 persons, and 6.1 nurses for each of the state's doctors.

Robert W. Wales

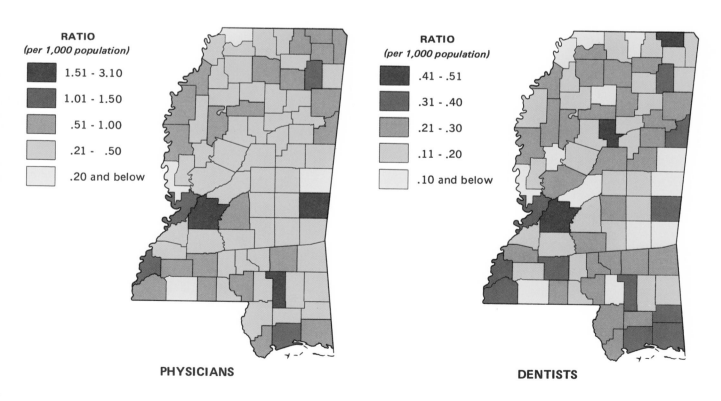

RATIO
(per 1,000 population)

1.51 - 3.10
1.01 - 1.50
.51 - 1.00
.21 - .50
.20 and below

PHYSICIANS

RATIO
(per 1,000 population)

.41 - .51
.31 - .40
.21 - .30
.11 - .20
.10 and below

DENTISTS

Source: Miss. State Board of Health, 1973

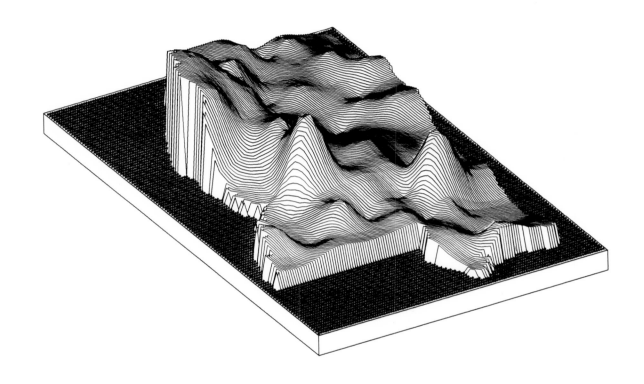

TOTAL EMPLOYMENT IN NATURAL RESOURCES

NATURAL RESOURCES AND RESOURCE UTILIZATION

Colonial Mississippi abounded in such natural resources as forests, water, productive soils, and wildlife, giving rise to the erroneous notion that these resources were fixed, inexhaustible, and indestructible. It was not until late in the state's history that Mississippians became alarmed at the erosion of the soil due to widespread, intensive, row-crop agriculture and at the destruction of large portions of timberland by ax and saw. Other resources were meeting similar fates. And Mississippians were not unique in their spendthrift's tolerance and blindness to waste—such occurrences were of a national scale.

The lessons of the past have been learned well. Over the last forty or fifty years, Mississippi has focused attention on developing a resource-use philosophy more in line with both the short- and long-range social and economic aims of the state. Although much work remains, much has been achieved.

Terracing, strip-cropping, and contour farming have replaced up-down hill row-cropping. Cotton is no longer king, and corn acreage is declining. Soybeans are of major importance, both industrially and as a soil builder, and other acreage is being converted to trees and improved pastures. The numbers and quality of beef and dairy cattle and of poultry are on the rise.

Comparatively, the state's mineral resource base is small. Nevertheless, this reserve directly or indirectly provides considerable employment and earnings, especially from oil and gas.

Mississippi is a national leader in timber products; commercial forests cover over half of the state. Water resources have received considerable attention in recent years. Improvements have been made in navigation, flood control projects have been implemented, and watershed drainage areas have become integral units of planning. The state's forest and water resources provide vast habitats for birds, animals, and fish—and therefore excellent opportunities for hunting, fishing, and camping. Mississippi's marine resources are economically important, and freshwater fish farming is becoming a significant industry.

Robert W. Wales

SOIL RESOURCES

Mississippi is blessed with a variety of soils with great production potentials yet to be fully realized. With slightly over 30 million acres of land in the state, Mississippi has more acreage of highly fertile soil than most other states in the South. However, to increase present farm incomes and to meet future agricultural needs, good soil management will be needed on every acre of land whether it is in the fertile Delta area or in the less productive hill section.

TYPES AND USES

Geology (providing parent material), topography, climate, and vegetation have been the primary factors in the development of Mississippi's soils. The great number of soil groups, families, series, and types resulting from these and other minor factors precludes the possibility of discussing them in detail here. However, a general categorization of the state's soils is made on the basis of eight recognized land resource areas reflecting certain inherent characteristics of soil groupings.

MISSISSIPPI DELTA—Soils of the Delta Area occupy the floodplains and other depressional or basin-like areas subject to seasonal saturation with water. Comparatively, these are young soils. Having been deposited by river action, they are generally high in organic matter, plant nutrients, and weatherable minerals. These soils are contained in a region of about 5 million acres and comprise one of the nation's more highly productive land areas. The major Delta soils include Sharkey, Dundee, Commerce, Alligator, Dubbs, Forestdale, Robinsonville, Tunica, and Tutwiler.

The Delta is a prosperous and highly specialized agricultural area. Soil tests indicate that when this land is drained and fertilized, the soils are productive and well adapted to a wide range of crops. Leading crops are cotton, soybeans, grain sorghum, and rice. Vegetable yields are increasing, and this region has the potential for becoming one of the leading vegetable-producing areas of the country. It is probable that the Delta will remain a highly specialized and mechanized farming area.

BROWN LOAM (THICK LOESS)—The soils of the Brown Loam Area are developed from loess, or windblown material, generally over four feet thick. This is the most uniform soil material found in Mississippi. Because of this uniformity, the number of different soils in the Brown Loam region is small in com-

parison with other land resource areas. Soils of this area are all high in silt content and, especially when slopes are steep, are subject to severe erosion. The uniform parent material contains sufficient native fertility for rapid plant growth, a fact reflected in the production of forage and other crops throughout the Brown Loam Area. Hardpans or impervious layers are common in these silty soils and are classified as fragipans. The major Brown Loam soils are Loring, Memphis, Collins, Calloway, Falaya, Grenada, and Natchez.

THIN LOESS AREA—The soils of this area have developed from thin loess (less than four feet) over sandy and clayey coastal plain materials. The nearly level to sloping soils are formed in silty substances overlying loamy materials; steeper soils are formed in mainly loamy materials. The dominant soils of this type include Gillsburg, Providence, Smithdale, Arkabutla, Ariel, Bude, Ealaya, Lexington, Ruston, and Sweatman.

Soils of the floodplains, when drained, along with the gently sloping soils of the uplands are well suited for row crops. All require applications of complete fertilizers. The primary crops grown in the Thin

SOIL TERRACING   USDA

Loess Area are cotton, soybeans, corn, and grain sorghum. The soils are also well suited for forage and pasture crops. About 40 percent of the area is in woodland, primarily mixed hardwood and pine.

BLACKLAND PRAIRIES (BLACK BELTS)—The major portion of the Blackland Prairie is located in northeastern Mississippi, though a smaller area extends from Jackson southeastward to Wayne County. Most of these soils are clayey or fine in texture and many are high in lime. The sloping soils are subject to severe erosion when cultivated without adequate conservation measures. In general, they are best suited to perennial grasses and legumes, since most are difficult to cultivate because of texture and wetness. These finer textured soils which easily bog in winter months are somewhat droughty during midsummer, a disadvantage for grazing. The leading Blackland Prairie soils are Okolona, Leeper, Brooksville, Catalpa, Kipling, and Vaiden.

UPPER COASTAL PLAIN—The soils of this area are formed in loamy, clayey, and sandy materials. Their fertility status is generally low and complete fertilizers are necessary for high crop yields. The floodplains, when drained, and the gently sloping uplands are well suited for such row crops as cotton, soybeans, corn, and grain sorghum. Beef cattle, dairying, vegetable crops, and pine timber also contribute to the agricultural economy of the Upper Coastal Plain. The major soils of the area include Smithdale, Ora, Sweatman, Cahaba, Iuka, Mantachie, Prentiss, Providence, and Ruston.

INTERIOR FLATWOODS—The Interior Flatwoods is a narrow area in northeastern Mississippi, extending from Tippah County southeastward into Alabama. The soils of this area have formed in silty and clayey materials. Their fertility level is generally low and complete fertilizers are necessary for high crop yields. The soils are level to sloping, and many need draining. Major Interior Flatwoods soils are Wilcox, Falkner, Mayhew, Adaton, Arkabutla, Providence, Savannah, and Smithdale.

The Flatwoods is well suited for loblolly pine, and much of the area is used for timber production. A general type of farming is also practiced, yielding cotton, corn, soybeans, pasture grasses, and hay. Sweet potatoes are produced in small areas as a specialized crop, and, in recent years, soybeans have become the most valuable row crop.

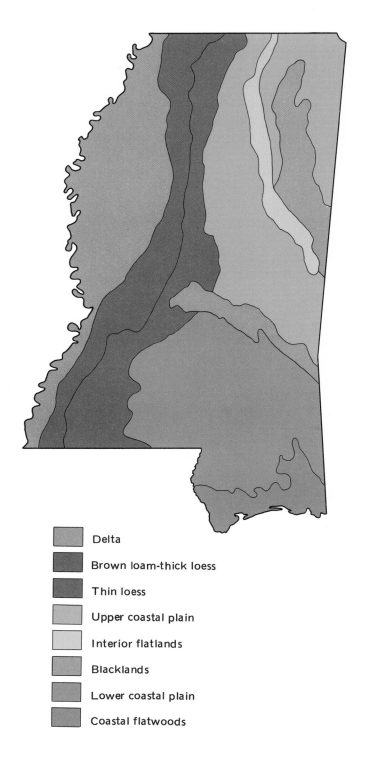

	Delta
	Brown loam-thick loess
	Thin loess
	Upper coastal plain
	Interior flatlands
	Blacklands
	Lower coastal plain
	Coastal flatwoods

GENERALIZED SOIL REGIONS

LOWER COASTAL PLAIN—The soils of this area have formed in loamy, clayey, and sandy materials, and range from nearly level to steep. They are low in natural fertility, necessitating fertilization, especially lime (most soils are highly acidic). Principal soils of the Lower Coastal Plain include Ruston, Savannah, Susquehanna, Benndale, Leaf, McLaurin, Ora, and Smithdale.

The topography, the loamy texture, and the good internal drainage of most of these soils support vegetation suited for grazing of livestock. About 60 percent of the Lower Coastal Plain is in pine trees and mixed hardwoods. Cotton, corn, sorghum, small grains, and pasturage are the main yields of this land in open areas.

GULF COAST FLATWOODS—Soils of this narrow area along the highly developed and populated Gulf Coast are formed in loamy and sandy sediments. Most of the Gulf Coast Flatwoods is used for trees and pastures; approximately 80 percent of the land is in pine woodlands or used for urban, industrial, and recreational purposes. Some of the better drained soils are used for pastures and forage crops production. Because of favorable rainfall in late summer and early fall, soybean production is on the increase. Livestock numbers are also rising because of the suitability for winter grazing. Major area soils include Harleston, Atmore, Poarch, Alaga, Benndale, Eustis, Leaf, and Ocilla.

SOIL CAPABILITIES

One of the most widely used systems of land classification is the Land Capability Classification developed by the Soil Conservation Service. This system is based on the capacity of land to produce cultivated crops without erosion losses or deterioration. The groups are classified according to the problems involved when the soils are used for adapted crops and to the response of the soils to treatments.

In this system the soils are grouped into major classes ranging from I to VIII, based on the limitations or problems involved in the production of row crops. Subclasses are made by adding the letters e, w, or s, which indicate, respectively, erosion problems, water or wetness problems, and soil property problems. Characteristics of the eight major classes are as follows:

Class I. Good land that can be cultivated continuously without major problems.

Class II. Good land that can be cultivated most of the time with only minor problems (such as erosion control and proper drainage).

Class III. Fairly good land that can be cultivated part of the time with good management practices.

Class IV. Land with major problems and limitations, but can be cultivated part of the time with intensive management practices.

Class V. Land that should not be cultivated because of wetness, rocks, etc., and is generally used for grazing or forestry.

Class VI. Land that is suitable for grazing or forestry with minor problems and limitations.

Class VII. Land suitable for forestry and some grazing with major limitations.

Class VIII. Steep and rough land suitable for wildlife and recreation only.

No map outlining the exact distribution of capability classes for Mississippi is available, but the accompanying table does indicate the land area in the state as divided into capability classes.

LAND CAPABILITY CLASSES

Class	Acres	Total by Classes
I	756,299	756,299
IIe	2,483,833	
IIs	63,242	
IIw	3,922,673	6,469,748
IIIe	2,348,693	
IIIs	179,371	
IIIw	3,538,881	6,066,845
IVe	2,042,018	
IVs	129,086	
IVw	2,804,965	4,976,069
Vw	722,525	722,525
VIe	2,598,962	
VIs	57,640	
VIw	17,312	2,673,914
VIIe	5,011,916	
VIIs	198,555	
VIIw	404,839	5,614,310
VIIIe	195	195

TOTAL USABLE LAND	27,279,905
Other land	2,970,095
TOTAL IN STATE	30,250,000

H. B. Vanderford

WATER RESOURCES

Precipitation in Mississippi annually averages approximately 50 inches in the north and about 60 inches near the coast, with a statewide mean of 53 inches. The amount of precipitation received in Mississippi and adjacent areas has, over the years, been adequate to keep the state well supplied with water. Annually, approximately 40–48 precipitation-equivalent inches of water are evaporated from open surfaces. Annual average runoff throughout most of Mississippi ranges between 15 and 30 precipitation-equivalent inches. Only in the extreme southeastern corner of the state does the mean runoff rate exceed 30 inches per year. The apparent paradox of evaporation plus runoff exceeding total precipitation per year is easily explained. First, a large percentage of evaporated moisture comes from water body surfaces having water storage from more than one year's accumulation. Second, all Mississippi streams are effluent. That is, the stream beds intersect the water table (zone of saturation) and are fed largely by ground water, especially during periods of droughts. Third, part of the ground water is derived by subsurface flow from aquifers originating outside the state.

SURFACE WATER

Today, an estimated 38 percent of fresh water used by Mississippians comes from surface water supplies. Of course this figure excludes such surface water uses as navigation and recreation.

Mississippi contains all or parts of eleven river basins, including small stream watersheds, which drain water directly into the Gulf of Mexico. The largest, the Mississippi River, directly drains only a small portion of the state. But several of the state's river basins are tributary to the Mississippi; through them over one-half of the state's land area is drained westward into the Mississippi River. Other than the above noted streams, and, with the exception of the streams of Region 1 (including the Tuscumbia, Hatchie, and Wolf rivers) and Region 5 (the Tennessee River) which trend northward out of the state then westward to become part of the Mississippi, the remaining river systems of the state generally flow south or southeastward to eventually reach the Gulf of Mexico.

Of the eleven river basins in Mississippi, there are five river systems which can be considered major ones on the basis of the size of area drained and the

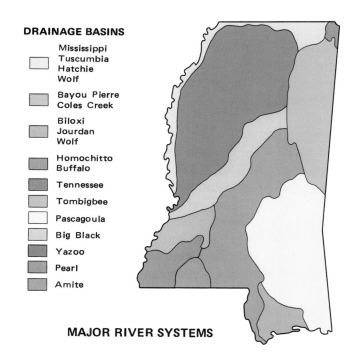

DRAINAGE BASINS

- Mississippi Tuscumbia Hatchie Wolf
- Bayou Pierre Coles Creek
- Biloxi Jourdan Wolf
- Homochitto Buffalo
- Tennessee
- Tombigbee
- Pascagoula
- Big Black
- Yazoo
- Pearl
- Amite

MAJOR RIVER SYSTEMS

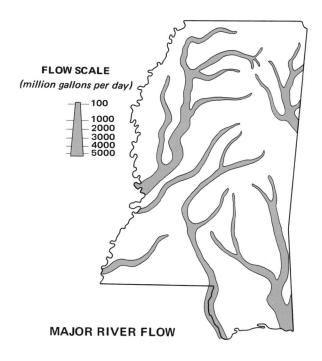

FLOW SCALE
(million gallons per day)

- 100
- 1000
- 2000
- 3000
- 4000
- 5000

MAJOR RIVER FLOW

Source: U.S. Department of the Interior, 1970

Source: Mississippi Research and Development Center, 1972

rate of channel flow. These basins in order of percentage of land area drained are: the Yazoo River (29 percent), the Pascagoula River (15 percent), the Pearl River (14 percent), the Tombigbee River (12 percent), and the Big Black River (9 percent).

The Yazoo River as measured at Greenwood, Mississippi, had a 49-year average discharge rate of 9,821 cfs (cubic feet per second) or 4,407,665 gpm (gallons per minute) as of 1972. The maximum discharge rate recorded occurred on January 14, 1932, at 72,900 cfs with a gauge height of 40.10 feet. The minimum flow rate of 536 cfs was recorded on October 20, 1943. The maximum gauge height was 41.20 feet which occurred in 1882 and was caused by the Mississippi River overflowing into the Yazoo Basin. The discharge rate at the time this stage was reached is not known.

The Pascagoula River as measured at Merrill, Mississippi, had a 41-year average discharge rate of 9,250 cfs (4,151,400 gpm) in 1972. The maximum recorded discharge of 178,000 cfs occurred on February 27, 1961, with a gauge height of 30.66 feet. The minimum recorded discharge, 696 cfs, was reached on November 3, 1936. An absolute maximum gauge height was recorded at 32.50 feet in April of 1900. No discharge rate figure for the year 1900 is available.

The Pearl River as measured near Bogalusa, Louisiana, had a 33-year average discharge rate of 8,582 cfs (3,851,602 gpm). A maximum discharge rate was recorded at this gauging station on February 23, 1961, at a gauge height of 21.70 feet. A minimum discharge rate was charted during the period October 29–November 1, 1963, at 1,020 cfs.

The Tombigbee River near Cochrane, Alabama—just across the Mississippi border—had a 32-year average discharge rate of 8,194 cfs (3,677,467 gpm). The maximum flow rate at this gauging station was 163,000 cfs and occurred on January 9, 1949, at a maximum gauge height of 46.90 feet. The minimum discharge rate was recorded on September 21, 1954, at 165 cfs with a gauge height of 2.34 feet.

The Big Black River near Bovina, Mississippi, had a 35-year average discharge rate of 3,346 cfs (1,501,685 gpm). The maximum discharge rate was experienced on December 20, 1961, at 63,500 cfs at a gauge height of 40.43 feet. The minimum flow rate was recorded here on October 2, 1954, at 65 cfs with a gauge height of 5.98 feet.

Mississippi's natural lakes, another form of surface water, are located almost exclusively in the old meander belts in the immediate floodplain of the Mississippi River in the form of oxbow lakes. Lakes Beulah, Bolivar, Eagle, and Washington are among the largest in the state.

Stream reservoirs are also important forms of surface water in Mississippi. The largest reservoirs are situated in the northern part of the state. The Arkabutla Reservoir on the Coldwater River, the Sardis Reservoir on the Tallahatchie River, the Enid Reservoir on the Yocona River, and the Grenada Reservoir on the Yalobusha River are all a part of the Yazoo River system. The main purpose of these reservoirs is flood control for the Delta, but they also serve as a water source for streams during periods of low flow. Moreover, they furnish some of the finest recreational sites in the state. Pickwick Lake, a reservoir on the Tennessee River in the northeastern corner of the state, provides excellent opportunities for outdoor activities, although the lake is primarily an electric power and flood control facility. Ross Barnett Reservoir on the Pearl River near Jackson, Mississippi, is one of the more recently constructed (1963) large reservoirs. It serves primarily as a recreational site for people in and around Jackson. There are many additional smaller reservoirs scattered throughout the state designed primarily for recreational purposes and/or for municipal or industrial water supply. Finally, there are numerous small farm ponds which serve recreational and stock watering functions.

GROUND WATER

Ground water is the water occupying the saturated pore spaces and fractures of rocks and sediments beneath the land surface. Beds of rocks and sediments which contain water and yield it readily to wells and springs are known as aquifers. The geographical distribution of ground water and the quantity of available water depend on the nature and the location of the geologic formations. Loose sands and gravels, cavernous limestones and conglomerates are the most prolific and are capable of producing several thousands of gallons of water per minute.

There are two classes of ground water in aquifers. In the first, water is confined in rock interstices under hydrostatic pressure; the pressure on the water is sufficient to cause the water to rise in a well to a level

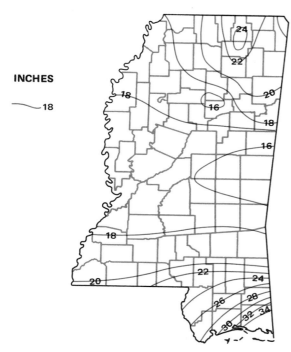

INCHES

—18

AVERAGE ANNUAL SURFACE RUNOFF

Source: Miss. Board of Water Commissioners, 1964

above the water table. If the water in such a well reaches the surface it is called a flowing well. Little or no pumpage is involved with these artesian wells. In the second type, water in an aquifer is not under pressure. In this circumstance the water in a well will not rise above the water table and has to be pumped to the surface.

Due to its geologic structure, Mississippi, located almost entirely in the Gulf Coastal Plain Province, is one of the most prolific ground water resource areas in the country. Important aquifers are widespread and occur beneath the surface at varying depths throughout the state. There are seven basic regions in Mississippi based on the uniformity of availability of ground water.

In western Mississippi (Region 1), the aquifers are principally unconsolidated alluvium—clay, sand, and gravel—of the Delta. The depth of this material ranges from just a few feet to about 200 feet, averaging a mean depth of 140 feet. The area encompasses approximately 7,000 square miles, and the water table varies from a few feet beneath the surface to about 30 feet below the surface. Of course, the water table is not fixed and is capable of fluctuating continuously. The alluvial area produces large quantities of cool,

hard water. Beneath the alluvium lie several artesian aquifers which yield water to some 2,000 flowing or near-flowing wells throughout the Delta.

Region 2 features parts of the Eutaw formation, the Ripley formation, and the Wilcox group—all sandy soils. Water supplies in this region range from small to moderate quantities of cool, medium-hard water.

Region 3 is underlain by most of the important aquifers of the state. Included in this region, beginning in the southern part of the state, are the Pascagoula and Hattiesburg clays which contain thick beds of sand interbedded in clays. Just north of this formation, trending from Copiah County to Wayne County, is an important zone of Catahoula sandstone. Still farther to the north, trending northwestward from Clarke County to Holmes County, is a significant band of the Cockfield formation. This formation consists of beds of sand interbedded with lignitic-clay and lignite. Paralleling this is an interrupted crescent of Sparta sand, originating in Clarke County, trending northwestward, and terminating in Grenada County. A narrow segment of Sparta sand is also present in Yalobusha County, then a larger zone begins again in Panola County and reaches the Tennessee border in Marshall County. Originating in the northeastern corner of Clarke County is the Wilcox group, which extends northwestward into Grenada County, then turns northeastward, and reaches the Tennessee border in Tippah County. This group consists of beds of fine to coarse sand interbedded with clays and includes the important Meridian sand. Next is a thin crescent of the Ripley formation starting in Kemper County, swinging westward through Chickasaw County, and running through Alcorn County. The Ripley formation is composed of sand, sandstone, sandy chalk, and clay. Finally, along the Alabama border in northeastern Mississippi are the Eutaw formation and the Tuscaloosa formation—the latter encloses the former on the Mississippi side. Both formations begin in Lowndes County and extend northward through Tishomingo County. The Eutaw formation is composed of fine to medium cross-bedded sand with clay belts. The Tuscaloosa formation is made up of irregularly bedded clay, sand, and gravel. These aquifers produce moderate to large quantities of soft water throughout most of Region 3. In local areas the water contains excessive iron in solution. Interspersed among these outstanding bands of aquifers are less productive ground water sources. These areas usually consist of rock strata or sediments of the same groups or formations as that of the aquifers lying adjacent to them.

Region 4 is underlain almost entirely by the Wilcox group. However, it is a region of little or no potable ground water.

Region 5 is covered primarily by loess and brown loam surficial materials. These materials are not water-bearing formations. But underlying the loess and brown loam at depths varying from 10 to 50 feet are water-bearing aquifers of the Pascagoula and Hattiesburg formations, Sparta sand, Cockfield formation, and Catahoula sandstone. This region has moderate to large supplies of soft water interspersed with small areas of little or no potable ground water.

Region 6 contains parts of the loess and brown loam area, Catahoula sandstone, Cockfield formation, and Sparta sand. Region 6 has moderate to large quantities of essentially hard water.

Region 7 is underlain primarily by the Pascagoula and Hattiesburg formations. Here a moderate supply of water ranging from very soft to hard is available.

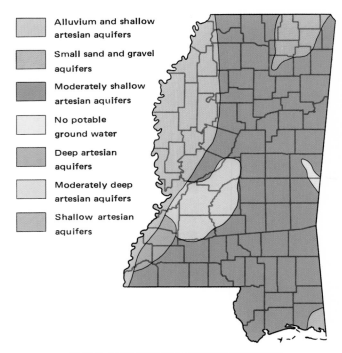

AVAILABILITY OF GROUNDWATER

Source: Board of Water Commissioners

WATER UTILIZATION

Public and industrial water withdrawals in Mississippi in 1971 amounted to about 1,512 mgd (million gallons per day). Surface waters supplied about 1,122 mgd, including 544 mgd of brackish water extracted from the Back Bay of Biloxi and the Pascagoula River estuary. The remaining supply of water, 390 mgd, came from ground water withdrawals.

SURFACE WATER—Surface water, chemically suitable for most uses, is available throughout most of Mississippi. Currently, the main sources are the Mississippi, Pearl, and Pascagoula rivers in the southern half of the state, and only Luxapalila Creek in the northern half.

Surface water is used primarily for irrigation, cooling, electric power generation in steam plants, product or raw material washing, or incorporation of water as a part of a final product. The paper, petroleum, and electric power industries are the main users of surface supplies. Only three cities (Jackson, Meridian, and Columbus) depended on surface water for public supply in 1971. It is anticipated that expanded use of surface water for public supply as well as for rising industrial needs will increase surface demand in the near future. Such cities as Hattiesburg and Pasca-

goula are already exploring the possibilities of increasing surface supply sources as the water demand rapidly grows. Other important uses of surface waters are for recreational purposes—boating, fishing, and swimming—and for navigation.

GROUND WATER—Most Mississippi municipalities depend on ground water as a public supply source. Public supply pumpage of ground water averages about 199 mgd, whereas industrial supplies averages only 191 mgd—a considerable difference from the amount of surface water used in industry. Of the total amount of ground water pumped annually in Mississippi, slightly over 49 percent is used in public supply. Industry is the second largest consumer of ground water using just over 35 percent of the total.

The remaining categories of ground water use are relatively insignificant when compared with those of public supply and industry. They are, in rank order by percentage of total utilization: electric power, 9 percent; institutional, 3 percent; irrigation, 2 percent; air conditioning, 0.32 percent; and miscellaneous (commercial, fire, and unused water), 1 percent.

Ralph D. Cross

MINERAL RESOURCES

Mississippi is not one of the nation's leading mineral producing states. Nevertheless, a considerable number of commercially valuable minerals has been found and developed, and other known or suspected concentrations can be expected to be developed when markets warrant or when technological improvements are made in the mineral industry.

MINERAL TYPES

PETROLEUM AND DERIVATIVES—Two major areas in the state have potential for petroleum production—the Mississippi or Interior Salt Basin in the south, and the Black Warrior Basin in the northeast.

The salt basin has produced commercially since 1930 with current production coming from strata of Tertiary, Cretaceous, and Jurassic ages. Most of the present production is associated with petroleum traps formed by faulting, anticlines, salt domes, igneous intrusions, stratigraphic anomalies, or various combinations of these. The salt domes are especially important in creating traps where petroleum pools can accumulate in the microscopic holes of porous rocks. Many fields have already been discovered in association with salt domes, and probably more will be found in the future.

Petroleum traps are formed by salt domes in several ways. Differential solution of the salt often leaves a cap rock of limestone which may be porous enough to trap and accumulate petroleum. In another case, as a salt plug slowly rises, local patterns of sedimentation are altered so that a stratigraphic pinchout of a porous bed occurs. In a third method, porous sandstone or other rocks are abruptly sheared and sealed off by the slowly rising salt mass. This may be called a structural pinchout. Under different conditions of stress, the beds of porous rock may be sheared and displaced to form fault traps either above, near the flanks, or quite a distance out from the flanks of the salt plug. In yet another situation, the beds of porous rock above the salt dome are arched to form anticlinal traps for oil and/or gas.

The Black Warrior Basin, which includes about 7,000 square miles of northeastern Mississippi, also extends into the neighboring states of Alabama and Tennessee. The basin consists of approximately 12,000 feet of rock ranging in age from Cambro-Ordovician to Pennsylvanian. So far, the production from the beds of Silurian, Mississippian, or Pennsyl-

vanian age has been commercially insignificant. Nevertheless, it is one of the few remaining undeveloped potential petroleum provinces of North America.

There are several indications that the Black Warrior Basin would be a favorable area to explore for oil and gas: the numerous shows of oil and gas in wells, the many sharp uncomformities, the marked lateral lithologic changes, and the many fault and anticlinal structures. In recent years, oil companies have spent large sums of money on exploration and drilling in the basin.

Petrochemicals are byproducts of the petroleum industry which have great significance in their own right. Petrochemicals, as commonly defined, include products based on ammonia, organic chemicals, and their derivatives. All types of petrochemicals are produced in Mississippi.

Ammonia is derived from natural and refinery gases and is used in the manufacture of nitric acid and fertilizers. Petrochemicals, which have a petroleum base, are used in the manufacture of paraxylene, toluene, and hydrocarbon resins. Natural gas and petroleum gas are also used to manufacture phosphoric acid,

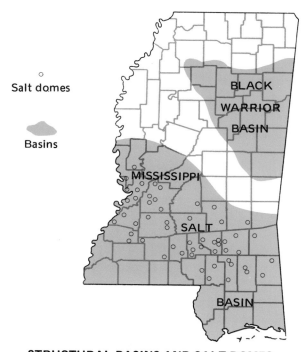

Salt domes

Basins

STRUCTURAL BASINS AND SALT DOMES

Source: Mississippi Geological Survey, 1972

sulfuric acid, formaldehyde, ammonium nitrate, flour-carbon resins, and polytetraflourethylene.

Hydrogen sulfide (H_2S) is another byproduct of oil and gas refining and is used to produce sulfur. Potential sources of hydrogen sulfide occur in the petroleum fields of Greene, Perry, Rankin, Stone, and Yazoo counties.

GRAVEL AND SANDS—Gavel production has been reported in forty-three counties. Ninety-five gravel pits are commercial operations, two are federal operations, and one is a local government operation. In addition, many other pits are maintained for local construction and county road maintenance. The principal gravel sources include the Tuscaloosa formation of Cretaceous age, and the Citronelle formation of the Pleistocene, plus numerous recent terrace and alluvial deposits.

Immense quantities of quartz sand are also widespread within the state. These are post-Paleozoic in age and may be fine- to coarse-grained. The chief impurities are clay, silt, and ironoxide; additional impurities include glauconite, kaolinite, lignite, mica, and heavy minerals.

Heavy minerals are found in many formations, but the largest known concentrations are the Recent beach sands of the Gulf Coast area and the associated offshore islands. They also occur in Cretaceous and Eocene formations. A concentration is usually 2–6 percent, but the Gulf side of the offshore islands has concentrations of heavy minerals as high as 60 percent. Of chief interest in sands rich in heavy minerals are ilmenite, kyanite, staurolite, and zircon.

Radioactive minerals are also present in Mississippi. They have been reported from several sources, but the largest known concentrations occur in the Recent beach sands of the Gulf Coast area and the associated offshore islands.

IRON ORE, COAL, AND LIGNITE—The iron deposits of Clarke, Benton, Kemper, and Webster counties have been of intermittent interest since 1881. These deposits consist chiefly of siderite and limonite along with small amounts of hematite. The Midway Group and Wilcox iron beds are most promising because they have 48–50 percent iron content. The Claiborne iron beds typically have 29 percent iron.

Some coal also occurs in Mississippi. The beds nearest to the surface occur in Chickasaw, Clay, and

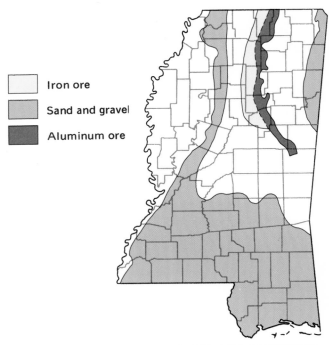

Iron ore

Sand and gravel

Aluminum ore

SAND AND GRAVEL, IRON, AND ALUMINUM

Source: Mississippi Geological Survey, 1972

Monroe counties where coal beds are about 1000 feet below the surface and are 2 feet in thickness. Lignite, a soft grade of coal, holds most promise for utilization in the immediate future. Unknown quantities have been mined spasmodically in various and most extensive beds of lignite. Choctaw County contains lignite beds which are consistently 7–8 feet in thickness. The lignite of the Claiborne Group is thickest in Holmes County and is also 7–8 feet thick. Minor amounts of lignite are known in the Tuscaloosa, Eutaw, Midway, Forest Hill, Vicksburg, and Miocene

LIMESTONE AND CEMENT—Marls and limestone, which are suitable for the manufacture of agricultural lime, are widespread in Mississippi. Localities worthy of special note occur in Clay County, Noxubee County, and the outcrop area of Vicksburg limestone in eastcentral Mississippi.

The raw materials for Portland and masonry cements are also found throughout the state. Deposits of both limestone and clay or shale are needed to produce the mixture which can be manufactured into cement. Substantial deposits have been noted in Rankin and Warren counties. The Oligocene limestones, marls, and clays of the Vicksburg formation also are good sources, but the outcrop belt of the Selma chalk is best. From the standpoint of markets and rail and water transportation, the hard limestones of the Paleozoic in northeastern Mississippi are especially promising.

CLAYS—Clays are abundant in Mississippi and have great commercial potential. In fact, Mississippi is one of the chief sources of the clay-type known as bentonite. Current production is confined to Itawamba, Monroe, and Smith counties, but other potential areas occur primarily in Attala and Pearl River counties. About 69 percent of the bentonite is used in foundrywork and other steelwork.

Mississippi is third in the nation in production of ball clay. Ball clay is mainly kaolinite, but has more silica and less alumina than typical kaolinite. Products fired from ball clay are generally not as white as kaolin products. The chief ball clay source is from the Eocene Zilpha formation of Panola County. All of the other known deposits are in northern Mississippi at the base of the Cretaceous Wilcox formations.

Mississippi ranks third in the nation in the production of fire clay. These clays are basically kaolinitic, although they also include other clay minerals and

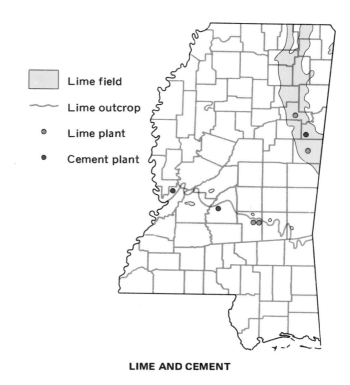

LIME AND CEMENT

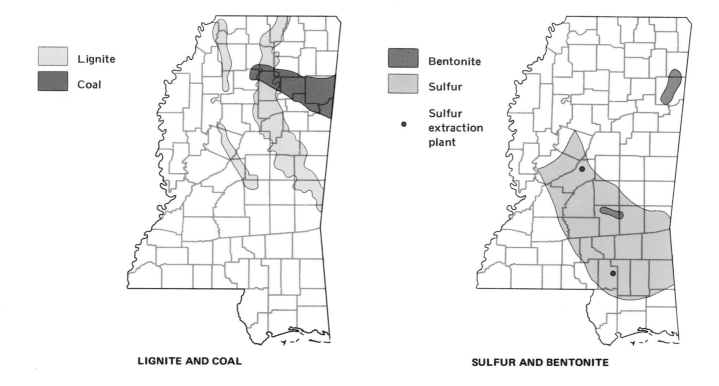

LIGNITE AND COAL

SULFUR AND BENTONITE

Source: Mississippi Geological Survey, 1972

91

impurities. Fire clays, used primarily for refractories, heavy clay products, and stoneware, are mainly produced near Byhalia and Holly Springs.

Fuller's earth, another Mississippi clay, consists primarily of montmorillonite; it is found chiefly in Tippah County. This clay may be used as an absorbent in mineral and vegetable oil refining, although it also has a potential in the manufacture of lightweight aggregate. Kaolinite and montmorillonite, clays used for making brick, are found throughout the state.

OTHER MINERALS—Chert is abundant in the Paleozoic area of northeastern Tishomingo County in solid layers, nodules, and as stringers of chert in other rocks. A few of these chert-bearing strata have weathered to form chert masses which are more than 100 feet thick, some of which is in the form of a soft, fine-grained type of silica called tripoli.

Dimension stone has also been produced in Tishomingo County. The Highland Church sandstone is quarried at several locations in beds 15–30 feet thick. It is a light colored, fine- to medium-grained quartz sandstone which has been used for rubble, ashlar, flagstone, and mantle cuts. Its excellent durability also makes it an attractive building stone.

Crushed stone can be used for concrete aggregate, road metal, or the base course of highways. The best locational possibilities for this stone are in the Paleozoic limestones which crop out in Tishomingo County. The Glendon member of the Vicksburg group, which outcrops in a narrow belt extending east–west across central Mississippi, also shows some development potential.

Production of shell from dead oyster beds began in 1951 from Mississippi coastal waters. These oyster shells are usually overlain by mud. The shells are used for cement, road aggregate, cattle feed, agricultural lime, whiting, soil conditioners, and for seeding live oyster beds.

The supply of salt and brines is tremendous but none is presently produced in Mississippi. The 100,000 tons used annually in the state come from sources outside Mississippi. Most of the salt occurs in subsurface salt domes in the southcentral part of the state. A total of sixty-one domes are known, twenty-five of which have salt less than 3,000 feet below the surface.

Karl A. Riggs

MINERAL UTILIZATION

The chief mineral products of Mississippi are, in order of economic importance, petroleum, natural gas, sand, and gravel.

PETROLEUM AND NATURAL GAS—The first attempt to discover oil or gas were wells drilled in 1903 in Clarke and Tishomingo counties. Numerous shows of oil and gas were found in succeeding years, but the first commercial gas well was not drilled until 1926 in Monroe County. The first commercial oil well was not brought into production until 1930 in the Tinsley Field of Yazoo County.

As of the beginning of 1973, approximately 423 oil pools and 70 gas pools were producing in 412 fields. In all, thirty-eight counties produced some oil and/or gas in 1972. That year, petroleum and natural gas constituted slightly over 91 percent of all mineral production in Mississippi.

Early oil and gas production was from strata of Cretaceous age with later production, including the Wilcox formation, of Eocene age. In 1964, production was discovered in strata of Jurassic age. This Jurassic "play" is still of great importance in current Missis-

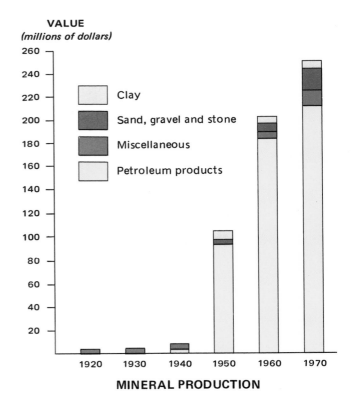

VALUE
(millions of dollars)

MINERAL PRODUCTION

Source: Mississippi Geologic Survey

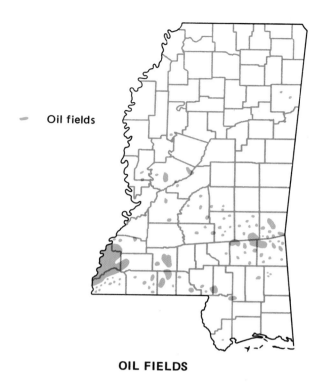

OIL FIELDS

Source: Mississippi Oil and Gas Board, 1972

sippi exploration. Minor production is known from Paleozoic strata and the Kosciusko formation.

The Baxterville field in Lamar and Marion counties is the largest oil producer in the state with over 7 million barrels of oil per year from upper Cretaceous and Wilcox strata.

Four counties account for about 72 percent of Mississippi's gas production—Jefferson Davis, Marion, Walthall, and Forrest. The upper Cretaceous produces 34 percent, the lower Cretaceous produces 42 percent, the Wilcox produces 15 percent, and the Kosciusko, Jurassic, and Paleozoic strata combined produce the remaining 9 percent.

The average field price in 1972 was $3.16 per barrel of crude oil. Cumulative value of all crude oil production in Mississippi was $3,525,758,473 at the end of 1972. That year the total value of petroleum production in Mississippi broke down as follows: oil, $192,-850,473 for 60,976,435 barrels; gas, $20,381,017 for 115,013,695 cubic feet. The combined total value of production for 1972 was $213,231,490.

At the end of 1972, the total number of producing wells in the state was 3,447, of which 3,106 were oil wells and 341 were gas wells. The approximate proved reserves of Mississippi as of January 1, 1973, were

1,100,000 million cubic feet of gas and 357,300 thousand barrels of crude oil.

Twenty-two percent of the state's area was leased for petroleum exploration as of early 1973. In 1971, the total number of people employed in crude oil and gas production was 13,700. Petroleum exploration continues in Mississippi. In 1972, the average exploratory well depth was 9,205 feet. The deepest well in the state went to a depth of 22,736 feet in the Mississippi Salt Basin. Of these exploratory wells, 111 produced oil, 11 were gas wells, and 324 were dry holes.

All classes of petrochemicals are produced at one or more of the ten plants in the state. These plants produce chemicals or derivatives for synthetic rubber and fibers, resins for paints and adhesives, plastics, plasticizers, solvents, adsorption agents, and acids.

Some petroleum products are stored in porous rocks underground during periods of light demand and withdrawn during periods of heavy demand. For example, Amory field, abandoned in 1937, and Jackson field, abandoned in 1954, have both been reworked for storage of natural gas.

SALT—Mississippi's salt supply is practically unlimited. Salt is found in rock domes deep beneath

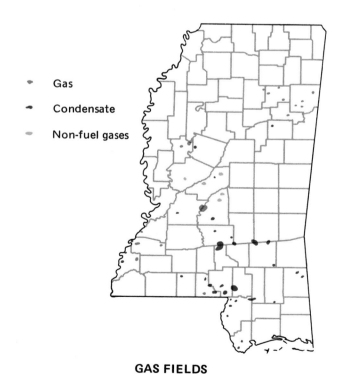

GAS FIELDS

Source: Mississippi Oil and Gas Board, 1972

the surface of southcentral Mississippi. Present Gulf Coast salt production, however, comes from about twenty-four salt domes in Alabama, Louisiana, and Texas. Except for one, these producing domes lie less than 3,000 feet below the surface. Although no salt is produced from them, there are twenty-five domes in the state situated less than 3,000 feet below the surface. There are additional salt domes at depths greater than 3,000 feet; natural gas could be stored in the porous cap rock of some of these.

SULFUR—Sulfur is a byproduct of oil and gas production. In Lamar County, Cretaceous beds produce gas and oil which can be processed to yield 25 long tons of sulfur per day. Likewise, Jurassic gas production in Rankin County yields 400 long tons of byproduct sulfur per day. The sulfur is derived from hydrogen sulfide gas (H_2S), a common constituent in crude oil and natural gas.

DIMENSION STONE AND LIMESTONE—Dimension stone has been produced in Tishomingo County, but currently most stone produced in the state is limestone, which is used for cement and agricultural lime. Although eighteen Mississippi counties contain ample supplies of agricultural lime, much is shipped in from other areas. Tishomingo County is a source of hard, crystalline, high calcium, Paleozoic limestones suitable for the manufacture of agricultural lime. Another lime area is the Cretaceous belt of Selma and Prairie Bluff chalks in eastern Mississippi. The Vicksburg formation has both marls and the hard, high-calcium limestone used for agricultural lime.

Cement sources are widely distributed throughout Mississippi. The carbonate rocks are artificially blended with shales or clays, fired to fusion, and then ground to make Portland cement.

CLAYS—Clays are playing an increasingly important role in the state's economy. Bentonite, an altered volcanic ash, is commercially produced in Smith, Itawamba, and Monroe counties. Bentonite is used in the manufacture of bleaching clay for refining and similar processes and of foundry molding sands.

Ball clays are used for pottery. These are commercially produced from the basal Wilcox and part of the Claiborne formations. Other miscellaneous clays are used for common brick and some face brick. Mississippi plants are capable of a combined production of about 1,800 bricks per hour.

SAND AND GRAVEL—At least forty-three coun-

SAND MINING   USDA

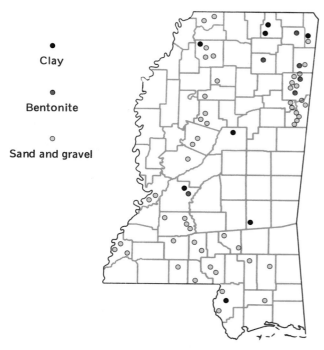

Clay

Bentonite

Sand and gravel

**SAND AND GRAVEL, BENTONITE,
AND CLAY PLANTS**

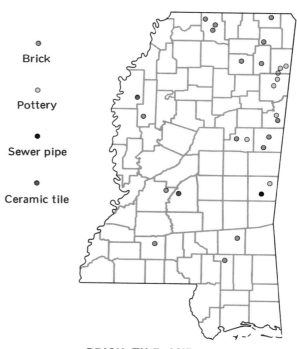

Brick

Pottery

Sewer pipe

Ceramic tile

**BRICK, TILE, AND
POTTERY PLANTS**

Source: Mississippi Geological Survey, 1972

OIL DRILLING   Delta Drilling Co.

ties in Mississippi record commercial production; other counties undoubtedly produce unreported amounts. Accurate figures are unavailable, but approximately 8 million tons of gravel and 4 million tons of sand are produced annually in the state. Much of the sand is mined in conjunction with gravel productions in the Citronelle gravels, the drainage basins of larger streams, and the alluvial plain of the Mississippi River. Most of the sand and gravel is used in the construction industry, although, in the past, glass sands for out-of-state shipment have been dredged from the Mississippi Sound of Hancock and Harrison counties.

SHELLS—Dredging the shells of dead oysters is a significant Mississippi industry concentrated in the Pearl River Estuary of Hancock County and the Mississippi Sound off Harrison County. The shell is used for road aggregate, cattle feed, agricultural lime, whiting, soil conditioners, and as cultch material for seeding oyster beds. The shell is usually found in water depths of eight to ten feet. Some of the shell is pure, but much of it is mixed with silt and clay.

Karl A. Riggs

FOREST RESOURCES

Mississippi and the South are entering a stage of forestry development unlike that of any previous period. In recent years, this era has become known as the Third Forest. Unlike its predecessors—the virgin forest and the second-growth forest that emerged from it—the Third Forest will encompass a large acreage of scientifically managed man-made woodlands.

FOREST TYPES

Mississippi was heavily forested in colonial times. Today, after generations of land clearing and logging, woodlands still dominate the landscape. Southern Mississippi, where nearly three of every four acres are in forest, is the most widely timbered region of the state. The Delta, with its highly mechanized agricultural economy, is the least timbered—only one acre in four supports any forest. Elsewhere the extent of woodland ranges between these extremes. In 1973, forests occupied almost 17 million acres, or 56 percent of the state's total land area.

The forests of Mississippi may be classified into six major resource types. Each type reflects the prevalence of certain key tree species:

FOREST

Forest Type	Acres (Thousands)
Longleaf–slash pine	1,337
Loblolly–shortleaf pine	4,247
Oak–pine	3,382
Oak–hickory	4,311
Oak–gum–cypress	3,284
Elm–ash–cottonwood	352
Total	16,913

LONGLEAF–SLASH PINE—Longleaf–slash pine forests are found on sandy soils of the lower Coastal Plain. Longleaf pine originally maintained itself on the drier sites, whereas the less fire-resistant slash pine was confined to the moister locations on which fire was less common. Cutting of the old growth and establishment of modern fire protection methods have enabled slash pine to seed into many areas formerly dominated by longleaf.

LOBLOLLY–SHORTLEAF PINE—Extending north from the lower coastal region, forests characterized by loblolly and shortleaf pines are found on several million acres. When intermixed, loblolly pine usually predominates and outgrows shortleaf on the wetter soils. Together these two species make up most of the

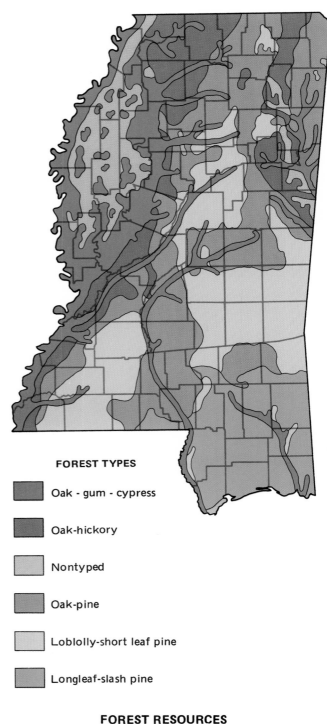

FOREST TYPES

- Oak - gum - cypress
- Oak-hickory
- Nontyped
- Oak-pine
- Loblolly-short leaf pine
- Longleaf-slash pine

FOREST RESOURCES

Source: U. S. Forest Service, 1969

standing pine volume in the state. Along with the long-leaf and slash pines, loblolly and shortleaf pines supply most of the raw materials for Mississippi's lumber, pulp, and veneer industries.

OAK–PINE–HICKORY—Throughout the loblolly-shortleaf pine forest, and to some extent in the long-leaf–slash pine belt, stands of upland hardwoods break up the continuity of the pines. Oak, hickory, and sweetgum commonly compose the principal cover in the forests. Much of the area dominated by the oak–hickory and oak–pine types is best suited for growing pines. But the uplands of Mississippi also have some deep, rich soils capable of supporting excellent hardwoods. The bluffs flanking the eastern edge of the Mississippi River's alluvial plain are a primary example. These loess bluffs, formed by the prehistoric deposition of windblown silt, support more than fifty species of trees. Among the economically preferred ones are cherrybark oak, Shumard oak, white oak, white ash, yellow poplar, black walnut, and black cherry.

OAK–GUM–CYPRESS— The Mississippi alluvial plain and the margins of secondary waterways throughout the state are typified by bottomland forests, mainly oak–gum–cypress. These forests vary considerably in composition from one area to another. Sweetgum, for example, is most common on the first bottoms or newer alluvium, where it is usually found in association with water oaks. The older soil formations or terraces are variously characterized by cherry bark oak, swamp chestnut oak, hickory, white ash, black-gum, and winged elm. Cypress is the only softwood of importance in the bottomlands. Stands of tupelo and cypress occur in the deep swamps and on the fertile but very heavy "buckshot" soils of low, wet flats and deep sloughs. Cypress forests are considered the most productive game habitat in the South.

OTHER TYPES—Generally speaking, timber grows rapidly in southern bottomlands. But a few localities, such as the poorly drained clay flats on first bottoms within the great backwater basin of the Yazoo River, have inherently low productivity. These sites are occupied mainly by overcup oak and bitter pecan, though the stands often include a workable nucleus of more desirable species, notably nuttal oak and green ash.

Herbert S. Sternitzke

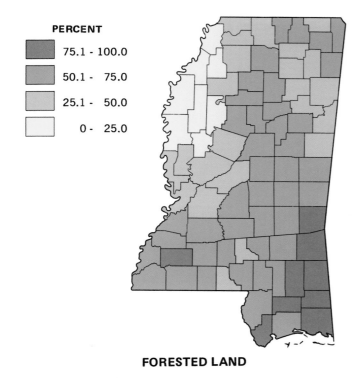

PERCENT

75.1 - 100.0

50.1 - 75.0

25.1 - 50.0

0 - 25.0

FORESTED LAND

Source: U.S.D.A., Forest Service, 1973

PINE TREES

Masonite Corp.

FOREST UTILIZATION

Primary forest industries using roundwood have been prominent in Mississippi for at least a century. In early years, forests were logged mainly to support sawmills, though cooperage and veneer plants were also important. Lumbering reached a peak in 1925, when a record 3 billion board feet were cut. After 1929, the Great Depression and the depletion of the forests kept production low for a decade or more. Large sawmills were replaced by numerous little ones that could operate on trees of small diameter.

After World War II, timber-growing practices began to improve and to provide the resources for industrial expansion. Pulpmills gained in number and in size. The small sawmills began to close as the quantity of lumber manufactured at the larger, modern plants increased.

Within the decade of the 1960s, the introduction of southern pine plywood manufacture added healthy competition in the timber market. By 1973, Mississippi's output of posts, poles, and pilings outranked similar production in most other southern states, although considerably less wood went into these products than into saw logs or pulpwood. Additionally, most industries have made great advances in the use of residues.

Because they have extensive pine stands to draw upon, Mississippi's primary forest industries can continue to grow and thereby contribute increasingly to the state's economy. The trend is toward large complexes manufacturing a variety of products efficiently and with minimum waste of wood.

FOREST OWNERSHIP—Forests are the dominant form of land use in Mississippi. In 1967, forests occupied 16.9 million acres, 56 percent of the state's total land area. Farmland, including pasture, made up 34 percent of the total. The remaining 10 percent was in urban and miscellaneous uses.

Forest area in Mississippi increased for almost three decades after the economic depression of the early 1930s. Most of this increase was realized from the reversion of abandoned farmlands. Since 1960, however, total forest area has declined slightly. Moreover, land clearing in the Delta has more than offset reversions in other parts of the state.

Ninety percent of Mississippi's commercial forest acreage is privately owned. Until recently, farmers held most of this land. But as the number of farms de-

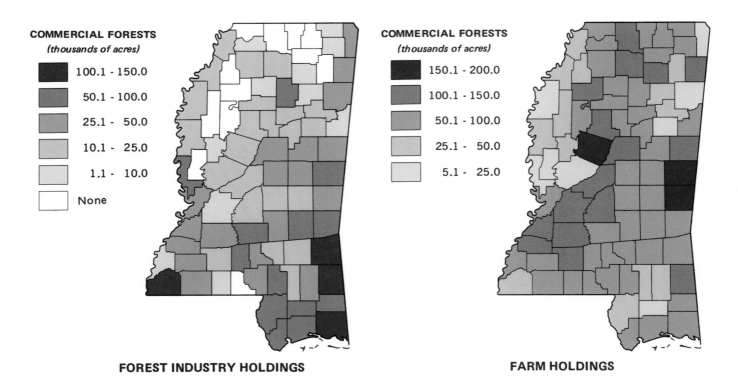

FOREST INDUSTRY HOLDINGS

COMMERCIAL FORESTS
(thousands of acres)

	100.1 - 150.0
	50.1 - 100.0
	25.1 - 50.0
	10.1 - 25.0
	1.1 - 10.0
	None

FARM HOLDINGS

COMMERCIAL FORESTS
(thousands of acres)

	150.1 - 200.0
	100.1 - 150.0
	50.1 - 100.0
	25.1 - 50.0
	5.1 - 25.0

Source: U.S.D.A., Forest Service, 1973

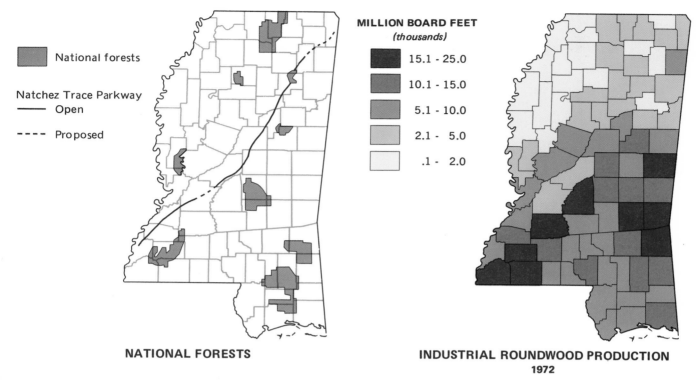

NATIONAL FORESTS

Source: Mississippi Research and Development Center, 1972

MILLION BOARD FEET
(thousands)

- 15.1 - 25.0
- 10.1 - 15.0
- 5.1 - 10.0
- 2.1 - 5.0
- .1 - 2.0

INDUSTRIAL ROUNDWOOD PRODUCTION
1972

Source: U.S.D.A., Forest Service, 1973

clined, so did the number of forest acres owned by farmers. In 1967, 6.2 million acres (36 percent of the total forest area) were farmer-owned, while miscellaneous private ownerships had risen to 6.4 million acres (38 percent). Forest industrial companies owned 2.5 million acres (15 percent) and leased 200,000 acres from farmers and other private owners. The remaining 10 percent was in public ownership. (Of this, 21,000 acres have been withheld from timber harvesting, most of the reserved land being in the Natchez Trace Parkway.)

By far the largest portion of public land in Mississippi is that composing the state's national forests. Slightly over 1.1 million acres are included in six such forests—Holly Springs, Tombigbee, Delta, Bienville, Homochitto, and De Soto.

In 1967, only nine of the state's counties had no land in forest industrial ownership. Industrial ownership among the remaining counties ranged from a low of 3,600 acres in Alcorn County to a high of 146,000 acres in Greene County. In addition to Greene, five other counties had industrial ownerships reaching approximately 1,000 acres each—Wilkinson (140),

Wayne (119), Jackson (100), Calhoun (94), and Clarke (92).

FOREST ECONOMY—Timber and timber-related activities are major sources of employment and income in Mississippi. In 1968, 64,280 full-time employees worked at timber-based jobs. Manufacturing was the largest employment category, providing jobs for over 59 percent of these workers. Manufacturing was followed by construction, transportation, and marketing (22 percent), by timber harvesting (16 percent), and by forest management (3 percent). Among those employed in the manufacturing sector (38,095), 57 percent worked in lumber and wood products, 18 percent in paper and allied products, 15 percent in furniture and fixtures, and the remaining 10 percent in miscellaneous activities.

These timber-based jobs paid an estimated $318 million in wages and salaries. As with employment, the manufacturing sector accounted for the larger portion of the wages and salaries earned, followed by construction, transportation, and marketing (22 percent), harvesting (12 percent), and forest management (4 percent). The manufacturing payroll, which

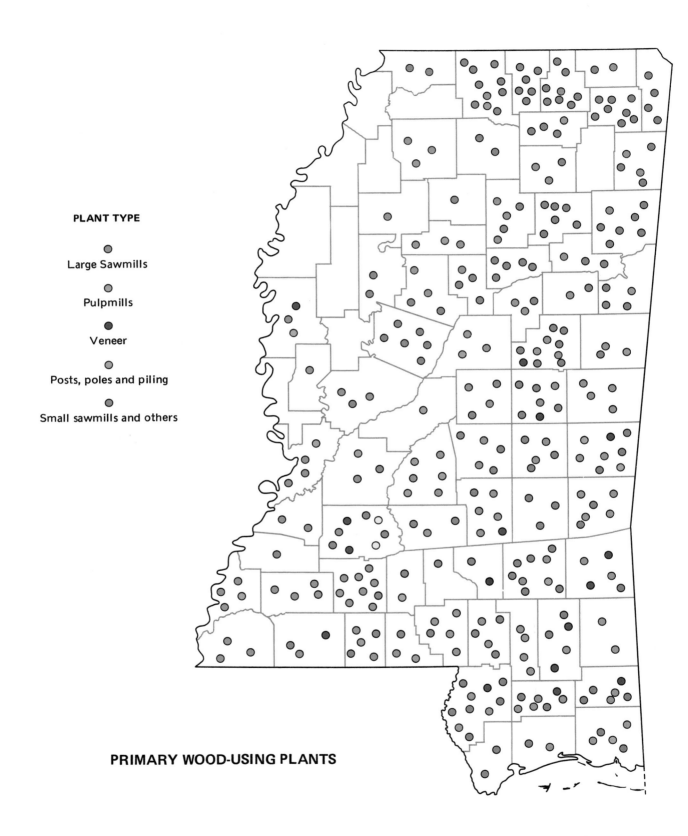

PLANT TYPE

Large Sawmills

Pulpmills

Veneer

Posts, poles and piling

Small sawmills and others

PRIMARY WOOD-USING PLANTS

Source: U.S.D.A., Forest Service, 1973

amounted to nearly $199 million, had as its components lumber and wood products (50 percent of the total), paper and allied products (26 percent), furniture and fixtures (13 percent), and miscellaneous activities (10 percent).

FOREST INDUSTRIES—In 1972 there were 318 forest industry plants throughout Mississippi, the Delta counties having fewer plants than elsewhere in the state. The 1972 volume of industrial roundwood harvested was 550 million cubic feet—383 million in softwood and 176 million in hardwood.

Pulpwood—Since the early 1960s, the pulp industry has been the major user of roundwood in Mississippi. In 1972, 51 percent of the timber harvested went into pulpwood bolts, as compared to 34 percent for saw logs. Eight mills, with a combined capacity of 6,050 tons per day, were in operation. Production capacity of the individual mills ranged from 80 to 1,620 tons daily. The two largest mills by employment are located in Jackson and Adams counties. Washington, Warren, Lauderdale, Jones, and Lawrence counties account for the remaining mills.

In 1972, production of round pulpwood totaled 3.5 million cords. In addition, mills used the equivalent of

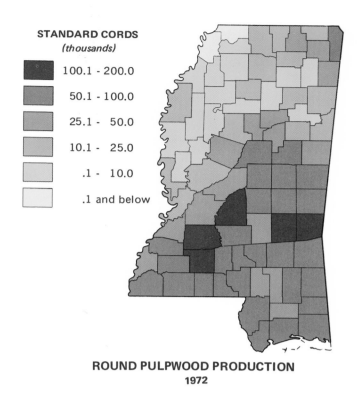

STANDARD CORDS
(thousands)

- 100.1 - 200.0
- 50.1 - 100.0
- 25.1 - 50.0
- 10.1 - 25.0
- .1 - 10.0
- .1 and below

ROUND PULPWOOD PRODUCTION
1972

Source: U.S.D.A., Forest Service, 1973

HARDBOARD PLANT   Masonite Corp.

one million cords of chips made from residues of plants manufacturing lumber, plywood, and other products. Until 1963, hardwoods were the main species cut for pulpwood; in 1972, two-thirds of the harvest was softwood.

Saw Logs—In 1972, Mississippi had 243 sawmills in operation. Output of individual mills ranged from 2,000 board feet to more than 54 million board feet. The average mill utilized 4.8 million board feet of saw logs. The 103 mills classed as large (cutting at least 3 million board feet annually) processed 90 percent of the lumber. Two-thirds of the large-mill production was softwood; in the small mills, almost two-thirds was hardwood.

Mississippi's 1972 saw log harvest was 1.1 billion board feet. Three-fifths of this total was softwood, mainly pine, but did include some cypress and eastern red cedar. Oaks accounted for more than half of the hardwoods cut for saw logs; gums were second. Sawmills are found in most Mississippi counties, but particular concentrations, especially among the larger operations, occur in the southern and northeastern parts of the state.

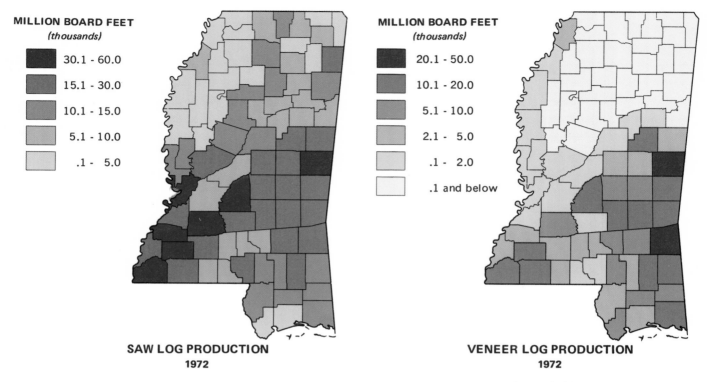

MILLION BOARD FEET
(thousands)

- 30.1 - 60.0
- 15.1 - 30.0
- 10.1 - 15.0
- 5.1 - 10.0
- .1 - 5.0

SAW LOG PRODUCTION
1972

MILLION BOARD FEET
(thousands)

- 20.1 - 50.0
- 10.1 - 20.0
- 5.1 - 10.0
- 2.1 - 5.0
- .1 - 2.0
- .1 and below

VENEER LOG PRODUCTION
1972

Source: U.S.D.A., Forest Service, 1973

Veneer—The first southern pine plywood plants in Mississippi opened in the mid-1960s. By 1972, seven plants were in operation. Together they processed 93 percent of the veneer manufactured in the state; the remaining 7 percent was produced in nine hardwood plants. The hardwood veneer industry in Mississippi reached its peak in the late 1940s, then began declining as supplies of large timber became scarce and as substitutes cut into the market. Only five of the remaining plants make face veneer; the rest turn out container stock. All of the state's veneer plants are located south of a line extending from Washington to Winston counties, and half of them are situated in the extreme southeastern part of the state.

The 372 million board feet of veneer logs harvested in 1972 comprised 11 percent of the state's total timber production. The ratio of softwood to hardwood cut for veneer logs that year was about ten to one.

Poles, Piling, and Other Products—All other products accounted for 4 percent of the total Mississippi roundwood harvest. More than 800,000 trees were cut for poles in 1972. The state also produced almost 8 million linear feet of piling and more than 3 million commercial posts. Small volumes went to plants manufacturing cooperage, furniture and handle stock, charcoal wood, excelsior, shuttleblocks, particleboard, and miscellaneous dimension.

Residue Utilization—In converting roundwood into primary products, Mississippi forest industries generated 145 million cubic feet of various wood residues in 1972. Seven-tenths of this volume was edging, cull pieces, and other coarse material suitable for conversion into pulp chips. The rest was comprised of such fine particles as sawdust and shavings. Almost 58 percent of these residues were sold to pulpmills. Another 23 percent were used for domestic and industrial fuel, charcoal, animal bedding, and soil mulch. Most of the remaining 19 percent were fine particles with no available market.

Utilization of residues can be expected to increase. But since most of the remaining volume is fine material, or is dispersed at small plants in quantities difficult to collect economically, the gains will be slower than heretofore.

Daniel F. Bertelson

RANGELAND RESOURCES

Grazing contributes materially to the economy of the South. In the area lying between Virginia and southwestern Texas there are approximately 200 million acres of forest land, much of which can be grazed. On most of this land timber production is considered the primary use, but native forage growing under the trees or in the clearings forms a great reservoir of food for livestock.

UPLAND HARDWOODS–BLUESTEM

This type extends over the northern and westcentral portion of the state, mainly in the areas where hardwoods and pine types intermingle. Most of the forage is furnished by several species of bluestem grass. The period of greatest nutritional value is during the spring and summer months. Excellent range conditions can support an animal unit on ten to twelve acres for twelve months, whereas poor range conditions often require twenty-five or more acres per animal unit.

BOTTOMLAND HARDWOODS–CANE

Bottomland hardwoods and native cane (includes giant and switch cane) are characteristic of the north-central Delta region. While both hardwoods and cane are found in the area, they do not necessarily occur together.

In this region, as in most of the state, the spring and summer months provide the best grazing; but, because of the wide variety of forages available, much of the area can also be grazed with little harm during the fall and winter. Common forage types under hardwoods include sedges, grasses, forbs, tree sprouts, and a variety of shrubs. The acreage needed to support a cow in hardwoods varies from about three acres on open grassy meadows to forty or more acres in densely wooded areas during the six-month spring and summer season when supplements are not needed.

In areas where native cane is the principal forage type, livestock can be maintained throughout the year when some supplement is provided during the winter. Stocking rates in the cane regions are usually higher than in hardwood areas, ranging from a high of two acres per cow on excellent range to fifteen acres on mediocre range.

PINE–BLUESTEM

Two broad forest–grassland types are included in the pine–bluestem category. Southern Mississippi, extending from Louisiana into Alabama, is dominated by the longleaf–slash pine–bluestem grass association. The remainder of the state, which includes most of the central and eastern portion, is predominantly of shortleaf–loblolly pine–bluestem grass associations. Together these two regions include most of Mississippi's rangeland and grazing area. Little bluestem is the dominant forage species throughout the area, but pinehill and other bluestem species, cutover muhly, pineywood dropseed, pancium species, native legumes, and some shrubs also provide important forage.

Progressive management usually calls for supplemental feeding or the provision of tame pasture during the fall and winter months in these pine–bluestem areas. Stocking rates for the months of April through November, when natural feeding occurs, range from eight acres per cow on grasslands with a few trees to as high as fifty acres per cow in heavily wooded areas. Since forests are the principal form of land use in these areas, care must be taken that livestock production does not interfere with timber production.

Robert W. Wales

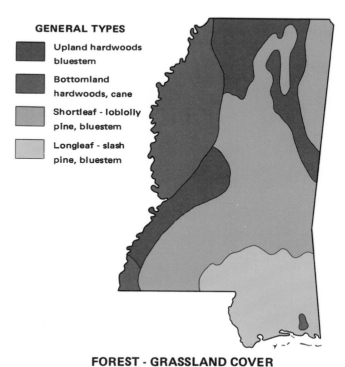

GENERAL TYPES

- Upland hardwoods bluestem
- Bottomland hardwoods, cane
- Shortleaf - loblolly pine, bluestem
- Longleaf - slash pine, bluestem

FOREST - GRASSLAND COVER

Source: American Society of Range Management, 1955

103

AGRICULTURAL RESOURCES

From even the most cursory examination of other sections in this Atlas concerning Mississippi's economy, the immensity of the industrial and commercial progress made in non-farm activities in the state since 1950 becomes quickly apparent. This dramatic progress tends to overshadow a corresponding and in many respects an even more remarkable advance in agriculture over the same period. Many Mississippians speak with justifiable pride of the "newly arising industrial Mississippi," but much of that industry is firmly based on a strong and steadily growing agriculture.

A high proportion of the state's industry is comprised of firms that process the output from farm and forest lands or that manufacture equipment and supplies essential to production on those lands. Much commerce is conducted by firms engaged in marketing, transporting, and distributing raw products from farms, or in providing the high volumes of supplies and services used in farm production. The farmer is therefore not only a dependable supplier of raw materials for industry and commerce, he is also a steady customer. In 1972, for example, Mississippi produced a raw product output valued at over $1.265 billion and moved a $1.084 billion share of it through channels of trade. In producing this record volume, the farmers put more than $800 million into the economy for production expenses. Most of the money went for products of industry—a vast array of production supplies ranging from tractors and similar equipment to fuel and oil, from fertilizers and other chemicals to milk pails and baling twine. It has long been the farmer's willingness to invest high percentages of his gross income into supplies that enabled him to realize such an increased production efficiency. Efficiency has been improved over the past two decades at a pace rapid enough to allow farmers to steadily increase annual output of farm commodities and, concurrently, to release vast quantities of manpower to the industries that complement their production.

Increased production efficiency has been reflected not only in an almost uninterrupted expansion of output, but also in changes in the composition of that output. These changes have increased the importance of Mississippi agriculture in both the state and national economy. For years Mississippi was known primarily as a cotton-producing state. Recently other enterprises have gained rapidly in prominence. In

1972, the state ranked ninth nationally and first among states east of the Mississippi River in beef cow production. Mississippi has become an important supplier of calves to cattle feeders throughout the nation. A massive expansion in poultry production has pushed the state to a national rank of fifth in broiler propagation and seventh in egg production. Cropwise, Mississippi remains second only to Texas in cotton production. It has also risen to a national position of fifth in rice production, eighth in soybeans, and tenth in peanut yield.

Other indicators of change, and ones partially reflecting production efficiency, are farm statistics. Farm numbers, for example, have shown a constant decrease for almost half a century, but the decline has been most pronounced since 1950. From a total of 251,383 farms operating in 1950, the number dropped to 72,577 in 1969. This decline was not accompanied by an equal decrease in total farm acreage, however. There were 20.7 million farm acres in 1950, 16 million acres in 1969. Much of the acreage held by those who left the farm scene was incorporated into the holdings of those who remained. Between 1950 and 1969 the average farm size increased from 82.4 acres to 221.0

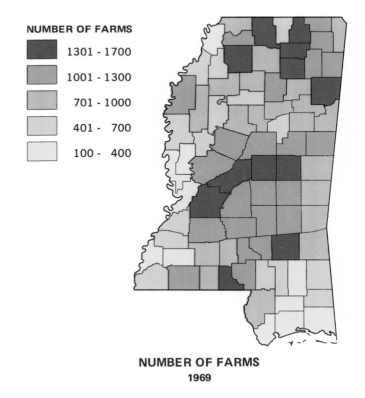

NUMBER OF FARMS

■	1301 - 1700
▣	1001 - 1300
▨	701 - 1000
▢	401 - 700
□	100 - 400

NUMBER OF FARMS
1969

Source: U. S. Census of Agriculture

acres. Also showing significant increases were the average farm value and average per-acre value. The average farm value in 1950 was $4,566; the corresponding figure in 1969 was $41,611. The average value per acre of farm land rose from $55.42 in 1950 to $233.53 in 1969.

CROP PRODUCTION

The year 1972 was a highly unusual one for Mississippi, perhaps best characterized as "good for growing" but notoriously poor for harvesting. Fortunately, at a time when farmers were planning to increase the planted acreage of cotton, an early warm, dry spring permitted faster-than-normal progress in cotton planting. But cool weather in May slowed early growth and delayed planting of soybeans, the state's second-ranking cash crop. Though most of the early growing season was favorable, by late August the dry, hot weather had damaged late planted acreages, slowing maturity of crops. Then the steady rains began in mid-October and continued throughout the winter, turning fields into seas of mud. Exceptionally poor harvest conditions plagued farmers through December, and by the first of the year about 10 percent of

the cotton acreage and at least 20 percent of the soybeans remained unharvested.

Yet, despite the latest, wettest, and most difficult harvest season in many years, the 1972 crop was a record-breaker. The output from the more than 5.2 million acres harvested was valued at over $719 million, an all-time high. Even when price differences are considered, there was a volume of commodities 9 percent larger than that of the previous year and about 42 percent more than that of five years earlier. Even though the number of farms had decreased by 15 percent and the number of farm workers had declined by 13 percent, nearly a tenth more acreage was harvested in 1972 than five years previously.

The largest cotton output in seven years had significant bearing on the record-breaking 1972 production, but the huge yield was attained without record production of any one crop. Rather, the feat was achieved through continuation of trends begun in Mississippi agriculture several years before. First, continued growth in farm size had justified the use of larger, more efficient equipment, thus enabling fewer farm workers to cultivate and harvest larger acreages. Additionally, much of the increase in volume was directly

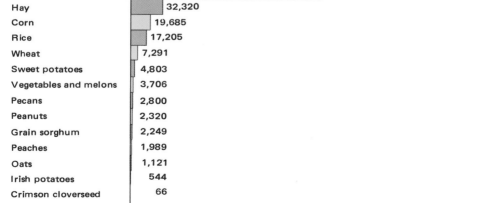

AGRICULTURAL CROP PRODUCTION BY FARM VALUE
(thousands of dollars)

Source: Crop Reporting Board, U. S. D. A., 1972

attributable to a shift away from low-yielding feed grains to the more productive (and more readily marketable) cash crops.

COTTON—Mississippi has long been America's second-ranking cotton-producing state, yielding an average 14–16 percent of the national cotton output. Mississippi's production is exceeded only by that of Texas, a state that normally devotes three to four times as much acreage to cotton as it does. Despite excessive rains throughout the 1972 harvest season, Mississippi farmers produced a 2 million bale, $426 million crop taken from 1.6 million acres.

The alluvial soils of the Mississippi Delta are some of the world's most productive for cotton, and more than half of the state's cotton acreage is planted in that region. In 1972, twelve Delta counties—including Yazoo but not Issaquena—harvested 54 percent of the state's cotton acreage and produced almost three-fourths of the total output. The counties of Sunflower, Bolivar, Coahoma, and Washington accounted for more than one-third of the cotton acreage and nearly 40 percent of the total production. Issaquena, a county with relatively few farms, was the only Delta county harvesting fewer than 35,000 acres or 50,000 bales in

1972. However, Issaquena did produce one of the highest yields in the state—765 pounds of lint per acre compared to an average of 640 pounds for other Delta counties and 599 pounds for the state as a whole.

Outside the Delta, cotton is most heavily planted in counties with loessial or brown loam soils. (In Panola, Madison, De Soto, and Marshall counties more than 28,000 acres of cotton were harvested in 1972, for a total of 154,300 bales. The remainder of the state's crop is produced largely in the northern half of the state. Only four northern counties harvested fewer than 5,000 acres or produced fewer than 5,000 bales in 1972. Accepting the 1972 production distribution as typical and excluding Madison County's production, less than 4 percent of Mississippi's cotton crop is produced in counties lying south of Noxubee, Winston, and Attala counties, and east of the Big Black River. Two percent of the cotton raised in this area is growing in Hinds, Rankin, and Leake counties. In recent years ten or more of the state's southernmost counties have harvested fewer than 50 acres of cotton.

SOYBEANS—The world-wide shortage of protein since the 1960s has made soybeans a crop of national significance. In response to the seemingly limitless demand for this versatile food and feed source, the acreage harvested for soybeans in the United States increased by more than 22 million acres or about 66 percent in a decade. In that period, production rose from 699 million bushels to almost 1.3 billion bushels, making the value of the 1972 national output $5.3 billion.

In Mississippi, soybean production has increased at a pace exceeding the national average. In 1962, slightly less than 21.6 million bushels were produced from 1.1 million acres. By 1971 state farmers were harvesting almost 56.6 million bushels of beans from 2.6 million acres. This increase is even more remarkable since in the South soybean production usually competes with cotton for land, labor, and other inputs. The trend toward a rising soybean output was reversed in 1972. Not only did fall and winter rains reduce yields that year, but some farmers also converted from soybeans to take advantage of higher cotton prices. The result was a 13 percent reduction in output from the level of the previous year—slightly less than 49.3 million bushels were harvested from about 2.5 million acres.

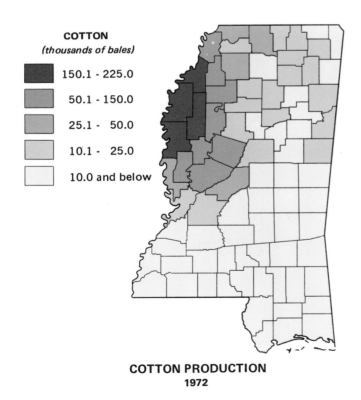

COTTON
(thousands of bales)

150.1 - 225.0
50.1 - 150.0
25.1 - 50.0
10.1 - 25.0
10.0 and below

COTTON PRODUCTION
1972

Source: Miss. Crop and Livestock Reporting Service

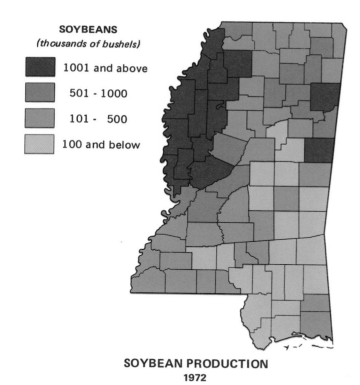

SOYBEANS
(thousands of bushels)

■ 1001 and above

▨ 501 - 1000

▨ 101 - 500

▨ 100 and below

SOYBEAN PRODUCTION
1972

At an average price of four dollars a bushel, the 1972 crop had a farm value of $197 million. The major portion of soybeans were processed in Mississippi oil mills; others were shipped to various states for crushing, and the remainder were transported to Gulf ports for export. Soybean exports in 1972 totaled approximately 1.7 million bushels, with an estimated value of $87.9 million.

Prior to the sixties, the state's soybean production was heavily concentrated in the Delta region. In 1962 the twelve Delta counties produced 84 percent of the state's 21.6 million bushel output. Nine counties harvested more than 1 million bushels, and three produced more than 2 million bushels. Five counties bordering the Delta and containing a high proportion of Delta-type soils, along with four counties in the northeastern corner of the state (Prentiss, Lee, Union, and Chickasaw), accounted for another 12 percent of the volume produced. The remaining 4 percent of the 1962 volume came from small acreages in fifty-six counties.

In 1972 the pattern of production within the state had changed significantly. An expansion of acreage outside the Delta was such that in 1972 the Delta

counties accounted for only 50 percent of total soybean output. The number of counties harvesting more than 1 million bushels of beans had increased from nine to fifteen, including the twelve Delta counties and the prairie counties of Monroe, Panola, and Noxubee. The second heaviest concentration of soybean production was in counties north of Highway 82 and in the loessial soils of Holmes, Madison, Hinds, and Warren counties. In thirty counties lying wholly south of Highway 80, production totaled only 4.4 million bushels, or less than 9 percent of the state total. In the eastern half of that area, production was particularly light.

RICE— Mississippi is one of six states in which rice is grown commercially. Rice, like cotton, is an allotment crop, its acreage being subjected to control under provisions of the Soil Conservation and Domestic Allotment Act of 1936, as amended. Mississippi's acreage allotment, and its contribution to the national rice output, is comparatively small. Still, rice makes a significant contribution to the agricultural economy, having become the state's third-ranking cash crop. In 1972, sales of more than 2.3 million hundredweight of rice from 51,000 acres exceeded $17 million.

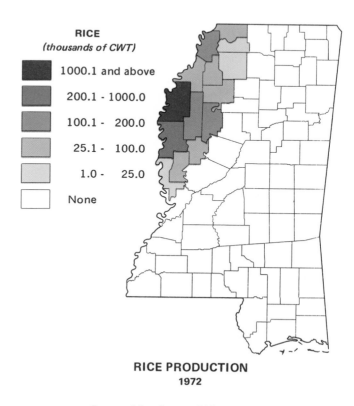

RICE
(thousands of CWT)

■ 1000.1 and above

▨ 200.1 - 1000.0

▨ 100.1 - 200.0

▨ 25.1 - 100.0

▨ 1.0 - 25.0

□ None

RICE PRODUCTION
1972

Source: Miss. Crop and Livestock Reporting Service

107

(Farm values of both corn and hay topped that figure, but in Mississippi these two crops are grown primarily for use on the farms where produced, rather than for the market.)

Rice production is restricted to the alluvial soils of the Delta and bordering counties. Bolivar County produces over 40 percent of the state's rice; Washington County produces an additional 20 percent. Other counties harvesting more than 3,000 acres and producing over 144,000 hundredweight in 1972 included Sunflower, Leflore, and Tunica counties. Issaquena, Panola, and Tate counties are less significant as rice-producing areas. Acreages harvested in these three counties have averaged about 300 acres annually with production at between 12,000–13,000 hundredweight.

Long-grain varieties of rice predominate in Mississippi. Fifty thousand of the 51,000 acres harvested in 1972 were planted to long-grain varieties. Only 1,000 acres were devoted to medium-grain types.

WHEAT—Farmers raised almost 5 million bushels of winter wheat on 160,000 acres in 1972. Value of production was approximately $7.3 million, and exceeded the previous year's crop by over $1 million.

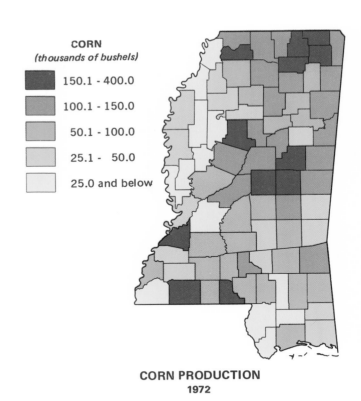

CORN
(thousands of bushels)

- 150.1 - 400.0
- 100.1 - 150.0
- 50.1 - 100.0
- 25.1 - 50.0
- 25.0 and below

CORN PRODUCTION
1972

Source: Miss. Crop and Livestock Reporting Service

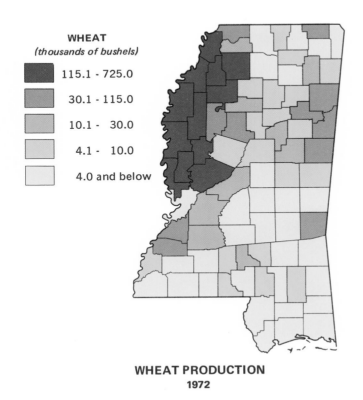

WHEAT
(thousands of bushels)

- 115.1 - 725.0
- 30.1 - 115.0
- 10.1 - 30.0
- 4.1 - 10.0
- 4.0 and below

WHEAT PRODUCTION
1972

Source: Miss. Crop and Livestock Reporting Service

The number of acres harvested fell sharply from a 1967 peak of 452,000 to 107,000 acres in 1969, but in recent years acreage has shown a slight increase.

Most of Mississippi's wheat production occurs in the Delta region. Twelve counties in that area, each harvesting 3,500 or more acres, produced better than 80 percent of the 1972 crop. Two counties, Bolivar and Washington, accounted for over one-fourth of the state's total output. Wheat is also grown in the loessial soils of the brown loam counties and in the Blacklands, or prairie counties near the Alabama border. Relatively little wheat is grown in the upper and lower coastal plain areas of the state.

Mississippi is one of only two southern states showing a long-term decline in corn production. The corn acreage for grain in Mississippi fell from over 2 million acres in 1950 to 1 million in 1960, and to only 163,000 acres in 1972. Concurrently, production fell from nearly 51 million bushels in 1950 to 7.3 million bushels in 1972. By far the greater part of that 7.3 million bushels, valued at about $19.7 million dollars, was used for feed on the farms where grown. Fewer than 1 million bushels entered commercial trade channels.

As recently as the late 1960s, over half of the coun-

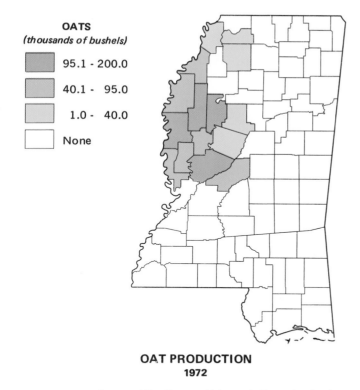

OATS
(thousands of bushels)

- 95.1 - 200.0
- 40.1 - 95.0
- 1.0 - 40.0
- None

OAT PRODUCTION
1972

Source: Miss. Crop and Livestock Reporting Service

ties in the state could each claim some 150,000 bushels of corn harvested. By 1972, only a dozen counties were producing as much. Corn is, at present, grown primarily in the northeastern quarter of the state, though not all of the twelve leading corn-producing counties are located in that area.

In addition to the acreage harvested for grain, 45,000 acres of corn were harvested for silage in 1972. At an average of 12 tons per acre, production totaled 540,000 tons.

OATS—The trend in Mississippi oat production has followed that of corn, albeit at a somewhat slower pace. Acreages of oats declined almost 100,000 acres in a decade, and by 1972 only 28,000 were harvested. With the decline, oats production in Mississippi has become primarily an enterprise of the Delta region. Four Delta counties—Sunflower, Washington, Leflore, and Yazoo—produced over 40 percent of the state's 1972 crop of 1.46 million bushels, valued at $1.2 million. A few non-Delta counties had acreages and productions sufficiently large to justify reporting of individual county estimates.

More than one-third of the oat volume produced in

the state and a much larger proportion of production in the non-Delta counties were used on farms where grown. Fewer than a million bushels of the 1972 production were marketed, and cash receipts from oats totaled only $713,000.

GRAIN SORGHUM—Prior to the 1970s, sorghum was grown in Mississippi primarily for silage or as a forage crop, and acreages exceeded that planted for grain. Following a cutback in cotton acreage and an increased demand for feed grains in 1970, sharp increases occurred in production of sorghum for grain. By 1971, Mississippi producers were harvesting 5.4 million bushels from 150,000 acres. Two limitations—the inadequacy of drying and storage facilities and the relatively low profitability of the crop—inhibited expansion, and in 1972 acreage harvested for grain declined to 33,000 and production to 1.4 million bushels.

In recent years grain sorghum production has been heavier in the northern hill portion of the state than in southern Mississippi or in the Delta region. A large proportion of the crop, particularly that produced in the southern half of the state, is used for feed on farms where grown. In 1972 less than two-thirds of the $2.2 million grain harvest was marketed. In addition to the 33,000 acres harvested for grain in 1972, about 45,000 acres were planted for silage and 6,000 acres for forage.

HAY—The long-term increase in beef cattle production on Mississippi farms has maintained a high production of hay. In only one year since 1964 did hay harvest fail to exceed a million tons. Although total hay acreage has been on the decrease, yields per acre have shown a significant increase. In 1965, for example, Mississippi farmers harvested 1.01 million tons of hay from 640,000 acres.

Traditionally, hay has not been considered a major cash crop in the state, but is produced primarily for consumption on farms where grown. In 1972 only one-eighth of the $32.3 million crop was marketed.

MINOR CROPS—Mississippi's 1972 crop yield included an $11.4 million harvest from about 41,000 acres of minor crops—peanuts, sweet potatoes, Irish potatoes, vegetables, watermelons, pecans, and peaches.

More than half of the 10,000-acre, 16-million-pound peanut output came from five Delta counties; harvested acreage in Coahoma County accounted for more than 27 percent of the state total. Although production value in 1972 exceeded $2.3 million, the peanut is of little commercial importance in most non-Delta counties.

Mississippi's 1972 sweet potato crop of 10,000 acres yielded 850,000 hundredweight, with a farm value of $4.8 million. Counties leading in production were Calhoun and Chickasaw in the north and Wilkinson in the southwest.

An estimated 2,000 acres of Irish potatoes yielded a harvest of 170,000 hundredweight, valued at slightly more than $.5 million. Growers in five counties— Panola, Coahoma, Monroe, Pontotoc, and Wilkinson —produced more than half of the crop.

Commercial vegetable production in Mississippi is limited primarily to cucumbers for pickling and fresh cabbage for markets. About 8,000 acres produced 21,000 tons of cucumbers valued at $2.3 million. Heaviest production is in the southern part of the state, particularly in that group of counties reaching from Copiah and Simpson south to the Louisiana line. A secondary concentration exists in Bolivar and Washington counties. Only about 700 acres of cabbage, yielding a crop valued at $178,000 were harvested,

with most of the acreage in Copiah County.

Although its contribution to the state's agricultural output is only minor, the watermelon crop is of some commercial significance. Leading in watermelon production in 1972 were Pearl River, George, and Smith counties, where most of the state's 10,500 acres of melon valued at $1.2 million were grown.

The average annual pecan production for the decade preceding the 1972 harvest was over 15 million pounds. However, an unusually small harvest throughout the nation's pecan belt in 1972 brought production down to 7 million pounds. The average farm price for the nuts that year rose to 40 cents a pound, for a total value of $2.8 million. Commercial pecan groves are concentrated in the Delta and in southern Mississippi.

Mississippi has three peach production belts. One is located in the Hinds–Copiah area, another lies in Lauderdale and Clarke counties, and the third consists of a narrow strip running approximately from Batesville to Clarksdale in the upper Delta. Peach production in 1972 totaled 17 million pounds for a farm value of approximately $2 million.

L. Dow Welsh

SOYBEAN HARVEST

USDA

LIVESTOCK PRODUCTION

Mississippi agriculture has been transformed from a largely labor-oriented activity to a mechanized enterprise. Moreover, the state has shifted from a two-crop agricultural scheme to a varied agricultural system emphasizing a balanced livestock program. Essentially, this change has occurred over the past hundred years with an accelerated transformation since World War II.

The greatest change occurring in Mississippi agriculture in the last thirty years has been the tremendous growth of the livestock industry. In 1960, the total agricultural farm income for the state was just over $626 million. Of that total, 17 percent (over $111 million) was derived from the sale of meat-producing animals. In 1972, the value of Mississippi farm products was in excess of $1.5 billion, of which over $329 million (20 percent) was derived from the sale of meat-producing animals.

BEEF CATTLE—Beef cattle production in the state has increased approximately 350 percent since 1950. Mississippi now ranks ninth in the United States in brood cow production with over 1.3 million head of brood cows, and fifteenth nationally in cattle and calves with an approximate total of 2.6 million head. During 1972, the state farm income from beef cattle was over $286 million. One of the major beef-producing activities in Mississippi centers around the sale of beef calves for fattening. Most of the beef calves produced are sold at weaning and shipped to major feeding areas in the western United States. In 1972 nearly 800,000 head of government inspected calves went to feeder farms in other states. Winter grazing of beef calves has been a rapidly growing enterprise within Mississippi; approximately 250,000 beef calves throughout the state are fattened on rye grass each year.

Although beef cattle production has expanded rapidly, there still remains room for continued growth. The state's adequate rainfall and moderately warm temperatures provide an optimum climate for the maintenance of 4 million acres of grass pasture for grazing beef cattle the year around.

There are a number of factors contributing to the development of the beef cattle industry in Mississippi. Among these are the state's potential for producing forage crops and the relatively recent decline in the number of small row-crop operators who have largely

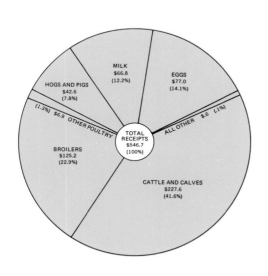

AGRICULTURAL LIVESTOCK PRODUCTION BY FARM VALUE
(millions of dollars)

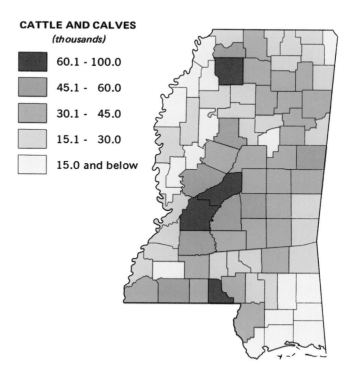

ALL CATTLE AND CALVES
1972
Source: Miss. Crop and Livestock Reporting Service

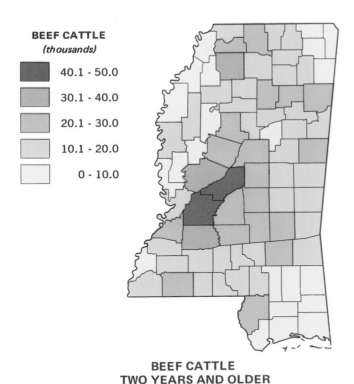

BEEF CATTLE
(thousands)

- 40.1 - 50.0
- 30.1 - 40.0
- 20.1 - 30.0
- 10.1 - 20.0
- 0 - 10.0

**BEEF CATTLE
TWO YEARS AND OLDER
1972**

Source: Miss. Crop and Livestock Reporting Service

converted their operations to cattle production. Also, the number of rural-nonfarm dwellers turning to cattle raising as a secondary income source has increased. These people live on farms but derive their primary income from industries or other urban-associated jobs in nearby towns and cities. All these conditions conducive to cattle production are present in the Brown Loam Region (see p. 83) and the counties in southeastern Mississippi where the heaviest concentrations of beef cattle exist.

DAIRYING—Mississippi lies well outside the traditional "dairy belt" of the northeastern United States. Dairying in Mississippi is not the dominant agricultural activity but exists primarily to service large urban markets lying, principally, outside the state. Within the state the dairy farmer is the base upon which the dairy industry is dependent. The dairyman furnishes the essential commodity—raw milk—for all dairy products eventually reaching consumers.

Location of dairy farms is primarily in response to positions of large urban centers providing markets for milk. Once it was necessary for producers to locate

BEEF CATTLE

USDA

near urban markets because of milk's perishability. However, technical advance in refrigerated transportation has made proximity to cities less significant. Nonetheless, most Mississippi dairy farms are situated on sites selected years ago and perpetuated to the present.

The largest concentrations of Mississippi dairy herds (a better indicator of dairying intensity than farms) are in the northwestern, central, and southern parts of the state. Counties with large numbers of dairy herds are oriented toward one principal market but also supply other markets, thereby resulting in overlapping milksheds. One such concentration is centered in De Soto County, but also includes Tate and Marshall counties. This area is a part of the Memphis, Tennessee, milkshed, with Memphis the primary market. Oktibbeha, Noxubee, Neshoba, and Newton counties, together with a large number of adjacent counties extending primarily to the northeast, form a part of the Birmingham, Alabama, milkshed. A third concentration includes Amite, Pike, Walthall, and Lincoln counties, together with several adjacent counties. This region is situated within the New Orleans milkshed, with New Orleans the primary market.

The physical environment, primarily topography and vegetation, also affects location of dairy herds. Normally, dairying is relegated to land not physically suited for other agricultural pursuits, or to areas where grass is abundant. In Mississippi, grazing often occurs on forest land having an undergrowth of grass.

The leading Grade A dairy area of the state includes the counties of Walthall, Pike, Lincoln, and Amite. Walthall County leads the state in both the number of Grade A dairies (151) and number of milk cows (10,000).

The total sales value of dairy products in 1972 was estimated at $86.3 million. Value of milk production alone that year was $66.8 million (this figure represents 78 percent of the combined value of dairy products plus dairy beef sales). Value of beef from sales of dairy cattle and calves was estimated at over $19 million in 1972 with cull dairy cows contributing the major portion.

The $86.3 million dairy income of 1972 was shared by almost 1,600 Grade A dairymen and about 1,800 producers of manufactured milk (products other than fresh milk). Grade A dairymen produce over 90 percent of all milk marketed in Mississippi and, therefore,

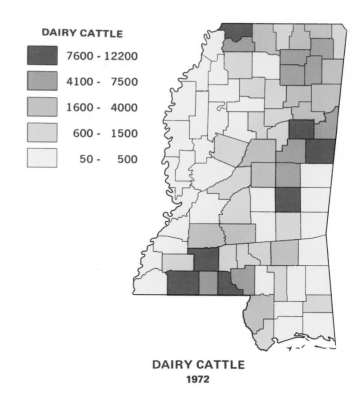

DAIRY CATTLE

■	7600 - 12200
▨	4100 - 7500
▧	1600 - 4000
▫	600 - 1500
□	50 - 500

DAIRY CATTLE
1972

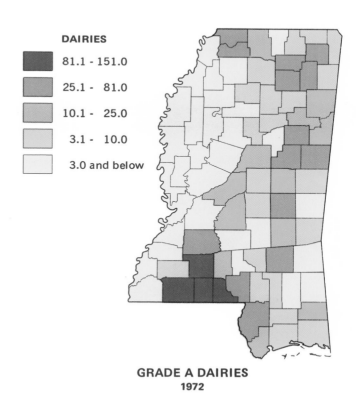

DAIRIES

■	81.1 - 151.0
▨	25.1 - 81.0
▧	10.1 - 25.0
▫	3.1 - 10.0
□	3.0 and below

GRADE A DAIRIES
1972

Source: Miss. Crop and Livestock Reporting Service

113

receive the major shares of dairy dividends.

In 1970 there were 44 milk processing firms reporting an average monthly employment of 1,974 persons. Total wages paid by dairy manufacturing plants in 1970 amounted to $13.4 million. In addition, there were 106 wholesale dairy product distributors. These distributors reported sales of about $63 million for the fiscal year ending June 30, 1971.

The firms noted above are classified as dairy processors. They are augmented by thousands of grocery stores across the state, employing several thousands of workers, and handling milk and milk products along with other food items. Workers in wholesale and retail grocery establishments amounted to some 15,000 persons and were paid annual wages amounting to $70 million in 1972.

POULTRY AND EGGS—Poultry ranks as the largest food producing industry in Mississippi. Nationally, Mississippi ranks fifth in broiler production and seventh in egg production. In 1972 a total of nearly 2 billion pounds of poultry meat and eggs—945 million pounds of poultry meat and 208 million pounds of eggs—were produced in Mississippi. In addition, hatcheries produced 260 million chicks for layers, breeders, and broilers. Mississippians consumed about 28 percent of the eggs and approximately 12 percent of the poultry meat produced.

Gross income from poultry in 1972 was $197.4 million, with egg sales accounting for $77.2 million. Investments of $4.7 million in such equipment and buildings as broiler, laying, and breeder houses, hatcheries, feed mills, and processing plants were the primary poultry industry expenditures.

The poultry industry in Mississippi arose from a need for additional income on the part of rural people, concentrating in areas where individuals were willing to invest personal and/or borrowed capital to ultimately resolve this need. As production increased, these areas became more concentrated due to reduced transportation costs.

In 1972, state feed mills turned out 1.75 million tons of feed for use in raising chicks for layers and broilers. Some mills averaged as much as 450 tons of feed per day, using corn, soybean meal, and other minor ingredients. For every ton of feed, an average 2¼ tons of poultry manure results. About 3 million tons of poultry manure was produced in 1972; its value as fertilizer was estimated between $16 and $25 per ton, for a total

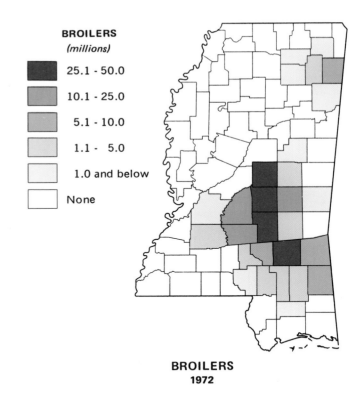

BROILERS
(millions)

- 25.1 - 50.0
- 10.1 - 25.0
- 5.1 - 10.0
- 1.1 - 5.0
- 1.0 and below
- None

BROILERS
1972

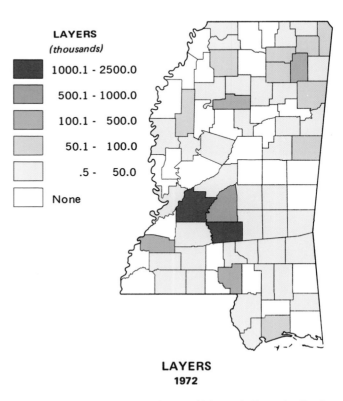

LAYERS
(thousands)

- 1000.1 - 2500.0
- 500.1 - 1000.0
- 100.1 - 500.0
- 50.1 - 100.0
- .5 - 50.0
- None

LAYERS
1972

Source: Miss. Crop and Livestock Reporting Service

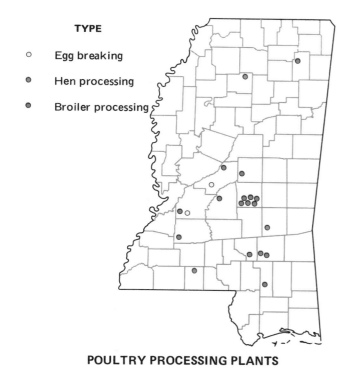

POULTRY PROCESSING PLANTS

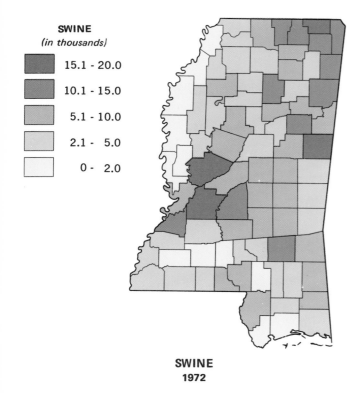

SWINE
1972

Source: Miss. Crop and Livestock Reporting Service

value between $56 million and $87.5 million, a substantial byproduct for the industry. Poultry fertilizer is used primarily on pastures and secondarily on cropland.

Mississippi poultry processing plants ship poultry to population centers throughout the nation and to several foreign countries. Poultry processing plants include broiler plants, hatcheries, egg grading plants, and egg breaking plants (where eggs are broken and frozen for use in such other food processing industries as bakeries, etc.).

The operating capital and working inventories of the poultry industry total half a billion dollars. Poultry's annual payrolls, which usually run well over a million dollars, include employees of farms (broiler, layer, and breeder), hatcheries, feed mills, and processing plants, truck drivers, administrative personnel, accountants, and many others.

SWINE—Since 1960, swine production has increased from the 639,000 pigs farrowed that year to over 797,000 pigs in 1972. During the same period, income from swine has increased from $20 million to $43 million. The production of feeder pigs has been one of the fastest growing segments of the swine industry. Feeder pigs are purchased by both in-state and out-of-state buyers. During 1972, a total of nearly 50,000 feeder pigs were sold for $1.3 million through organized sales.

Mississippi's potential for expansion of the swine industry in the 1970s appears quite good. Currently, a significant percentage of swine slaughtered by the Mississippi packing industry is imported from outside the state.

The heaviest concentrations of swine are situated in Hinds, Noxubee, Yazoo, and Alcorn counties, though the counties adjacent to these also contain large swine populations. Regionally, the heaviest concentrations appear to be in the northeastern and east-central parts of the state. Mississippi swine producers are usually owners of small farms, employed in urban jobs, who use swine production as a means of increasing income.

Charles E. Lindley

GAME AND FISH RESOURCES

Mississippi is fortunate to possess an abundance and variety of environments—marshes, coastal and inland waters, forests, and grasslands. Each of these offers habitats for a large number of game and fish resources. The significance of this fact cannot be overlooked. Wildlife is a major source of aesthetic and recreational enjoyment. Wildlife is also big business in the state not only in terms of earnings derived from hunting, fishing, and other recreational pursuits, but from fish farming and the rich Gulf Coast marine industries as well.

GAME ANIMALS

SQUIRRELS—Squirrel hunting is the most popular of all hunting sports in Mississippi. Well over 50 percent of the resident licensed hunters hunt squirrels, and the harvest usually averages 2–3 million annually.

Two distinct species of squirrels inhabit Mississippi—the gray and the fox squirrel. Gray squirrels are more abundant and more evenly distributed throughout the state. There are two races of fox squirrel: the hill fox squirrel, which has a white nose and ears and a black crown, and the Delta fox squirrel, native to the Yazoo Delta and counties bordering the Mississippi River, which occurs commonly in both red and black color phases, but lacks the white nose and ears of the hill fox squirrel.

Squirrel hunting is best along the rivers and larger stream bottoms and in large, mature or maturing tracts of upland forest. Squirrels do not range into large, unbroken stands of pine. In general, the gray squirrel prefers large dense tracts of hardwoods, whereas the fox squirrel prefers open hardwoods or forest peripheries and the park-like stands of mixed pine–hardwoods in upland areas. Hardwood habitats supply shelter, escape cover, food, and nesting and playing sites. Preferred tree species for squirrels include oaks, pecans, cypress, ash, mulberry, elm, magnolia, maple, gum, dogwood, and ironwood.

WHITE-TAILED DEER—The white-tailed deer is the only big game animal present in Mississippi in sufficient numbers to justify hunting. Mississippi's deer herd numbers in excess of 300,000 animals, which are hunted in all of Mississippi's eighty-two counties. Deer numbers have benefitted from man's efforts at reforestation, stocking, protection, and management programs. As recently as the late 1920s, deer had been exterminated over most of the state, with only a

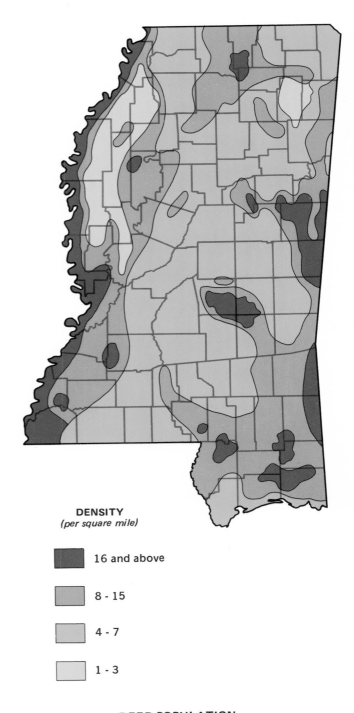

DENSITY
(per square mile)

16 and above

8 - 15

4 - 7

1 - 3

DEER POPULATION

Source: Mississippi Game and Fish Commission

few herds found in the larger floodplains. With the regeneration of timber stands, and a concentrated restocking effort over the past several decades, deer have been restored to abundance. In the 1971–72 hunting season, an estimated 35,000 deer were killed by hunters.

Bottomland hardwood forests contain the largest concentrations of deer within the state. The animals favor, in progressively lower order of tree density, the loblolly–shortleaf, pine–hardwood, oak–pine, and longleaf–slash pine forests. The greatest concentration of kill is along the Mississippi River Valley, particularly in the southwestern part of the state. Deer habitat is best where many and dispersed openings occur within the forest, and where timber thinnings are frequent and heavy. Timber management practices thus greatly affect the quality and quantity of cover and food.

Party hunting with dogs is the most popular form of hunting deer in Mississippi, although still and stalk hunting, without dogs, is increasing in popularity. Guns by far account for the greater kill during the two hunting seasons in November–December and December–January. Special seasons for bowhunters and primitive firearms hunters are also provided, and 11,000 and 5,000 such hunters, respectively, bought licenses for the 1972–73 season.

RABBITS—The cottontail rabbit, one of the most hunted game animals in the United States, in Mississippi ranks third in popularity among game animals. Two species of rabbits inhabit the state—the cottontail and the swamp rabbit. Their ranges overlap, but generally the cottontail is the more abundant; exceptions are in swampland or bottomland hardwoods where swamp rabbits sometimes exceed cottontails in numbers.

Mississippi hunters bag in excess of 1 million rabbits annually, a harvest generally well-distributed throughout the state. The best areas for rabbit hunting are recently burned-over or cutover lands with an abundance of treetops, briars, and brush. Hunting with beagles or hounds is the usual and most productive method. Interest in field trial beagling is increasing in Mississippi. Field trial clubs exist in most parts of the state, and many of these clubs manage their own running grounds for rabbits.

OTHER ANIMALS—The fraternity of hunters who keep hounds for the chase is quite large in Missis-

sippi. Raccoons, opossums, and foxes are classed by law as both game and fur-bearing animals and can be run with dogs the year around. Fox and 'coon hunt clubs are numerous, and field trials are held on running grounds. Raccoons and opossums are abundant throughout most of Mississippi, and red and gray foxes are plentiful enough to attract regional and national field trial events.

RESIDENT GAME BIRDS

EASTERN WILD TURKEY—The wild turkey, like the white-tailed deer, has experienced a fairly rapid population increase over the past several decades. By the late 1930s, wild turkeys were found only in the most remote areas of Mississippi in small numbers, with the entire state population numbering only about 1,500 birds. A slow recovery began in the late 1930s, and by 1941 the population had increased to around 5,000 birds. Experimental stocking with pen-reared, wild-strain turkeys in the thirties resulted in failure. A few wild-trapped turkeys became available in the 1940s from a private game preserve; these birds were used to stock state game refuges, and the increase and their progeny have provided breeding stock for other areas. Since 1954, over 2,000 live-trapped wild turkeys have been reintroduced to suitable habitats lacking breeding stock. As a result of this stocking, and subsequent protection and management programs, Mississippi in the early 1970s had almost 100,000 birds with an open hunting season in all or part of sixty-three counties. From these, hunter kill numbered over 9,000 turkeys in the 1972 season.

The regeneration and maturing of forest lands, the reversion of innumerable small farms from cropland to pasture and timber, and landowner and sportsman interest and protection have favored the restoration of wild turkeys. Much progress has been made toward turning public sentiment against illegal poaching, a practice which long made positive management programs difficult to implement.

Although turkey populations are influenced by many factors, weather conditions seem to play the most important role in affecting their increase. Cold, wet weather during that part of the season when nests are hatching and poults are small limits production success. Warm, dry weather during this season favors good poult production. Several successive good or below-normal production seasons can cause drastic fluctuations in the total population of turkeys over wide areas of the state.

Turkey populations within Mississippi and throughout the South are most numerous in bottomland hardwood forests. Conversion of these lands for agricultural purposes, reservoirs, or other uses will greatly affect future birds. The best habitats are found in stands of mixed hardwoods, groups of conifers with scattered clearings, well-distributed water, and freedom from disturbance. The usual range for a flock is 5,000 to 10,000 acres, though 500 to 600 acres may be sufficient.

Mississippi's highest density turkey populations are found in the land between the levees along the Mississippi River in the northern Delta counties. Southwestern Mississippi counties, the southern Piney Woods, and national forest and state management areas also support large turkey populations. Many other sections of the state have rapidly expanding and increasing flocks, particularly in the eastern and northcentral areas.

BOBWHITE QUAIL—The bobwhite quail is a popular Mississippi game bird. Although quail are fairly abundant throughout the state, they are often not sufficiently plentiful in most areas readily available to the average hunter to furnish satisfactory hunting. Nevertheless, even the hunter of moderate means can find good shooting if he keeps one or two good dogs, cultivates the good will of small-farm owners, and has the knowhow and interest to "beat the bushes" in the sub-marginal quail habitats. Although the number of quail hunters is on the decline, hunters still harvest a per capita average of 29 quail per season. Approximately 1.8 million quail are harvested annually by 63,000 resident Mississippi hunters.

Conversion of small farms to wood or pasture and large-scale, clean, mechanized farming are adverse to quail production and good quail hunting. Quail production responds to land management practices that provide good cover and food distribution. Such practices include food and cover plantings, controlled burning, discing for natural plant succession, and manipulation to provide cover for escape, roosting, and nesting.

MIGRATORY GAME BIRDS

Woodcock, common snipe, rails and gallinules, mourning doves, ducks, coots, geese, and mergan-

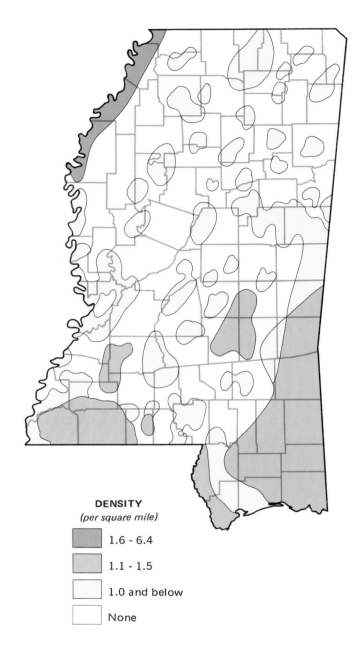

DENSITY
(per square mile)

　1.6 - 6.4
　1.1 - 1.5
　1.0 and below
　None

TURKEY POPULATION

Source: Mississippi Game and Fish Commission

sers are the migratory game birds most hunted in Mississippi. Hunting seasons and bag limits are set each year by federal regulations.

The mourning dove is the favorite target of migratory, upland game hunters. Mechanized, clean-farming practices favor both the production and harvest of doves. The Yazoo Delta and the Black Prairie belt in northeastern Mississippi are probably the most productive dove hunting areas, although hunting is successful in all sections of the state where planted or harvested grain attracts and holds concentrations of birds.

The woodcock is another upland game bird that is gaining popularity. Most bird hunters know the woodcock as an occasional bonus bird bagged while quail hunting. Even so, over 30,000 are probably taken in the state each year. Mississippi is the heart of the wintering grounds for woodcock. In most years, woodcock winter throughout the state, and at times during migration concentrations appear locally. Woodcock haunts are thickets in bottomlands near sloughs, spring seeps, cypress–tupelo–gum brakes, bayheads, and beaver ponds.

There are better than 20,000 duck hunters in Mississippi. More than a dozen different species of diving or surface-feeding ducks are sought, but the mallard and woodduck are the two species most often taken. The best duck hunting areas are the large reservoirs, oxbow lakes, sloughs, brakes, and flooded bottomland timber areas. The Yazoo Delta and Mississippi River areas of the Mississippi flyway are the most productive. Sardis Reservoir is the best reservoir for both surface-feeding and diving ducks. Goose hunting in Mississippi is limited to areas along the Mississippi River, Sardis Reservoir, and a few localities on the flood control reservoirs and islands of the Mississippi Sound.

W. H. Turcotte

QUAIL HUNT

State Game and Fish Commission

FRESHWATER SPORTS FISH

For both in-state and out-of-state residents, Mississippi provides some of the finest freshwater sports fishing in the South. With the increasing emphasis on recreation in Mississippi, freshwater fishing (which ranked tenth among all state outdoor recreation activities in 1972) can be expected to increase in popularity in the near future.

Mississippi's 493 square miles of fresh water contain some 157 species and subspecies of freshwater fish, plus an additional 38 kinds of salt and brackish water fish. The freshwater fishes range in size from the lowly minnows and shiners, which measure as small as two inches, to the large blue catfish, having been known to attain weights over 100 pounds, and some members of the gar family, which measure over eight feet in length and weigh in excess of 200 pounds.

Although the list of Mississippi freshwater fishes is long, there are only ten species generally classified as game fish of major importance—the channel, blue, flathead, and bullhead catfish, and six species of the sunfish family (including the largemouth and the spotted bass, bluegill, the black and the white crappie, and redear).

The sport of catfishing is well recognized by local fishermen. Surprisingly, however, anglers in many other sections of the country mistakenly think of catfish as a poorman's food and of catfishing as a dull match between man's wit and a sluggish fish which will eat anything dead or alive. However, catfish—mostly through commercial production of pond-reared fish—are reaching the tables of the best restaurants in the country as well as abroad; and any fisherman who has ever hooked a flathead would be hard to convince that it is not a fighting fish. While the Mississippi River and its immediate tributaries, lakes, and ponds are recognized as prime catfishing spots, the fish can be found in waters just about everywhere throughout the state.

The channel catfish is found principally in the larger streams and lakes. Averaging five pounds or less, it is probably the tastiest catfish species and is thus heavily sought after. The blue, or Mississippi, catfish is most abundant in the lower reaches of the Mississippi River and its larger tributaries. It is the biggest of the catfish discussed here, averaging from three to twenty pounds, with fifty-pounders not uncommon.

The flathead catfish generally averages five pounds or more and can reach five feet in length. It favors rivers; the wider and deeper the river, the larger the fish. Good flathead fishing is found below larger dams and above dams in river impoundments. The bullhead catfish are of three types—black, brown, or yellow. The black is by far the most numerous of the three, and can attain a weight of two pounds and a length of sixteen inches. Bullheads are the most ubiquitous of the catfish, ranging from small creeks and ponds to the larger rivers and reservoirs. Though probably most fished by younger anglers, they provide good sport for all age groups, and are excellent pan fish.

In the sunfish family, the largemouth black bass and the spotted bass are, in that order, the most important of the larger game fish in Mississippi. The largemouth bass is the bigger of the two, with one largemouth having been recorded at slightly over thirteen pounds. Shallow ponds, warm lakes, and sluggish streams provide excellent habitats for the largemouth. The cooler, spring-fed streams are more favored by the spotted bass. Both species, as well as other members of the sunfish family, can be taken by spinning rods, casting rods, fly rods, or poles with either artificial or live bait.

The bluegill bream, weighing as much as one and one-half pounds, is often considered the gamest of all sunfish. By virtue of its wide distribution in natural lakes, streams, and artificial impoundments, this bream is the most sought after Mississippi sports fish. Second only to the bluegill in popularity is the crappie, of which there are two species, the black and the white. Like others of the sunfish family, the crappie are abundant throughout the state and are known for their delicate flavor and tender meat. The last of the state's more popular game fish is the redear, also known locally as the "shellcracker" or "chinquapin." It is quite similar to the bluegill in habitat. Although not so prolific as the bluegill, it is heavier, sometimes weighing as much as two pounds.

Robert W. Wales

FISH FARMING

Although per capita consumption of fresh fish in the United States has remained relatively constant over the last five or six decades, the population growth and the increased use of fishery products in industry and in agriculture have strained the nation's ability to produce sufficient quantities of these products. In 1967, for example, 71 percent of the country's fishery products were imported, and it is estimated that this figure will reach 92 percent in 1974. The shortage of fishery products from traditional sources within the United States has been an important factor in the growth of freshwater fish farming. While this industry is relatively new in Mississippi, it has become widespread within the state in the last decade.

Catfish are the main "crop" harvested on Mississippi fish farms. Of the several catfish species available, the channel catfish is preferred by fish farmers because channel cats can withstand handling, survive relatively low oxygen levels, and are favored by catfish connoisseurs. Three hundred days of feeding are required to raise a catfish fry to food fish size of a little over a pound. The average growing season in Mississippi is over 200 days, but many days are too hot for catfish to feed. For this reason it normally requires two growing seasons to raise fry to the proper weight.

One major requirement of fish farming is clay soils. Ponds need to be constructed on clays in order to hold water at the surface and prevent it from percolating through. Much of Mississippi has soils with sufficient clay content for construction of good fish ponds. This is especially true of the Yazoo Basin, where old backswamps can be drained; the basin's "gumbo" clay makes excellent pond sites. Moreover, the water table in this area is close to the surface, and supply wells are relatively inexpensive to drill and bring into production.

Mississippi's Clay Hills region also offers excellent sites for fish ponds since the draw of a course on a small stream can be dammed off, and relatively large ponds made with little cost. Farmers in the Clay Hills can use their fish ponds to water livestock. This is an excellent arrangement, because livestock provides natural fertilizers for ponds and catfish seem to do much better under these conditions than when commercial fertilizers are used alone.

Many fish farmers have special ponds for brood fish and fingerling production. Young fish are usually kept in fingerling ponds until they reach a size of three to six inches; then they are placed in a production pond and kept until harvested. Some fish farmers specialize in brood stock. Production of brood stock is rather risky because these fish must be kept from three to

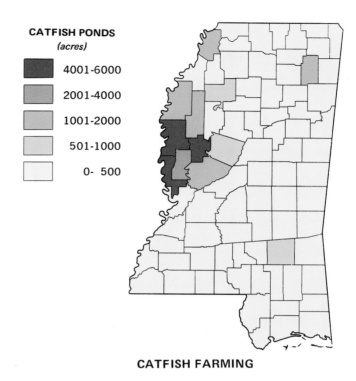

CATFISH PONDS
(acres)

4001-6000

2001-4000

1001-2000

501-1000

0- 500

CATFISH FARMING

Source: Soil Conservation Service, 1973

four years; therefore the chances of the fish dying or becoming diseased are much greater than in the production of food fish.

Good, high-quality water is another requirement for raising fish. While some fish farmers depend on runoff to fill ponds, most of them supply ponds from wells. Wells are very important during the hot season, since they can be used to supply fresh water to ponds with a low dissolved oxygen content during periods of high temperatures when oxygen depletion is likely. Moreover, the farmer is not dependent upon intermittent stream flow to fill ponds when constant flow is needed for production. Other advantages of wells are a lack of undesirable fish and a lesser possibility of chemical and industrial waste contamination, which might be contained in springs, streams, and surface runoff. These latter sources may also bring undesirable sediments into a pond.

Water quality control has to be maintained in stocked fish ponds. The water can be neither too hard nor too soft—a range in mineral content of 20–200 parts per million is desirable. The optimum pH range for catfish is between 6.5 and 8.5. However, in Mississippi an acid water condition is far more probable than any other condition, a factor which can be corrected by an application of lime to the pond.

Three types of fish cultures are in use in Mississippi—extensive, intensive, and highly intensive. In extensive culture, the fish are placed in ponds and left to fend for themselves; occasionally, supplemental feeding is used. The stocking rate is proportional to the natural support capability of a pond. Where extensive culture is used, the stocking rate is usually less than 1,000 fingerlings per surface acre. Extensive culture does not require much investment in such equipment as pumps and feeding systems.

Intensive culture of catfish requires a dependable source of water and a high degree of water quality control. The fish must be fed regularly, since ponds cannot supply enough natural food for them. The stocking rate in intensive culture is commonly 2,000 fish per surface acre, a number which can quickly deplete the dissolved oxygen in a pond. Therefore, lift pumps are usually essential to aerate pond water when the dissolved oxygen content reaches low levels.

Highly intensive culture, or raceway culture, was not in common use in Mississippi in 1973. In highly intensive culture, water must be run continuously through the pond because the high stocking rate (3,000–6,000 fish per acre) would otherwise quickly use the available dissolved oxygen in a pond.

Catfish farming provides a high yield of meat per acre. In intensive catfish culture, yields vary from about 1,000 pounds per acre to over 3,000 pounds per acre. In highly intensive culture it is possible to obtain yields as high as 10,000 pounds of fish per acre. In a world where the ratio of arable land to population is steadily decreasing, this type of farming has great promise for the future. Large amounts of high protein meat can be grown on a relatively small amount of land that is generally unproductive for other crops.

Catfish farming has been a rapidly growing farm enterprise in Mississippi. For all practical purposes there were no pond-grown catfish in the state in 1960. By 1969, there were 16,000 acres in catfish ponds in Mississippi; by 1973, there were 29,000 such acres. The center of catfish production lies within the Mississippi River floodplain. Over 80 percent of the total acreage in catfish production is found in Bolivar, Holmes, Humhpreys, Lee, Sharkey, Sunflower, Tallahatchie, Tunica, Washington, and Yazoo counties.

Even though catfish farming requires a large fixed investment in land, levees, pumps, boats, seines,

feeding stations, and other equipment, it is a profitable enterprise for many of the farmers of the state. The demand for catfish is so great that there is a continuous shortage of catfish on the market. As long as this shortage exists, it is reasonable to assume that more and more farmers will turn to the production of catfish. It is not uncommon for fish farmers using intensive culture to gross $800 to $1,200 per acre per year.

Although many farmers sell their fish to local markets, most of the catfish grown in Mississippi go to commercial processors, who kill, clean, and either pack the fish in ice or freeze them for shipment. Catfish can also be frozen and stored, since their storage life is up to one year. Some catfish processors have automated equipment that will skin and freeze a catfish as it goes through a production line.

Catfish farming started at an opportune time in Mississippi. The demand for fish is rising, and the traditional sources for fish are diminishing. While farm-raised fish have never been as inexpensive as ocean fish, conditions may soon become economically feasible for their worldwide distribution.

John W. Kilburn

MARINE SPORTS FISH

The marine sports fishery in Mississippi is divided into an inshore and an offshore component. The former is an all-year fishery, whereas the latter is seasonal.

In 1971, approximately 141,000 fishermen participated in the inshore fishery of the Mississippi coast. These fishermen landed a total of 1.44 million pounds of fish, averaging a catch per unit of effort of two pounds of fish per hour of fishing. There are three variations in the type of inshore sport fishing along the coast. These include "still" fishing, trolling, casting, or any combination of the three. Still fishing is by far the more popular method throughout the year. Only during the early winter months, when the large spotted sea trout move into the coastal rivers and bayous, is there any significant amount of trolling.

Baits used in the inshore fishery are of three types—live, dead, and artificial. Live and dead bait are notably the most popular, and only the most ardent sports fishermen and the winter spotted sea trout fishermen utilize artificial baits. Dead bait is commonly used during the warmer months; as the season progresses, and the weather cools, live baits are the more successful. Among the baits most commonly used by the inshore fisherman are shrimp, squid, menhaden, and bull minnows. Of these, shrimp, live or dead, are the most popular. Combinations of shrimp and squid or of shrimp and cut bait are also widely utilized. Menhaden, although a very successful bait, are not used by most anglers. During the cooler months, when the shrimp supply decreases, bull minnows become very popular in the quest for spotted sea trout, redfish, or flounder.

The inshore catch is composed of about twenty species of fish, the most sought after of which are the spotted sea trout, white trout, red drum, flounder, and ground mullet. The composition of the catch varies throughout the year with some predictability. White trout account for the greatest percentage of the catch on a year to year basis, followed closely by the croaker and the spotted sea trout. Together with ground mullet, these four species account for over 85 percent of the total sport fish catch in the inshore waters.

During the spring, summer, fall, and early winter the white trout and the croaker are the fish most apt to be hooked; during that period, they account for over 80 percent of the total catch. During the late fall and early winter the white trout and the croaker are replaced by the spotted sea trout, which accounts for 80 percent of the take during November and December. Ground mullet make up about 10 percent of the total catch throughout the spring, summer, fall, and early winter. The remaining 10 percent of the take is composed of sixteen different species of fish ranging from catfish to sharks. The inshore fishing is slow during the late winter months of January and February.

The inshore fishery is served by sixty-two fishing camps and marinas located in Jackson, Harrison, and Hancock counties. These establishments offer a variety of services, including boat and motor rentals, mooring facilities for personal boats, bait, tackle, ice, fuel, and lodging.

Approximately 83 percent of those persons engaged in the inshore fishery are from the three coastal counties. About 9 percent of the inshore anglers are from other Mississippi counties, 7 percent are from other states, and the remaining 1 percent are from countries as far away as Germany and Korea.

The offshore marine fishery of the Mississippi Gulf Coast is centered around the barrier islands lying

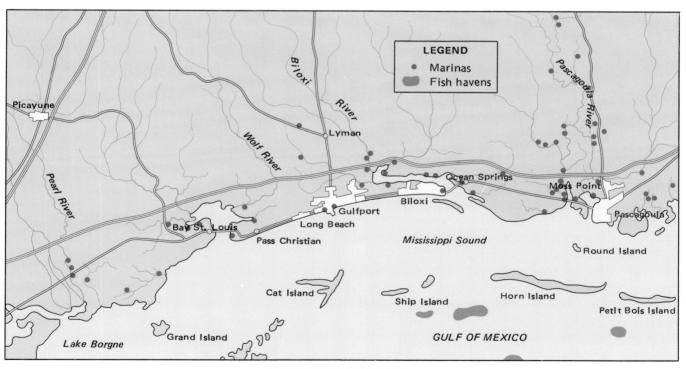

SPORT FISHING SITES

from ten to twelve miles off the coast. The waters surrounding these islands offer a variety of fishing, as do the Gulf waters lying to the south of the islands. From the beaches of the islands spotted sea trout, red fish, ground mullet, and pompano can be caught. From boats in the immediate waters around the islands the catch is mainly of Spanish mackerel, king mackerel, lemon fish, bonita, and blue fish. Still farther offshore to the south are found a variety of such big game fishes as blue and white marlin, wahoo, sail fish, and several varieties of tuna.

Over the past few years a number of oil wells have been drilled in the open waters a few miles south of the Mississippi Gulf Coast. The offshore drilling rigs offer some of the finest fishing to be found anywhere in the world. Although a variety of fishes are taken from around these rigs, the most frequently caught is the red snapper, one of the tastiest and most prized of fish.

The island fishery becomes active from late February to early March, when weather permits. By late April and early May, the island fishery is in full swing and continues until the first cold spell in the fall. During the spring, spotted sea trout and red fish are hooked by surf casting from both the north and south beaches of the barrier islands, including Ship, Horn, and Petit Bois islands. Anything from artificial lures to live shrimp will prove useful in landing these fish. Casting from the island beaches during the summer period can yield the pompano, blue fish, red fish, and spotted sea trout. These fish usually are hooked on artifical lures. A number of local fishermen have also introduced freshwater fly rod casting to the island fishery, providing one of the most challenging sports to be found anywhere.

In the shallow waters north of the barrier islands are extensive grass beds. Among these beds lemon fish can be caught in spring and summer. Lemon fish range in size from 15–90 pounds and offer the fisherman with a limited budget some excellent big game fishing. Normally, the fish are taken while "still" fishing, using baits ranging from artificial lures to live catfish. In the shallow waters just south of the barrier islands, trolling yields Spanish mackerel, king mackerel, bonita, and blue fish.

The deeper waters south of the Mississippi coast are fished mostly for red snapper, which are hooked on hand lines, using dead bait. Snapper are numerous around the offshore drilling rigs, as are blue fish, Atlantic croaker, Spanish mackerel, and lemon fish. Out in open Gulf waters, approximately 90 miles south of the coast near the edge of the continental shelf, the big game fishery is located.

The island fishery and near Gulf waters are readily available to most fishermen with an 18-foot or larger boat. Some of the finest sport fishing in the world is within 30 miles of any site on the Mississippi coast.

In addition to the many coastal fishing camps and marinas, there are also a number of charter boats for hire from Bay St. Louis to Pascagoula, with the greatest number located in the Biloxi–Gulfport area. These boats provide access to the big game fishery in the open Gulf. They can handle day parties of from one to fifty people and overnight trips for as many as twelve persons. The charter boats offer a day's fishing, including bait, tackle, and ice, for a nominal fee.

The Mississippi Fishing Banks Committee has been chartered as a non-profit group to improve upon the coastal fishing. This organization plans construction of artificial fishing banks out in the near Gulf waters to provide the same kind of fishing found around the offshore rigs. By 1973 one reef had been built, using old, abandoned car bodies left by Hurricane Camille. This reef is currently producing some fine red snapper fishing. The committee has also received several surplus liberty ships from the American government. These vessels will be towed to pre-selected sites outside the barrier islands and sunk, thereby creating additional fishing banks.

Currently, no license is required for sport fishing south of U.S. Highway 90 along the Mississippi Gulf Coast. Fishing around the Chandeleur Islands, which lie some 20 miles south of the Mississippi coast and in Louisiana waters, requires a Louisiana salt water fishing license.

By 1973, there were still no size or catch limits placed on the salt water fishes taken in Mississippi waters. Both sport and commercial fishermen vie for many of the same fishes. Figures are available on the commercial fishery catch, but there are no long term statistics for the sport fishery take. In recent years the number of fishermen participating in the marine sport fishery has increased dramatically; it is likely that the catch has also risen proportionately.

Thomas D. McIlwain

COMMERCIAL MARINE FISHERY

Mississippi's commercial marine fisheries play a vital role in the economy of the state's coastal counties. This is not a recent circumstance—early colonists in this area also earned their livelihood chiefly by fishing and farming. Even before the colonists came, the Biloxi and Pascagoula Indians supported themselves in part by the fish and shellfish they took from the coastal waters.

Coastal fisheries yield a more abundant harvest now than they did in the early days, primarily because of increased efforts. With a coastline of only 155 miles, the shortest of any of the Gulf states, Mississippi produces enormous quantities of the sea delicacies. In the period 1961–71, landings of fish and shellfish totaled 3.6 million pounds valued at $104 million. Approximately 3,000 fishermen, using 600 vessels of five net tons or greater, and 1,000 or more motorboats, annually land their catches at Mississippi ports. An additional 1,500 onshore employees convert this catch into processed products valued at more than $32 million. Fishing and processing directly support an employment of over 4,500 persons annually.

Many other industries are directly or indirectly dependent on the fishing industry. Net making, for example, annually employs about 30 persons. The marketing of nets is not confined to Mississippi or even Gulf coastal fishermen; some Mississippi net houses export their product to markets worldwide. Approximately ten shipbuilding firms making fishing vessels are located on the Mississippi coast. These firms employ about 100 persons total in the construction and repair of fishing craft. Fuel consumption is another important adjunct of the fishing industry; at least 25 persons are engaged in supplying fuel to the fleet. Other employment is to be found in local ice plants, where the product is used in preserving catches, and in stores supplying hardware and other miscellaneous items used in the fishing industry. Thus, fishing is indeed an important segment of the economy of the coastal counties, providing directly and indirectly for more than 4,700 jobs.

The commercial fisheries of Mississippi are drawn largely from fish and shellfish that are caught in and are dependent on the estuarine area. (The single exception is the red snapper fishery.) Within the estuarine areas are several distinct fisheries and means of catching fish. The purse seine and the trammel net are the most popular encircling gear used in Mississippi. The trammel net is principally used in the mullet fishery and for certain sciaenid fishes such as red drum and spotted sea trout.

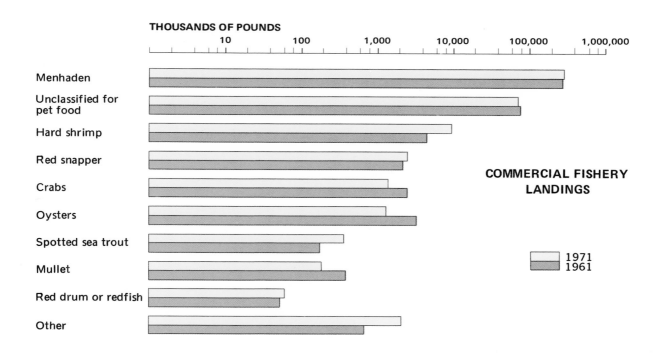

THOUSANDS OF POUNDS

COMMERCIAL FISHERY LANDINGS

1971
1961

The spotted sea trout is considered a choice fish on the Mississippi Gulf Coast. The catch of spotted sea trout has shown a rather steady increase except for the 1962–63 fishing season when net fishermen shifted to shrimping because of the higher price for shrimp. In 1971, more than twice as many pounds of spotted sea trout were taken than in 1961, despite the closing of areas to net fishing.

Mullet, also taken by trammel net, is a neglected resource. These fish are abundant, easily taken, and are nutritious, but not a popular item with fish buyers. There is room for expansion of the mullet market.

Trawling vessels also provide fish for the pet food industry. Landings of unclassified fish for pet food have fluctuated considerably since the early 1960s. This is a highly competitive business and changes are constantly occurring in the composition of the product and in merchandising. The processors of pet food are now preparing more of the so-called "gourmet" dinners for pets, using much less fish and more chicken and beef. The pet food industry annually employs about fifty-five vessels catching approximately 70 million pounds of mixed fish.

Menhaden are taken by large vessels using purse seines. The catch has fluctuated considerably in recent years, dipping to a low of 150 million pounds in 1968 from a high of 301 million pounds in 1961, then recovering to reach a record catch in 1971 of 308 million pounds. This fishery is sustained by one- and two-year-old fish. Menhaden are processed into meal and oil—the meal is used principally as animal feed, while the oil is largely exported. The menhaden fishery is an important feed supplier to Mississippi's broiler industry. Without menhaden the broiler industry would be forced to use other feed supplements, which do not provide the rapid growth that fish meal does and which are often more expensive.

The red snapper fishery of Mississippi is an offshore hand line fishery, carried out primarily by vessels specifically constructed for red snapper fishing. While its history in the Gulf of Mexico dates back to the Civil War, it is a comparative newcomer to Mississippi in volume, having grown up since the late 1950s. Very little research has been done on the red snapper, and available statistics cannot adequately assess participation in the fishery. During the 1960s the catch fluctuated between 1.8 (in 1965) and 3.7 million pounds (in 1968).

BLESSING OF THE FLEET

State A & I Board

Crabs, taken by lines, pots, or traps, annually yield nearly 2 million pounds. Mississippi's crab population probably is supported partially by the migration of crabs from Louisiana waters (principally Lake Borgne) on the west and from Alabama waters (principally Mobile Bay) on the east. Fluctuations appear in the catches because of the scarcity of crabs, economic conditions, or a combination of these factors. For example, the 1962 decline in landings of crabs was almost totally the result of the closing of one large crab packing plant at Pascagoula rather than due to a scarcity of crabs. Data are not available to determine whether or not the fishery is yielding to its capacity, but its ability to spring back to its former abundance after a bad year does not indicate any serious danger of depletion.

More controversy has revolved around shrimp than any other commercial fishery on the coast with perhaps the exception of the menhaden fishery. The shrimp harvest has increased only slightly since the early 1960s. Taking the three-year average for 1961–63, approximately 6.6 million pounds of shrimp were caught reflecting a value of $2 million. The 1969–71 average was 9.5 million pounds valued at $4 million.

During this time the number of shrimping vessels remained fairly constant. Unless new resources are discovered, shrimp fishing in Mississippi will probably not increase to any great extent.

The oyster fishery is the one marine resource in Mississippi that has declined in output in recent years. The reasons for this decrease are complex. In the period 1969–71 the average annual take was but 1 million pounds valued at slightly over $400,000. This low harvest was partially caused by Hurricane Camille, which devastated the Mississippi coast in August, 1969, and severely damaged all oyster reefs in state waters. Furthermore, oyster canning has declined somewhat due to heavy imports of canned oysters from other areas. Pollution has also been a serious drawback to oyster production on the Gulf Coast. If the state is successful in cleaning its coastal waters there will undoubtedly be enough oysters for the Mississippi raw trade without the necessity of importing from other states.

Charles H. Lyles
Thomas D. McIlwain

SHRIMP FLEET

State A & I Board

RECREATION AND TOURISM

Unlike many urbanized states, Mississippi has vast quantities of clean, unspoiled, readily accessible outdoor areas. Much of the land is in its natural state, free from human encroachment. The opportunities for outdoor recreation are directly related to the unspoiled condition of the natural resources and the relatively low population density of the state. Statistics from the 1969 Comprehensive Outdoor Recreation Plan for Mississippi indicate that there are slightly more than 1,500 acres of recreation per 1,000 people in the state.

Even urbanized areas have not experienced the overwhelming effects of crowding, pollution, and overuse encountered by several other states. The towns and cities of Mississippi have more open spaces and undeveloped areas than many cities found elsewhere. Those Mississippi cities possessing limited open spaces have access to such undeveloped areas within short distances.

Community and municipal recreation agencies offer a substantial amount of outdoor recreation opportunities to the citizens of Mississippi. There are twenty-four full-time recreation agencies in the state, and another forty-three communities which operate part-time recreation programs, usually during the summer months.

Federal and state agencies furnish many thousands of additional acres and millions of man-days of recreation, principally in the form of state parks and national forests. Other smaller but nonetheless popular spots consist of wildlife management areas, national landmarks, state lakes, historical sites, and Corps of Engineer Reservoirs.

Numerous tourist attractions and facilities also exist, and tourism is rapidly becoming an important state industry. During 1973, approximately 22 million out-of-state residents made pleasure trips to Mississippi. Public transportation, particularly the interstate highway system, has made most recreational, historical, and cultural attractions readily accessible to both out-of-state visitors and Mississippi citizens alike.

STATE AGENCIES

Governmental institutions in Mississippi provide much of the recreation available to the public. Several administrative agencies are responsible for recreation planning and development.

PARKS SYSTEMS—The Mississippi State Parks System administers fourteen state parks, encompassing 15,355 acres, and four historical sites. Ten of the parks have reservoirs or lakes within their boundaries, providing a total of 1,676 surface acres of water. The remaining four parks are located adjacent to major reservoirs.

The Mississippi parks system began in 1933 as a part of the federal government's economy measures to curb the effects of the depression. Civilian Conservation Corps camps were established in nine locations in the state, and during the following three years the basic facilities for the first nine of Mississippi's fourteen parks were constructed under the Federal Emergency Conservation Work Program. Today these nine parks attract approximately 60 percent of the state park visitors. In all, over 2 million people visited this park system in 1972, and over 50 percent of these visitors were from out-of-state.

MISSISSIPPI STATE PARKS AND HISTORICAL SITES

State Parks	Total Acres	County
Clarkco	815	Clarke
Holmes County	400	Holmes
Hugh White	745	Grenada
J. P. Coleman	1,474	Tishomingo
Lake Lowndes	750	Lowndes
Leroy Percy	2,442	Washington
Paul B. Johnson	808	Forrest
Percy Quin	1,500	Pike
Roosevelt	562	Scott
John W. Kyle	740	Panola
Tombigbee	822	Lee
Tishomingo	1,500	Tishomingo
Wall Doxey	800	Marshall
Yacona Ridge	2,000	Yalobusha

Historical Sites	County
Golden Memorial	Leake
Nanih Waiya	Neshoba and Winston
Sam Dale Memorial	Lauderdale
Winterville Mounds	Washington

GAME AND FISH COMMISSION—Fishing and hunting are among the most popular of the traditional outdoor activities in Mississippi. Approximately 493 square miles of fresh water and 202 miles of coastline are available for fishing. More than 1.5 million acres of land (federal, state, and private) are available for hunting.

A statewide survey conducted in 1972 illustrates the popularity of hunting and fishing in the state. Among all outdoor recreation activities in Mississippi, freshwater fishing ranked tenth, saltwater fishing was six-

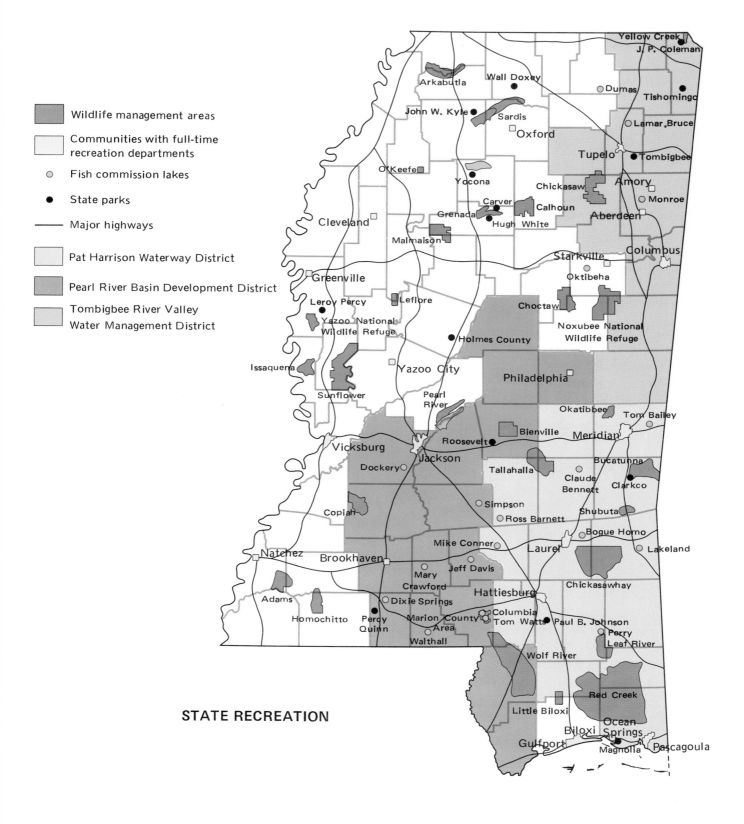

Legend:

- Wildlife management areas
- Communities with full-time recreation departments
- Fish commission lakes
- State parks
- Major highways
- Pat Harrison Waterway District
- Pearl River Basin Development District
- Tombigbee River Valley Water Management District

Yellow Creek
J. P. Coleman
Arkabutla
Wall Doxey
Dumas
Tishomingo
John W. Kyle
Sardis
Lamar Bruce
Oxford
Tupelo
Tombigbee
O'Keefe
Amory
Yocona
Chickasaw
Monroe
Carver
Calhoun
Grenada
Aberdeen
Hugh White
Cleveland
Columbus
Malmaison
Starkville
Greenville
Oktibeha
Leflore
Choctaw
Leroy Percy
Noxubee National Wildlife Refuge
Yazoo National Wildlife Refuge
Holmes County
Issaquena
Yazoo City
Philadelphia
Sunflower
Pearl River
Okatibbee
Tom Bailey
Bienville
Meridian
Roosevelt
Vicksburg
Jackson
Bucatunna
Dockery
Tallahalla
Claude Bennett
Clarkco
Simpson
Shubuta
Copiah
Ross Barnett
Bogue Homo
Mike Conner
Lakeland
Natchez
Laurel
Brookhaven
Jeff Davis
Chickasawhay
Mary Crawford
Hattiesburg
Adams
Dixie Springs
Columbia
Homochitto
Marion County
Tom Watts
Paul B. Johnson
Percy Quinn
Area
Perry
Walthall
Leaf River
Wolf River
Red Creek
Little Biloxi
Ocean Springs
Biloxi
Gulfport
Pascagoula
Magnolia

STATE RECREATION

129

teenth, small game hunting was thirteenth, and big game hunting was twenty-seventh.

The Mississippi Game and Fish Commission is one of the greatest contributors to outdoor recreation areas and recreation opportunities in the state. The commission owns or leases twenty prime fishing lakes with a total of 5,202 acres of fresh water, ranging in size from 12 acres to 1,200 acres. These lakes provided 133,676 man-days of fishing during 1970–71, primarily for bass, bluegill, crappie, and channel catfish.

Many of the lakes provide overnight camping facilities for a nominal fee. Restrooms and showers are also available in some areas. Most of the lakes are open for boating and water skiing at least one or two afternoons a week. Approximately 500,000 man-days of non-fishing recreation were provided on these lakes during 1971.

MISSISSIPPI FISH COMMISSION LAKES

Lake	Acres	County
Dumas	32	Tippah
Lamar Bruce	330	Lee
Monroe	111	Monroe
Tom Bailey	234	Lauderdale
Claude Bennett	71	Jasper
Ross R. Barnett	87	Smith
Simpson County Legion	94	Simpson
Dockery	55	Hindes
Bogue Homa	1,200	Jones
Mike Connor	88	Covington
Jeff Davis	164	Jefferson Davis
Mary Crawford	135	Lawrence
Dixie Springs	100	Pike
Walthall	62	Walthall
Columbia	90	Marion
Tom Watts	12	Marion
Perry	125	Perry
Lakeland Park	12	Wayne
Oktibbeha County	700	Oktibbeha

Mississippi has more than 1.5 million acres of prime game habitat open to public hunting. These areas are uniformly distributed over the state and are easily accessible to sportsmen. Many of the areas are on U.S. Forest Service lands; others are under corporate and private ownership.

Almost .5 million hunting and fishing licenses were purchased by sportsmen in Mississippi during 1971–72. Slightly over half of the 328,057 resident licenses sold were combination hunting and fishing. The remainder were about equally divided between licenses sold separately for hunting or for fishing. Of the 137,632 non-resident licenses sold, 104,313 were for fishing and the remainder for hunting.

Squirrel hunting ranks first in terms of hunter participation, with deer hunting second. Deer hunting expenditures, however, are more than two and one-half times greater than those of squirrel hunters. Other game species popular in Mississippi are wild turkey, woodcock, dove, quail, opossum, raccoon, and various species of ducks.

MISSISSIPPI REFUGE AND PUBLIC HUNTING AREAS

Area	Acres	Counties
Adams County	16,000	Adams
Bienville	40,000	Scott
Bucatunna	100,000	Clarke
Calhoun	9,000	Calhoun
Chickasaw	27,000	Chickasaw, Pontotoc
Chickasawhay	135,000	Jones, Wayne
Choctaw	50,000	Choctaw, Winston
Copiah	6,500	Copiah
Homochitto	51,500	Amite, Franklin
Issaquena County	13,000	Issaquena
Leaf River	42,000	Perry, Greene
Little Biloxi	19,400	Harrison, Stone
Marion County (Hugh White)	7,200	Marion
Red Creek	360,000	Harrison, Stone Jackson, George
Sardis (Upland)	47,000	Lafayette
Shubuta Creek	8,000	Clarke
Sunflower	70,000	Sharkey
Tallahala Creek	35,000	Jasper, Scott, Smith Newton
Wolf	300,000	Lamar, Marion, Pearl River
Arkabutla Waterfowl	28,000	De Soto, Tate
Grenada Waterfowl	75,000	Yalobusha, Grenada, Calhoun
Indian Bayou	500	Sharkey
Leflore County	350	Leflore
O'Keefe	5,000	Quitman
Pearl River	2,200	Madison
Sardis Waterfowl	51,800	Lafayette, Marshall
Sunflower Waterfowl	1,600	Sharkey
Yellow Creek	250	Tishomingo
Okatibbee	5,000	Lauderdale
Malmaison	7,933	Grenada, Carroll
Total acreage	1,521,133	

WATERWAY DISTRICTS—Three district agencies administered by the state of Mississippi assume water and shoreline development responsibilities, including development and operation of recreation areas and facilities.

The Pat Harrison Waterway District, with headquarters in Hattiesburg, manages six water parks, and has several others scheduled for future development.

This agency manages approximately 5,500 acres of land and 2,100 acres of water. During fiscal year 1972–73 more than 140,000 people visited these six parks, and more than 11,000 of these were overnight campers.

The Pearl River Basin Development District, headquartered in Jackson, encompasses most of the southcentral portion of Mississippi, and administers and manages twelve major recreational facilities. It provides 30,000 acres of water for public recreation facilities in addition to a public golf course, a pleasure boatway, and an equestrian trail. These outdoor facilities accommodate 50,000–75,000 visitors each weekend.

The Tombigbee River Valley Water Management District, with headquarters in Tuepelo, was created in 1962 and presently includes twelve counties in the northeastern section of the state. One of this district's primary objectives is to provide public parks and recreation facilities. Feasibility studies for recreational development have been completed in most of the member counties for multi-purpose lake and recreational area development. Land acquisition for facilities has in many instances been completed and preliminary construction has begun.

FEDERAL AGENCIES

The United States government provides substantial park and recreation acreage in Mississippi. Agencies with recreation functions are the U.S. Forest Service,

the U.S. Army Corps of Engineers, the U.S. Fish and Wildlife Service, and the National Parks Service. Together these agencies contribute approximately 12 percent of the state's developed park and recreation acreage.

FOREST SERVICE—There are more than 1.1 million acres of national forest lands in thirty-four of the state's counties. These lands also include a total of 4,942 acres of freshwater impoundments. In 1972, 770,100 visitor-use-days were enjoyed in Mississippi's national forests.

NATIONAL FORESTS IN MISSISSIPPI

Name	Acres
Bienville	176,800
Delta	59,000
DeSoto	500,900
Holly Springs	123,000
Homochitto	189,000
Tombigbee	85,600

National forests in Mississippi are designated for multi-purpose use, including recreational use. In all, there are fifty-five developed recreation areas available for public use on national forest lands. In addition to the developed camping and picnicking areas, the Forest Service also provides and maintains a 50-mile floating stream on Beaverdam and Black creeks and an 11-mile hiking trail (Tuxachanie Hiking Trail), all in the DeSoto National Forest.

BOATING
S. Jean Busbee

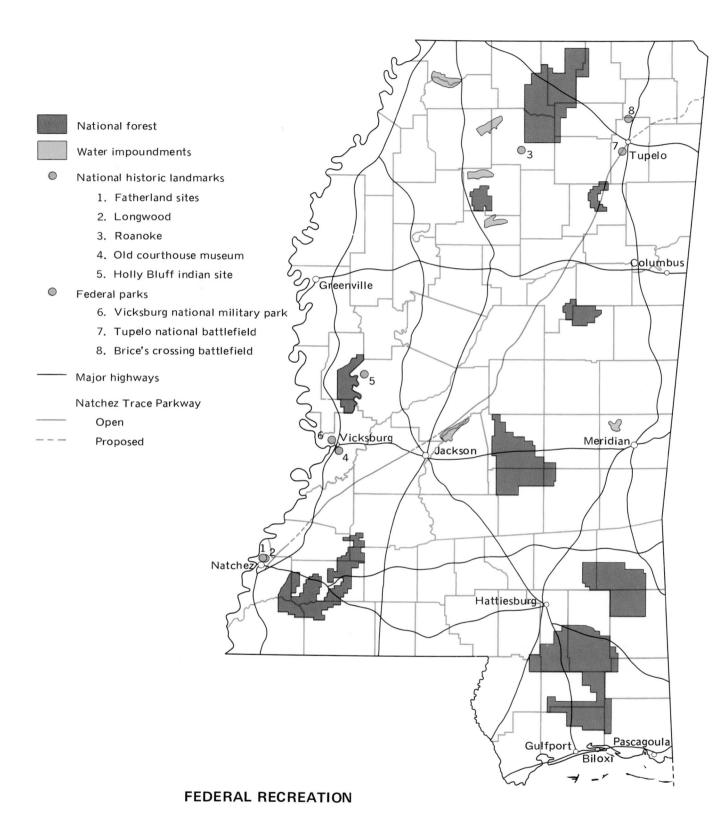

Legend

National forest

Water impoundments

National historic landmarks
1. Fatherland sites
2. Longwood
3. Roanoke
4. Old courthouse museum
5. Holly Bluff indian site

Federal parks
6. Vicksburg national military park
7. Tupelo national battlefield
8. Brice's crossing battlefield

Major highways

Natchez Trace Parkway
Open
Proposed

FEDERAL RECREATION

ARMY CORPS OF ENGINEERS—The corps has constructed five major reservoirs in the state. The largest of these is Grenada with 29,789 acres; the smallest is Okatibbee with 3,800 surface acres of water. Basic recreational facilities such as paved boat-launching ramps, access roads, picnic grounds, parking areas, comfort stations, swimming beaches, tent and trailer spaces, and rental cottages are available at most of the areas.

FISH AND WILDLIFE SERVICE—The U.S. Fish and Wildlife Service operates two national wildlife refuges in Mississippi. These are the Noxubee Wildlife Refuge in Noxubee and Winston counties, and the Yazoo National Wildlife Refuge in Washington County. Noxubee Refuge has 50,000 acres, and Yazoo Refuge encompasses 9,351 acres.

These refuges are primarily for waterfowl, with certain sections closed to hunting. The service has a working agreement with the Mississippi Game and Fish Commission that permits large portions of the refuge acreage to be open for fishing and hunting. Developed recreational facilities are limited in the refuges, but public use of the land is not discouraged. Some facilities provide for picnicking and wilderness-type camping.

NATIONAL PARK SERVICE—The National Park Service maintains and operates four historical interpretation areas within the state. The administration of these areas is "dedicated to conserving the scenic, scientific, and historical heritage of the United States for the benefit and inspiration of the People."

Probably the most scenic of the four is the Natchez Trace extending 450 miles, from just west of Nashville, Tennessee, to Natchez, Mississippi. Approximately 238 miles of the Trace Parkway has been completed in Mississippi. The trace began as a series of wilderness trails utilized by Indians and later by white settlers. In 1801 President Jefferson assigned U.S. Army troops to begin construction of the road as a supply route into the western territory. The road was also heavily used by merchants as a return route after delivering their goods to Natchez or New Orleans by flatboat.

Today the Natchez Trace is a major tourist and recreational highway, attracting some 10,665,000 visitors each year. Each mile of the completed trace is flanked by approximately 100 acres of land which is in a completely natural setting with no roadside signs or other distractions. Numerous facilities such as camp grounds, picnic areas, visitor centers, historical sites, and trails are located along the entire length of the highway. Two major park developments are also located on the trace.

The Vicksburg National Military Park and Cemetery is an 1,800-acre Civil War battle site located at Vicksburg. This is one of the largest military parks in the National Park System. Memorials from each state which had troops at the Battle of Vicksburg are located throughout a 16-mile network of park roads. Interpretive facilities include a museum and battlefield plaques portraying the siege and battle of the river city.

An act of Congress on February 21, 1929, established Brices Cross Roads National Battlefield Site. This site contains one acre of federal land located in Lee County, six miles west of Baldwyn.

The last site operated by the National Park Service is the Tupelo National Battlefield, a one-acre site located on Mississippi Highway 6 within the city limits of Tupelo. It was established in 1929 as a national battlefield site and changed to the Tupelo National Battlefield in 1961.

NATIONAL HISTORICAL LANDMARKS

Mississippi has five sites that have been declared Registered National Historical Landmarks. These attractions are maintained and operated by private individuals or agencies, and include:

1. Rowan Oak—William Faulkner's home, 1930–62. Located at Oxford, Mississippi. Faulkner wrote most of his novels and short stories here.
2. Warren County Courthouse, Vicksburg. The old courthouse now serves as a Confederate museum which is maintained by the Vicksburg and Warren County Board of Supervisors.
3. Longwood—antebellum home. Located in Natchez and operated by the city's Pilgrimage Garden Club. This is a classic example of southern plantation elegance and grandeur.
4. Grand Village of the Natchez Indians. This site, located in Adams County, is considered to be one of the most thoroughly documented archeological sites in the nation. It contains the remnants of three temple mounds, a plaza, and one mound that has been restored.
5. Lake George—Holly Bluff site. This site con-

tains twenty prehistoric temple mounds as well as encircling wall and ditch.

COMMUNITY RECREATION AREAS

Community recreation in Mississippi is usually conducted through the auspices of a city or county recreation department. A variety of recreational opportunities and facilities are provided by these agencies, and are primarily utilized by the local citizens. Natural areas, gardens, picnic grounds, swimming areas, playgrounds, and organized sports areas are among the facilities provided. Most agencies also offer a variety of indoor recreational opportunities for citizens of all ages.

Community recreation programs in Mississippi are divided into three classes:

Class I. Municipalities with full-time park and recreation directors. Financial assistance for the agency is obtained primarily from city or county resources.

CLASS I RECREATIONAL DEPARTMENTS

Location	Population Served	Acres
Jackson	153,000	1,500
Biloxi	48,400	120
Meridian	45,000	300
Gulfport	40,700	197
Greenville	39,648	242
Hattiesburg	38,277	100
Pascagoula	27,264	35
Columbus	25,700	80
Vicksburg	25,400	50
Laurel	24,135	200
Clarksdale	21,600	14
Tupelo	20,400	250
Natchez	19,700	250
Moss Point	19,321	40
West Point	18,000	44
Oxford	13,800	51
Cleveland	13,300	30
Starkville	11,300	14
Yazoo City	10,700	33
Brookhaven	10,700	40
Ocean Springs	9,500	21
Amory	7,500	60
Philadelphia	6,274	80
Aberdeen	6,100	22

Class II. Municipalities with part-time or seasonal recreational programs which are financed by the community.

Class III. Municipalities with the private sector serving as the primary source of recreational opportunities. Little financial support is available to these programs, and the leadership is usually the result of volunteer action.

There are twenty-four Class I municipalities in Mississippi, which together own and operate 3,773 acres of recreational land and facilities, and serve a population of approximately 655,228 people. There are twenty-six Class II and eighteen Class III municipalities in Mississippi; these own or lease 906 acres of recreational land.

TOURISM

The level of tourism in Mississippi has been significant since the end of World War II. However, only in recent years has tourism become a dynamic state business. Those areas experiencing the most rapid growth in tourism include the Natchez–Vicksburg area, the Gulf Coast, and that region of the state south of Memphis, Tennessee. Much of the increase in tourism can be directly attributed to the 601 miles of interstate highways and improvements in other roads in Mississippi. It is estimated that more than 80 percent of all tourist travel in the state is by automobile.

A 1972 survey conducted for *Better Homes and Gardens* revealed that 1.5 percent of all vacation trips in the United States were taken to Mississippi and that these trips generated $77.2 million in income for the state. Approximately 952,500 family vacation visits occurred in Mississippi during 1972, with each family staying an average of 2.3 days (28 percent of their total vacation) and spending $81 while in the state.

An additional increase in tourism in Mississippi will be realized upon establishment of the Gulf Island National Seashore which will include four Mississippi offshore islands. It is estimated that visitations to these islands will exceed 3.5 million by the fifth year of operation and will eventually reach 10 million annually. In 1971 the Gulf Coast area received slightly more than 67,000 tourist visitations.

Tourism in Mississippi is generated, to a significant degree, by numerous special events and attractions which occur throughout the state during the year. The more significant of these events, their locations and scheduled times are listed below.

Raymond Busbee

SPECIAL EVENTS AND ACTIVITIES

ACTIVITY	LOCATION	DATE	DESCRIPTION
Choctaw Indian Fair	Philadelphia	4 days in July	Tribal programs, arts and crafts, stickball championship, Choctaw Princess contest.
Mississippi Deep Sea Fishing Rodeo	Biloxi	July	Trophies awarded to winners of various fishing events, queen of the rodeo contest.
Annual Blessing of the Fleet	Biloxi	June	Ceremonies commemorating deceased fishermen, boat parade, and religious services.
National Tobacco Spitting Contest	Raleigh	Last Sat. in July	Coondog field trials, tobacco spitting contest, guest speakers.
Natchez Pilgrimage	Natchez	Spring	Antebellum home tours, Mississippi's oldest and best-known pilgrimage.
Mississippi State Fair	Jackson	October	Exhibits, carnival midway, livestock.
Natchez Trail Festival	Kosciusko	3rd Sat. in April	Old-fashioned country fair.
Vicksburg Pilgrimage	Vicksburg	Spring	Historic sites, Vicksburg Military Park and Cemetery, river cruises.
Dixie National Livestock Show	Jackson	February	Contests, shows, livestock sale, rodeo.
Neshoba County Fair	Philadelphia	August	Exhibits, horse races, political speeches, midway rides, beauty pageant, and livestock shows.
Woodville Pilgrimage	Woodville	March	Nine antebellum homes.
Canton Flea Market	Canton	1st Thurs. of May and October	Flea market, arts and crafts sale.
Mississippi Arts Festival	Jackson	May	Seminars, performing arts, workshops, exhibits.
Jackson Pilgrimage	Jackson	Spring	Mynelle Gardens, Petrified Forest.
Lively Arts Festival	Meridian	April	Entertainers, Meridian Symphony Orchestra, plays, art show, exhibits.
Mainstream Festival	Greenville	July	Exhibits, air show, antique car show, fireworks, boat and balloon races.
Columbus Pilgrimage	Columbus	Spring	Friendship Cemetery—origin of Memorial Day.
Greenwood Arts Festival	Greenwood	May	Musical entertainment, jazz festival, puppet theatre, performing artists, exhibits.
Oxford Pilgrimage	Oxford	April	Home of William and John Faulkner.
McComb Lighted Azalea Trail	McComb	March–April	Arts festival, lighted home tours, beauty pageant, open house.
Cross Roads Jubilee	Corinth	May	Historical tour, reenactment of the Battle of Corinth, exhibits, turkey shoot.
Clinton Arts and Crafts Fair	Clinton	April	Arts and crafts exhibits, country store.
Central Mississippi Fair	Kosciusko	September	Exhibits, rides, rodeo.
Holly Springs Pilgrimage	Holly Springs	April	Tours of beautiful southern homes.
Carrollton Pilgrimage	Carrollton	Spring	Tours of Delta plantations and antebellum homes.

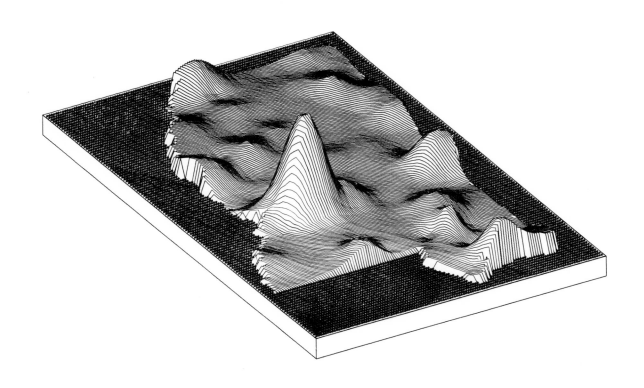

**TOTAL EMPLOYMENT IN
TRANSPORTATION AND COMMUNICATION**

TRANSPORTATION AND COMMUNICATION

One measure of an area's economic development is its communication and transportation system. The social and economic growth of a county, state, or nation depends on the ability of its people to communicate and trade with people in other areas. The transportation and communication systems of a region can be compared with the vital systems of the human body. The human nervous system, circulatory system, alimentary system, and respiratory system are coordinated networks of communication and transportation that enable the body to sustain life. Likewise, the movement of ideas, people, and goods depends on the connectivity of several types of transportation and communication systems—highways, waterways, railways, pipelines, airways, radio and television broadcasts, telephones and telegraphs, and newspapers and magazines. This network is the circulatory system that provides for economic growth. Without transportation and communication an area cannot take advantage of its natural and human resources; its citizens cannot grow intellectually nor economically.

Any analysis of circulation in a given area must consider the following: (1) an *inventory* of route mileage and number of vehicles; (2) the geometric *pat-* *tern* or network of circulation; (3) the intensities of movement—the *flow* pattern; (4) the *modes* or types of transportation and communication. The degree of interrelationships among the four components provides an area with its characteristic functional circulatory system.

Mississippi is fortunate to have a well-developed, integrated circulatory system. An inventory of Mississippi's transportation and communication facilities reveals that its citizens have ready access to both modern transportation modes and routes, and that public utilities, radio and television facilities, and newspapers are available in all sections of the state. Mississippi's geographic location in the Gulf South gives manufacturers and agricultural producers excellent access to imported commodities as well as giving them an advantage over other areas for outshipment and transhipment of products. The interconnected transportation and communications network characteristic of Mississippi provides the state's citizens with the circulatory system necessary for dynamic economic and intellectual growth.

W. T. Mealor

TRANSPORTATION

Transportation enables people to enjoy the benefits of an industrialized economy. It provides not only the means through which agricultural commodities and industrial raw materials are moved to market but also the means by which finished products are distributed to the consumer. An efficient and effective transportation system, interconnected and balanced, is a necessity for economic development.

Mississippi's location is advantageous for external trade, both national and international. Atlanta, New Orleans, Houston, Dallas, St. Louis, Memphis, and Mobile, the major regional centers of the Mississippi Valley, the southeastern United States, the Gulf South, and the southwest, are located within 400 miles of Jackson. Mississippi is the crossroads of east–west highways, railroads, and pipeline traffic between the Atlantic seaboard and the oil-rich Gulf South and southwest. The state is on the nation's major river system, which connects the Midwest with the Gulf of Mexico. Paralleling the Mississippi River are railroads, highways, and pipelines that give the industrial and agricultural activities of the Midwest easy and efficient access to ports on the Gulf Coast.

Mississippi not only is fortunate in having excellent transportation routes connecting it with the rest of the nation, but the state also is blessed with excellent ports on the Gulf of Mexico which provide outlets for international trade. Complementing these coastal ports are inland port facilities as far north on the Mississippi as Greenville that can accommodate ocean-going vessels.

Internal transportation within Mississippi is characterized by a well-developed interstate, federal, state, and local highway system, coupled with a railroad net that serves every county. The inland waterway system provides access to the western tiers of counties and to the extreme northeastern corner of the state. The federally approved Tennessee–Tombigbee waterway, when completed, will open to waterborne traffic additional areas in the eastern portion of the state.

Supplementing the ground transportation network is a feeder airline system that provides all sections of Mississippi with scheduled service. Through interconnecting flights at Jackson, Meridian, Biloxi–Gulfport, and at Memphis, New Orleans, and Mobile, all points in the state are within one-half day's travel of the nation's major metropolitan areas.

MOTORIZED HIGHWAY TRANSPORTATION

The flexibility and adaptability of motor transportation makes it the most important link in an interconnected transportation system. Many rural areas are not served by railroads, water traffic, or aircraft, but are located on roads. Compared with railways, highway construction is less expensive and can serve a greater variety of needs. Highways and roads vary in quality and size, just as the need for them varies. Feeder roads, such as farm and county roads, act as collectors of traffic from rural and more isolated areas. Traffic from the feeder system is channeled into secondary roads that focus on either primary highways and/or towns. There are two types of primary highways in the United States. One is the interstate system that connects the major metropolitan areas of the nation but either bypasses or provides limited access to smaller cities and towns. The second type of primary highway is the system that connects the major towns and cities of a state, designated as part of the "U.S." or "State" highway system.

Dependability of motorized traffic on highways compares favorably with other forms of transportation. Vehicular breakdowns normally are quickly repaired, and blockage of routes by weather or road repair is infrequent and seldom prevents the flow of traffic from reaching its destination. Both the speed (particularly over short hauls) and dependability of trucks is greater than that of railroads. Trucks can avoid all terminals between their points of origin and their destination, while trains must stop at intermediate terminals. Because expensive terminal operations are avoided, the truck is more flexible. The truck does not require as large a payload as a train to be economically operational, and it uses the public highways in which the truck owner has no financial investment other than taxes. Therefore, operations can be increased by adding another vehicle and routes can be changed without loss of funds vested in rights-of-way.

Mississippi's highway system of 66,000 miles is a well-developed, integrated network of local, state, and federal roads. The Mississippi county road system provides feeder routes to both federal and state highways and to local trade centers. The county road system, coupled with the local farm road system, provides farmers with all-weather routes to market and it

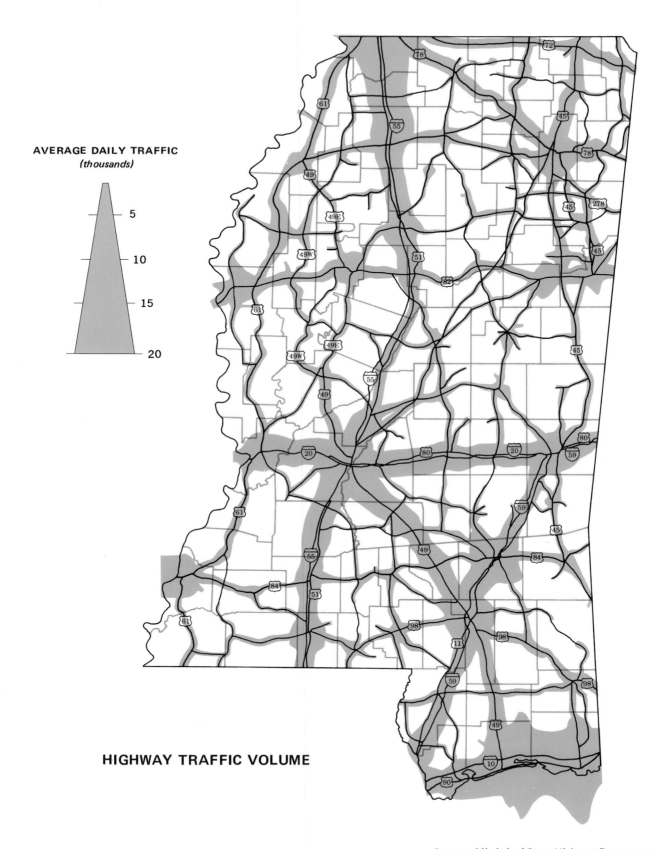

AVERAGE DAILY TRAFFIC
(thousands)

5
10
15
20

HIGHWAY TRAFFIC VOLUME

Source: Mississippi State Highway Department

139

provides rural nonfarm residents with an efficient way to work. The state-aid county road system consists of more than 14,000 miles of road, about 11,000 miles of which are part of the federal aid secondary system. More than 60 percent of the county road system is paved. Local farm roads total approximately 36,000 miles, of which less than 6,000 miles are paved, and roads in cities and urban areas total 5,700 miles. The state highway system is comprised of those routes so designated by the Mississippi legislature. It consists of approximately 11,000 miles of routes, including interstate, federal aid primary, and federal aid secondary highways. The system is composed of all intercity routes having load limits equal to or greater than 57,650 pounds. (The maximum weight limit on Mississippi highways is 73,280 pounds.)

The major traffic arteries in Mississippi focus on Jackson, the Gulf Coast, and the Mississippi River cities of Natchez, Vicksburg, and Greenville. Among the busiest highways are U.S. 90 along the Gulf Coast, U.S. 80 and I-20 between Vicksburg and Meridian, U.S. 51 and I-55 between Jackson and the Tennessee state line, U.S. 49 between Jackson, Hattiesburg, and Gulfport, and I-59 from the Alabama state line to the Louisiana state line. Each of these highways carries an average of more than 4,000 vehicles daily.

There are approximately 1.2 million vehicles registered in the state to 1.9 million people, or one vehicle per 1.1 licensed drivers. Total miles driven annually by Mississippians is in excess of 1.2 billion miles, with the average Mississippian traveling more than 5,200 miles each year.

Since the mid-1960s there has been a general decline in the percentage of fatalities per 100 million miles of vehicle travel in the state. In 1967, 888 people lost their lives on Mississippi highways. A total of 9.7 billion miles were traveled on Mississippi roads in 1967, with a fatality rate of 9.1 percent. During 1971, a total of 12 billion miles were traveled, and 951 persons lost their lives in 34,446 state accidents. The fatality rate per 100 million miles of vehicle travel decreased to 7.9 percent in that year.

Contributing to the increased mileage traveled and to the decrease in fatalities per mile has been a vigorous highway construction and improvement program. Between 1961 and 1972, Mississippi's expenditures on highway construction increased by 140 percent while disbursements for maintenance increased 80

percent. Total disbursements by the Mississippi State Highway Department now exceed $150 million annually, with an average of more than $98 million spent per year for construction over the past five years and an average of $11.5 million spent on maintenance over the same time period.

Mississippi is served by more than twenty commercial common truck lines plus many contract truckers. Truck terminals are found in all areas of the state, with scheduled common carrier terminals located in more than one-half of Mississippi's counties. Normal truck delivery time to most areas of the southeastern United States, Gulf South, and Midwest is by the second morning. All points in the conterminous United States are within five days travel of Mississippi.

RAILROADS

Railroads often have been described as the backbone of America's transportation system. In terms of ton-miles of freight carried (number of tons carried one mile), railroads are the dominant mode of transportation in the United States. Unlike most motor carriers, aircraft, and water vessels that use publicly financed rights-of-way or terminal facilities, railroads are privately owned and operate over privately owned property. Capital investment in rights-of-way development and in maintenance, including land purchase, construction, and other operational needs, is high.

In 1973 there were approximately three hundred railroad companies operating over 200,000 miles of mainline track in the United States. In Mississippi, eleven railroads are operative over more than 3,600 miles of mainline track. More than 3,500 miles of that mainline track are owned by five Class I railroads (railroads having a gross operating revenue exceeding $5 million annually)—the Illinois Central Gulf (3,070 miles), the Alabama Great Southern (part of the Southern Railway System, 171 miles), the Louisville and Nashville (74 miles), the St. Louis–San Francisco (the "Frisco" line, 180 miles), and the Southern Railway Company (also part of the Southern Railway System, 46 miles). Class II railroads, those lines with less than $5 million annual gross revenue, operate approximately 125 miles of trackage and include Corinth and Counce (11 miles), Meridian and Bigbee (20 miles), Mississippi Export (42 miles), the Mississippian (24 miles), the Mississippi and Skuna Valley (22 miles), and the Pearl River Valley (5 miles). Com-

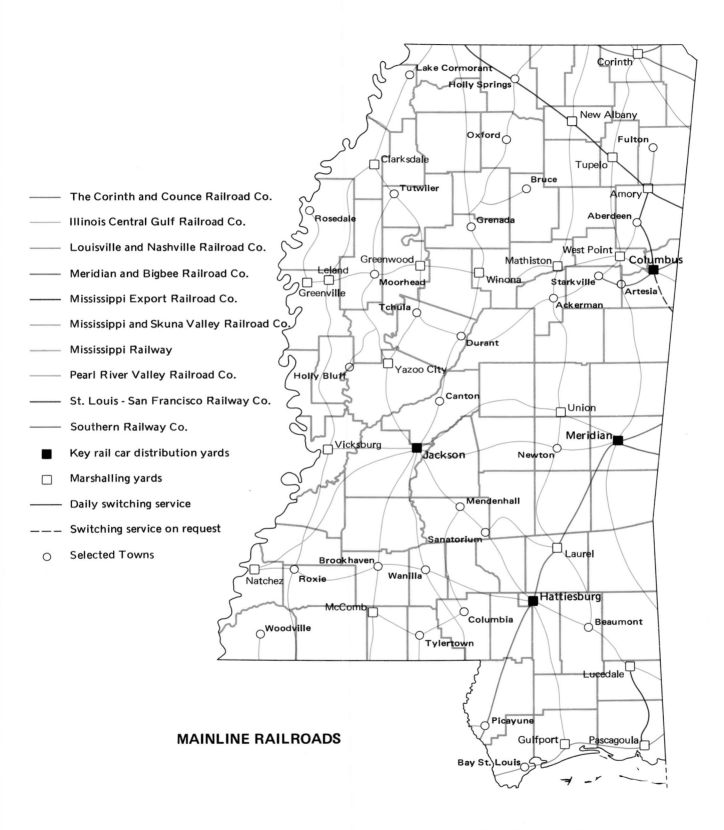

The Corinth and Counce Railroad Co.

Illinois Central Gulf Railroad Co.

Louisville and Nashville Railroad Co.

Meridian and Bigbee Railroad Co.

Mississippi Export Railroad Co.

Mississippi and Skuna Valley Railroad Co.

Mississippi Railway

Pearl River Valley Railroad Co.

St. Louis - San Francisco Railway Co.

Southern Railway Co.

■ Key rail car distribution yards

□ Marshalling yards

— Daily switching service

– – – Switching service on request

○ Selected Towns

MAINLINE RAILROADS

Source: Mississippi Research and Development Center, 1973

141

bined, these eleven railroad companies serve every county in Mississippi.

The Class I railroads provide Mississippi with excellent rail connections to all parts of the nation. Most of the industrial South is within second morning delivery time from any part of Mississippi, and the major industrial areas of the Midwest and the eastern seaboard are within four days travel. No place in the conterminous U.S. is more than six days travel time by rail from any part of Mississippi. Key rail car distribution yards and marshalling yards are found in Hattiesburg, Meridian, Columbus, and Jackson.

The Illinois Central Gulf Railroad, founded in 1972 through the merger of the Illinois Central Railroad, the Gulf Mobile and Ohio Railroad, and several short lines, is the largest railroad in the state in terms of miles of mainline track, gross revenue, and traffic ton-miles. Based upon 1971 figures, the ICG carried well over one-half of the traffic ton-miles recorded by all railroads operative in the state. The next two largest rail carriers in the state, the Southern Railway System (including the Alabama Great Southern) and the St. Louis–San Francisco Railroad, combined did not equal one-half of the ton-miles carried by the ICG. Although the ICG does not serve every county in the

state, its mainline trackage penetrates all sections of Mississippi, providing an interlinking system. The other Class I railroads provide excellent daily service to specific areas of Mississippi. The Southern Railway (including its service offered over the right-of-way of the Alabama Great Southern) serves southeastern and extreme northeastern Mississippi. Southern's route between Meridian and Picayune, part of the Washington, D.C.–New Orleans run, is served by a daily passenger train. The Frisco (St. Louis–San Francisco) serves northeastern Mississippi, while the L & N (Louisville and Nashville) serves the Gulf Coast.

Mississippi railroad companies, in cooperation with the State Public Service Commission, are constantly striving to improve their safety record. During fiscal year 1971, there were 94 derailments in Mississippi, costing the railroad companies more than $3.1 million. Although the number of derailments increased to 102 during fiscal year 1972, the total cost was reduced almost two-thirds, to $1.3 million. In order to further reduce derailments, the state legislature implemented a railroad safety inspection program in 1970 under the auspices of the Public Service Commission. Inspectors regularly check equipment, rights-of-way, grade crossings, and service.

RAILROAD ACTIVITY IN MISSISSIPPI, 1971

Class I Railroads	Car Miles	Train Miles	Ton-Miles
Alabama Great Southern	51,195,574	691,231	1,377,197,000
Southern Railway Co.	10,547,752	147,934	262,378,000
Total Southern System	61,743,326	839,165	1,639,525,000
Gulf Mobile and Ohio*	NA	NA	NA
Illinois Central*	NA	NA	4,791,584,000
Louisville and Nashville	23,061,069	314,838	590,770,000
St. Louis—San Francisco	54,924,079	769,123	1,298,300,000
Class II Railroads	Car Miles	Train Miles	Ton-Miles
Bohomie and Hattiesburg*	305,732	16,740	7,063,909
Columbus and Greenville*	2,603,614	100,441	46,851,655
Fernwood, Columbus, and Gulf*	177,181	24,256	3,451,803
Corinth and Counce	513,615	21,224	16,067,984
Meridian and Bigbee	3,024,789	72,442	77,410,898
Mississippi and Skuna Valley	138,994	13,200	2,713,238
Mississippian	110,826	12,192	2,439,776
Mississippi Export	1,019,385	22,953	23,116,642
Pearl River Valley	12,966	2,228	277,385

* Part of the 1972 merger forming the Illinois Central Gulf Railroad.

AIR TRANSPORTATION

Air transportation provides a fast, dependable means for delivery of high quality and time-dependent commodities and for safe and speedy movement of passengers. Most people and goods move to and from Mississippi by scheduled commercial aircraft, although private and chartered services are available.

Scheduled commercial airline companies are classified as either trunk or regional air carriers. A trunk carrier is one that offers multiple service and routing between major metropolitan centers throughout the nation. A regional carrier, sometimes referred to as a feeder line, provides services primarily to smaller cities within a defined geographic region. The regional carrier provides rapid transportation from the smaller cities to the major regional city served by a trunk airline.

Mississippi is served by one trunk carrier (Delta) and two regional airlines (Texas International, serving the Gulf South and southwestern United States, and Southern, serving the South). These three airlines provide service to all areas of Mississippi through eleven airports. During 1972, more than 455,000 passengers boarded scheduled air flights in Mississippi. That same year, the three commercial airlines carried more than 10,500 tons of mail, air express, and air freight.

Jackson airport, Thompson Field, is the largest and busiest commercial aviation airport in the state. The number of enplaned passengers at Jackson has increased 190 percent since the early 1960s. The tonnage of air freight, air express, and air mail handled by the scheduled airlines through Thompson Field more than tripled for 1971–72. Scheduled airlines serving Jackson provide daily direct flights to thirty-two out-of-state cities, including Atlanta, Chicago, New York, Philadelphia, Washington, Houston, Dallas, and Miami.

There are more than fifty-five general aviation airports (airports not having scheduled commercial air service) presently available for public use, with another twenty slated for construction by 1975. Upon completion of this building program, the number of counties without airports will be reduced from eighteen to three. Regional airports are also being developed. The regional airport is designed to serve a great number of people with better commercial schedules and with a greater variety of aircraft, in-

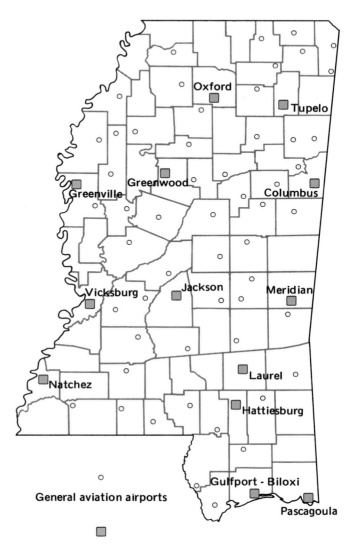

General aviation airports

Air carrier airports

PUBLIC AIRPORTS

Source: Mississippi Aeronautics Commission, 1973

143

COMMERCIAL AIR TRAFFIC IN MISSISSIPPI, 1972

Airport	Enplaned Passengers	Actual Departures	Mail (Tons)	Express (Tons)	Freight (Tons)
Jackson	306,570	*	4,422.05	388.45	4,893.16
Gulfport	80,289	5,422	122.95	22.08	4,368.89
Golden Triangle	29,177	2,393	33.17	35.74	125.09
Meridian	28,363	2,420	40.06	12.45	321.19
Greenville	25,104	2,215	10.79	13.18	263.72
Tupelo	11,064	1,999	24.77	10.86	61.09
Hattiesburg	3,217	1,114	0	8.24	17.81
Natchez	3,005	982	5.13	5.14	73.72
Laurel	2,157	1,158	7.82	2.23	31.11
Greenwood	2,022	1,130	13.97	15.09	34.23
Oxford	1,405	1,113	14.55	.55	5.99
Pascagoula **	1,201	1,022	16.74	16.74	8.21
TOTAL	493,574	20,968	4,712.00	531.08	6,132.70

* There was a total of 83,060 aircraft operations, including scheduled airlines, from the Jackson airport.
** Scheduled service to Pascagoula was discontinued at the end of 1972.

cluding jets, than could the older community airports. The Golden Triangle Regional Airport, serving Columbus, West Point, and Starkville, is already completed and the Pine Belt Regional Airport, serving Laurel and Hattiesburg, is under construction.

WATER TRANSPORTATION

Integral to the interconnected transportation system of the United States and of the world is water travel. One of the oldest means of transportation, navigable waterways provide a cheap, flexible, and efficient means for moving large loads of raw materials, fuels, and other commodities that can be bulk loaded. Bulk commodities such as gravel, grain, and coal are easily accommodated on barges that are towed along inland coastal waterways. Petroleum, such bulk raw materials as bauxite, and semifinished and finished products are carried on large tankers and freighters that ply the oceans between deep water ports in the United States and in other nations.

Mississippi is fortunate to be astride the largest inland waterway in the United States and to have direct access to both the navigable coastal waterway system and to the world's major ocean shipping lanes. River ports include Natchez, Vicksburg, and Green-

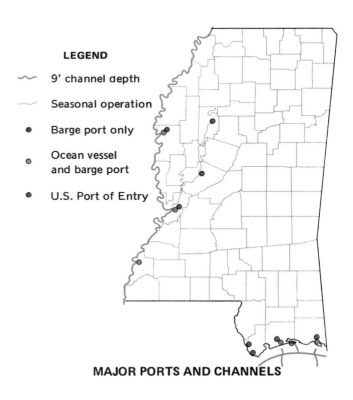

LEGEND

⌒ 9' channel depth

⌒ Seasonal operation

● Barge port only

◉ Ocean vessel and barge port

● U.S. Port of Entry

MAJOR PORTS AND CHANNELS

Source: Miss. Research and Development Center

144

ville on the Mississippi, Yazoo City and Greenwood on the Yazoo, and Yellow Creek on the Tennessee–Tombigbee waterway. Pascagoula, the busiest port in Mississippi, Biloxi, Gulfport, Pass Christian, and sites along the Pearl, Wolf, and Jordan rivers serve as ports for coastal and ocean-going vessels. Gulfport is only 12 miles from deep water shipping lanes, making it Mississippi's most accessible port on the Gulf of Mexico for ocean traffic.

Ports on the Mississippi River can handle both ocean-going vessels and barges with drafts (depths of water a ship displaces) up to nine feet. Yazoo City has facilities to handle barge traffic with drafts of less than nine feet, and Greenwood can handle barge traffic on a seasonal basis. The Pearl and East Pearl rivers have water depths that can accommodate vessels with drafts of less than nine feet. Pascagoula can accept ships having drafts up to thirty-nine feet, while Gulfport can handle vessels with drafts up to twenty-nine feet. Biloxi can accommodate ships with drafts of twelve feet or less. Port Bienville, a new waterfront industrial park near the mouth of the Pearl River, is connected to the Intracoastal Waterway via a twelve-foot barge canal.

Pascagoula is the largest port in Mississippi both in terms of vessels served and in terms of tonnage handled. During 1971, more than 8,300 ships entered Pascagoula harbor and more than 10 million tons of cargo were handled. By comparison, Vicksburg, the second leading port, handled 3,800 ships and 2.3 million tons of cargo.

River shipments and internal shipments (those along the inland waterway) account for 68 percent of Mississippi's port tonnage. The vast majority of internal shipments (85 percent) are handled through the three river ports. Of these, 83 percent is incoming cargo. Exports to foreign nations total approximately 20 percent of all cargo handled by Mississippi ports, and more than half of these exports go through Pascagoula. Only 6 percent of the commodities entering Mississippi ports are foreign imports. Almost two-thirds of the state's foreign imports are bananas, entering through the state port facilities at Gulfport, the nation's leading banana port.

With the completion of the Tennessee–Tombigbee system, connecting the Ohio and Tennessee rivers with the Gulf of Mexico, northeastern Mississippi will have access to inland water shipment. The "Tenn-Tom" project will provide channels nine feet in depth in the Tombigbee River and twelve feet in depth in the canals. A series of locks will provide a total lift of 341 feet to overcome the difference in elevation between the Tennessee River and the Tombigbee.

PIPELINES

Pipelines are the most highly specialized mode of transportation in the state. They are limited almost entirely to the transport of liquid and gaseous products. Pipelines are unique when compared with other modes of transportation because the *pipe* is both right-of-way and vehicle.

Advantages of pipelines rest in their ability to pro-

ACTIVITIES IN MISSISSIPPI PORTS, 1971

Port	Drafts	Tons of Cargo	Vessels Served**	Leading Commodity
Pascagoula	39'	10,098,504	8,346	Gasoline
Vicksburg	9'*	2,370,389	3,804	Agricultural products
Greenville	9'*	1,793,974	—	Agricultural products
Gulfport	29'	1,315,431	551	Chemicals/bananas
Natchez	9'*	646,174	—	Paper/pulp
Biloxi	12'	609,818	4,448	Coal
Jordan and Wolf river ports	8'	134,894	304	—
Yellow Creek		42,174	—	—
Pearl River ports	9'	31,781	66	—
Pass Christian	8'	29,712	227	—

* Authorized draft by the Corps of Engineers is nine feet, however each of these ports can accommodate vessels of greater depth except during periods of low water.
** For coastal ports, vessels served are inbound. For Vicksburg, it is the number of vessels passing the mouth of the Yazoo River.

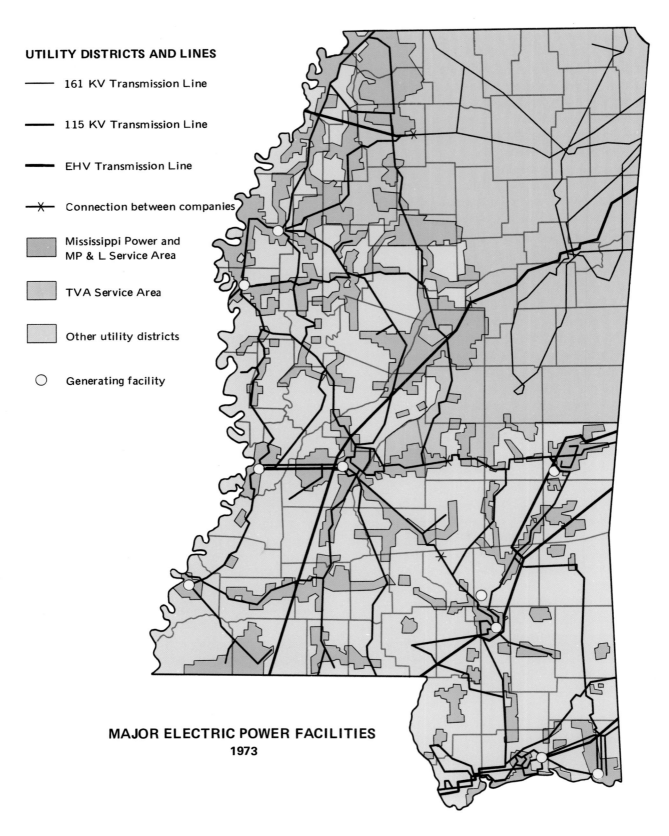

UTILITY DISTRICTS AND LINES

——— 161 KV Transmission Line

——— 115 KV Transmission Line

▬▬▬ EHV Transmission Line

—✕— Connection between companies

■ Mississippi Power and MP & L Service Area

■ TVA Service Area

□ Other utility districts

○ Generating facility

MAJOR ELECTRIC POWER FACILITIES
1973

Source: Mississippi Research and Development Center

vide low-cost bulk service. Transportation of liquid products (petroleum) by pipeline is ten to fifteen times cheaper than by railroad tank car and up to one hundred times cheaper than by motor truck. Only ocean tankers compare favorably in cost with pipelines. Cost per ton-mile of pipeline transport of petroleum products is estimated to be three-quarters of one mill.

Pipelines have characteristics other than cost that give them a comparative advantage over other transportation modes. First, they are almost totally unaffected by weather; seldom is a pipeline product prevented from reaching its destination because of inclement conditions. Also, there are few stoppages due to accidents or leakages. Third, "deadheading," or the return of empty vehicles, and the routing of vehicles is not a problem with pipelines as it is with other modes. Finally, labor requirements for operation and maintenance of pipelines are relatively low.

Utility of pipelines is limited to products in liquid form or as slurry (mixture of pulverized solids and water). Slurries, however, have not proved practical for long distance movement. Construction costs of pipelines may run into tens of thousands of dollars per mile.

Mississippi has a total of 2,950 miles of petroleum pipelines and 9,350 miles of natural gas pipelines. Diameters of pipelines vary from two inches to forty inches. More than two-thirds of the gas pipelines have diameters twenty inches or larger, while one-third of the petroleum pipelines are larger than eighteen inches.

Distribution of pipelines in Mississippi emphasizes the importance of the state's geographic position between the Texas–Gulf Coast producing area and the consuming areas of the northeastern United States. Pipelines traverse the state in a general southwest to northeast pattern. Gas pipelines dominate in the central and northern portions of the state, while petroleum pipelines are confined primarily to southern Mississippi. Every county and large city in Mississippi and many small communities are served by natural gas pipelines. Petroleum pipelines pass through nearly two-thirds of Mississippi's counties.

UTILITIES

Electrical power, furnished by both private and public companies, is available in every county in Mississippi. The primary suppliers of electrical power are the Mississippi Power and Light Company, the Mississippi Power Company, and the Tennessee Valley Authority. Each of these companies supplies electrical power directly to consumers, to municipal electric systems, and to rural electric power associations. Mississippi Power and Light Company serves western Mississippi. Mississippi Power Company furnishes electrical power to the southeastern quadrant of the state, and the Tennessee Valley Authority supplies electrical power to northeastern Mississippi. Of these three companies, only the TVA does not have electrical generators in Mississippi. There are fifteen municipal electric utility systems and twenty-eight rural electric power associations operating in Mississippi, several of which have generating systems. The two power companies and one rural electric power association generating electricity within the state have a combined capacity of more than 3,330 megawatts. An additional 4,330 megawatts of generating power was either under construction or announced for development in Mississippi as of January 1, 1974.

W. T. Mealor

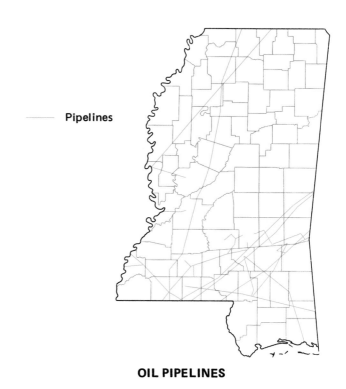

Pipelines

OIL PIPELINES

Source: Mississippi Oil and Gas Board, 1973

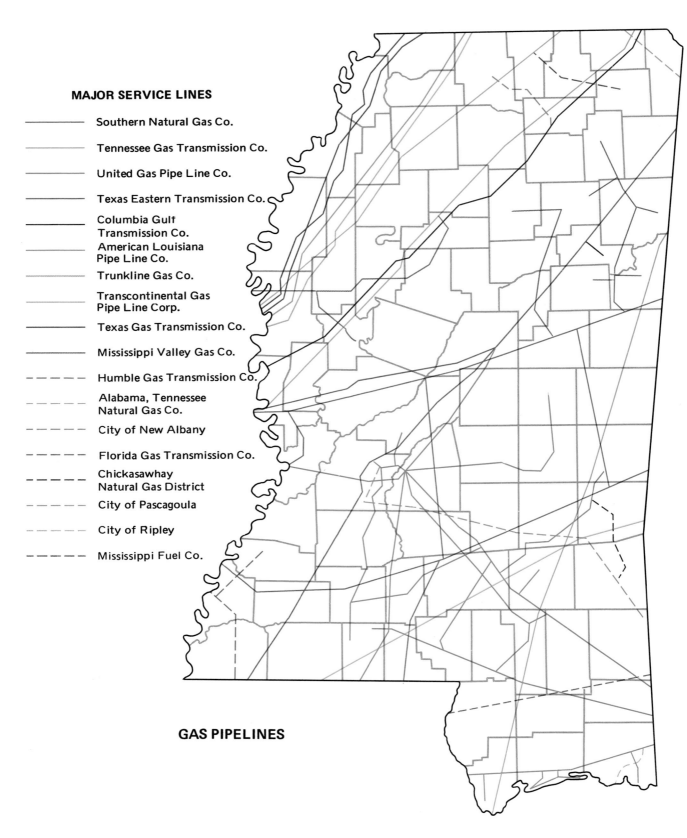

MAJOR SERVICE LINES

————————— Southern Natural Gas Co.

————————— Tennessee Gas Transmission Co.

————————— United Gas Pipe Line Co.

————————— Texas Eastern Transmission Co.

————————— Columbia Gulf
Transmission Co.

————————— American Louisiana
Pipe Line Co.

————————— Trunkline Gas Co.

————————— Transcontinental Gas
Pipe Line Corp.

————————— Texas Gas Transmission Co.

————————— Mississippi Valley Gas Co.

– – – – – – Humble Gas Transmission Co.

– – – – – – Alabama, Tennessee
Natural Gas Co.

– – – – – – City of New Albany

– – – – – – Florida Gas Transmission Co.

– – – – – – Chickasawhay
Natural Gas District

– – – – – – City of Pascagoula

– – – – – – City of Ripley

– – – – – – Mississippi Fuel Co.

GAS PIPELINES

Source: Mississippi Research and Development Center, 1969

148

COMMUNICATIONS

NEWSPAPERS

Every county in Mississippi, with the exception of Issaquena, is served by an in-county daily or weekly newspaper. Twenty-two of the state's 140 papers are published daily. Of these, all but five are owned by in-state proprietors. All daily general circulation newspapers are printed in their own plants in standard size. Print styles and sizes vary, however, with five (four of which serve the largest population areas) using letterpress and the remainder offset print. Of the 118 weekly papers, 33 are letterpress publications and 85 use offset. Most of the weekly publishers who do printing in their own plants also do commercial printing, a practice which is rare with daily publishers. In addition to the 140 newspapers serving a general audience within the state, there are also 17 papers published by universities and colleges. These are weekly, monthly, or quarterly publications, with the exceptions of the University of Mississippi's *Mississippian* which appears five days a week and the twice-weekly *Student Printz* of the University of Southern Mississippi.

The majority of weekly newspapers have local circulations seldom extending beyond the several counties surrounding their place of publication. The largest circulation involves daily publications; however, even these vary considerably in number, ranging from a low of 3,600 to over 58,000. Eleven dailies have circulations over 10,000; five are over 20,000; and three—*The Daily Herald* from Biloxi–Gulfport (36,719), and the Jackson *Daily News* (47,918) and *The Clarion-Ledger* (58,585) from Jackson—are over 30,000. Several of these larger circulation dailies serve regional audiences, but only *The Clarion-Ledger* and the Joint Sunday edition of *The Clarion-Ledger* and Jackson *Daily News* (111,648) can be considered to have statewide circulation.

In addition to newspapers published in Mississippi, several out-of-state papers circulate to regional audiences in the state with Mississippi editions. The Memphis *Commercial Appeal* covers large areas of northern Mississippi; the New Orleans *Times-Picayune* serves the southern and southwestern portion of the state; the Mobile *Press-Register* covers the southeastern segment; and the *Birmingham News* serves the eastcentral sector.

Two wire services supplying both state and national news coverage are available to Mississippi

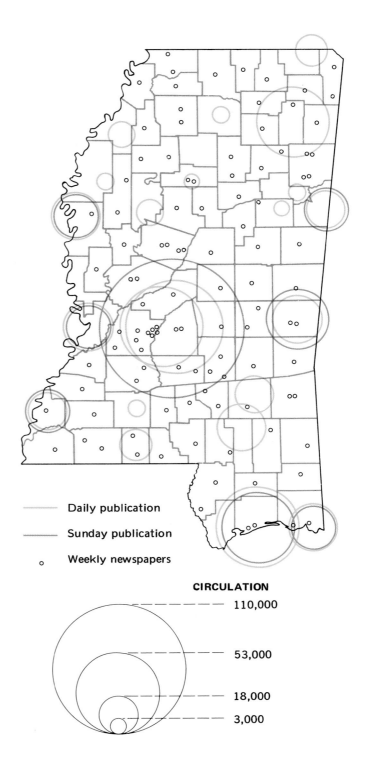

Daily publication

Sunday publication

o   Weekly newspapers

CIRCULATION

110,000

53,000

18,000

3,000

NEWSPAPERS

newspapers—the Associated Press and United Press International. Both maintain news bureaus in Jackson.

The interests of both Mississippi daily and weekly newspapers are served by the Mississippi Press Association, which has its offices in Jackson. The Mississippi Newspaper Advertising Executive's Association promotes the advertising aspect of daily newspapers. Sigma Delta Chi, a national journalism society, and the Mississippi Press Women's Association also have chapters in Mississippi.

Journalism is taught at the high school, junior college, and university levels in Mississippi. The University of Mississippi and the University of Southern Mississippi both offer degrees in journalism.

RADIO AND TELEVISION

The first radio station in Mississippi started broadcasting early in 1924 in Coldwater, under the direction of Hoyt Wooten. Call letters for this ten-watt station were KFNG. Four other stations also had their beginnings in the 1920s—WFOR in Hattiesburg

(1924), WCOC in Meridian (1926), WGCM in Gulfport (1928), and WJDX in Jackson. Radio station WQBC in Vicksburg (1931) cannot qualify as one of the oldest stations in Mississippi, but it was probably the first to put uniqueness into its call letter combinations: W (We) Q (Quote) B (Better) C (Cotton).

Most of the 155 AM and FM radio stations presently operating in Mississippi belong to the Mississippi Broadcaster's Association (MBA). The association was formed in 1940 with Charles J. Wright, Sr., then owner of WFOR, serving as its first president. Bob McRaney, Sr., owner of several broadcast properties, including WROB in West Point, Mississippi, was the second president of the MBA and has served as the association's executive secretary continuously since 1958. The Mississippi Broadcaster's Association serves both radio and television stations, promoting convention activities, sales clinics, and sponsored tours. It publishes a monthly newsletter and serves as liaison with the Federal Communications Commission in Washington, D.C.

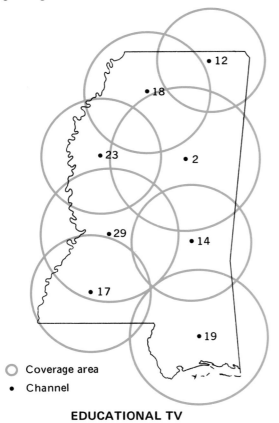

EDUCATIONAL TV

Source: Mississippi Authority for ETV

Mississippi's first commercial television station was WJTV in Jackson, which began telecasting in January, 1953. The station originally signed on as a UHF operation but later converted to VHF. WJTV was followed by WTOK-TV, Meridian, which began broadcasting in September, 1953, and WLBT-TV, Jackson, which went on the air in December, 1953. Six additional television stations have since begun operation in the state—WDAM-TV, Hattiesburg (1956); WCBI-TV, Columbus (1956); WTWV, Tupelo (1957); WLOX-TV, Biloxi (1962); WHTV, Meridian (1968), and WAPT, Jackson (1970). WHTV, Meridian, suspended operations in October, 1970, but was purchased in 1972 by WTWV, Tupelo, and is currently operating as a satellite of the Tupelo station.

Educational television (ETV) programming and broadcasting in Mississippi is unique; few other states can claim such complete and detailed statewide coverage. Work toward the development of the state's first ETV network in the 1960s was based upon a need to overcome the broad gap in educational achievements between the citizens of Mississippi and the rest of the nation. It was hoped that a comprehensive system of ETV broadcasting might provide more people with a better education in less time and at a reduced cost. The impact of ETV on the social and economic life of the state has yet to be measured. However, the very existence of statewide educational television coverage in Mississippi reflects today's trend toward self-improvement and the underlying shift to an industrialized economy.

Educational television was inaugurated in Mississippi by a 1966 act of the legislature, which authorized the Mississippi Authority for Educational Television (MAET). William R. Smith was hired as director, a position he still holds in 1974. Broadcasting on educational television channels began in February, 1970, with station WMAA, Channel 29 in Jackson. WMAA serves as the production center for all educational public television programs broadcast by the network. In 1971 and 1972 six satellite stations were added to the network—WMAB, Starkville, Channel 2; WMAH, Biloxi, Channel 19; WMAW, Bude, Channel 17; WMAV, Oxford, Channel 18; and WMAO, Greenwood, Channel 23. A seventh station is to be added to the ETV network in 1974 to broadcast from Booneville on Channel 12.

Stan P. Gwin

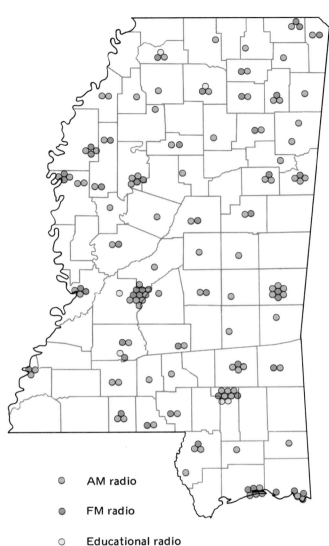

○   AM radio

◉   FM radio

○   Educational radio

RADIO STATIONS

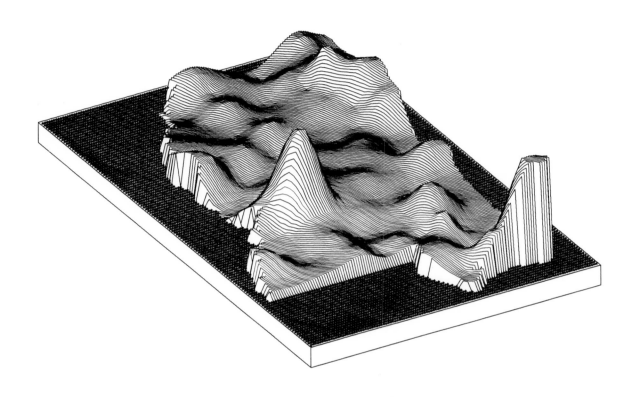

TOTAL EMPLOYMENT IN MANUFACTURING

MANUFACTURING

The most noticeable change occurring on the Mississippi economic landscape during the post-World War II period has been the shifting emphasis from farms to factories. As a result, since the mid-1960s manufacturing has become the single largest source of income and employment in the state. Over one-fourth of the Mississippi labor force is now employed in manufacturing industries; likewise, these industries provide over one-fourth of the state's total personal income.

Much of the growth and progress in Mississippi's manufacturing sector is related to the national trend of the 1960s and early 1970s with the relocation or expansion of many northern industries into the South. But considerable credit must also be given to the efforts of state officials, community leaders, and private individuals to create a progressive investment climate for manufacturing activities throughout Mississippi. At the state level, the Mississippi Agricultural and Industrial Board and the Mississippi Research and Development Center have been primarily responsible for encouraging and directing the growth of the manufacturing sector. The much publicized success of the state's 30-year-old BAWI Plan (Balance Agriculture with Industry) has prompted its adoption as a model by several other states in recent years.

Mississippi is an attractive location for manufacturing activities, due in part to geography. The state is centrally located with respect to both the raw materials and markets of the South and Midwest. Moreover, it enjoys an almost year-round frost-free climate, has plenty of good water, and has excellent accessibility by truck, railroad, and airline. But while the state can still provide an abundance of productive labor, it is evident that low wage scales and the lack of union activities, two earlier arguments for locating a manufacturing enterprise in Mississippi, will greatly diminish in importance by the late 1970s.

Several trends in Mississippi manufacturing are evident in the mid-1970s. The most obvious of these are:

- Although the manufacturing enterprise in Mississippi is still growing, its *rate* of growth is decelerating.
- There is a tendency toward larger plants and, in general, larger payrolls.
- The incidence of manufacturing activity in the state is spotty; many areas of the state are not favored at all with an industrial plant—of any size.
- The importance of the apparel industries is growing while the historically important lumber and wood product industries are playing a decreasing role in the state economy.
- There is a growing emphasis on capital-intensive industries (e.g., chemicals and metalworking) at the expense of labor-intensive industries (e.g., apparel).
- There is a directed trend toward achieving a better balance between the higher paying and lower paying industries.
- The heavier (more capital-intensive) industries are tending to locate on the Gulf Coast, on navigable water in the northeastern sector of the state, and at port towns and cities along the Mississippi River.

William M. Roberts

MANUFACTURING CHARACTERISTICS

In the production process man's activities can be subdivided into primary, manufacturing, and service categories. Primary activities include agriculture, forestry, fishing, and mining. Manufacturing and construction comprise that group sometimes known as secondary activities. Manufacturing is the process in which raw materials are assembled in an industry, upgraded in usefulness through a change in form, and shipped out as commodities more valuable than their original raw form. Service activities are those in which services are rendered to others and include such employment types as repairmen, teachers, housekeepers, government employees, and bankers.

EMPLOYMENT

Manufacturing employment in Mississippi has grown rapidly since 1940. While both state population and total employment decreased during 1940–60, manufacturing employment increased steadily. Manufacturing employment in 1940 was 3.1 percent of 727,245 total employment, or 66,610, whereas in 1970 it had risen to 25.9 percent or 185,896 persons of a total employed labor force of 718,948. During the period 1940–70, total manufacturing employment increased by 179.1 percent. Over this same thirty-year period the total population of the state increased by only 1.8 percent.

The pattern of employment by SEAs (U.S. Census State Economic Areas) shows a difference in emphasis on manufacturing vis-a-vis other employment sectors. The economic area with the largest manufacturing employment is SEA-4 (Tippah, Alcorn, Tishomingo, Prentiss, Itawamba, Union, Pontotoc, and Lafayette counties), the Mississippi Pine Hill Area, in which 38.5 percent of the labor force is occupied in manufacturing. The lowest percentage of manufacturing occupations occurs in SEA-A, Hinds County, which had 13.8 percent of employed persons working in manufacturing in 1970. The low percentage of manufacturing employment in Hinds County is due largely to the importance of service activities in Jackson. SEA-1, the Delta (Tunica, Coahoma, Quitman, Bolivar, Tallahatchie, Sunflower, Washington, Humphreys, Sharkey, and Issaquena counties), has the lowest absolute number engaged in manufacturing. In this region, agriculture provides employment for a large segment of the population.

Total employment as a percentage of state popu-

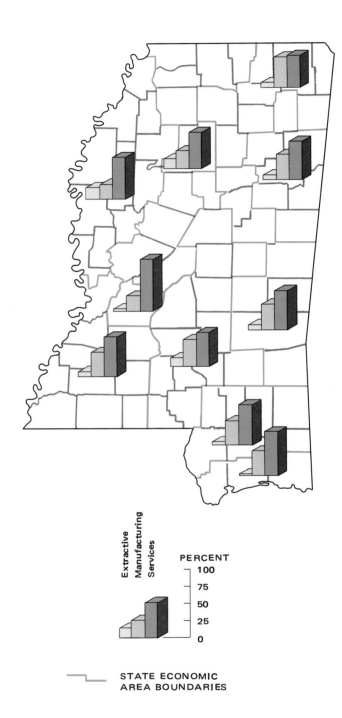

EMPLOYMENT IN MAJOR ACTIVITIES

lation has decreased from 33.3 percent in 1940 to 32.7 percent in 1970. As with total population, however, a downward trend has been reversed in the last decade, and total employment has grown by 6.2 percent during 1960–70. These changes are modest, but they do suggest significant alterations in the Mississippi population patterns and movements. If the earlier trend has ended, more important gains may be evidenced in the future.

The distribution by industry of Mississippi's manufacturing employment differs notably from the average patterns for the United States. Manufacturing and construction absorb 31.9 percent of total U.S. employment, whereas in Mississippi 33.3 percent of the employed labor force is engaged in these secondary activities. This contrast tends to negate the concept that the state is primarily an agricultural area. Only 7.5 percent of Mississippi employment was devoted to agricultural occupations in 1970.

As noted, the state has shown a rather marked rise in manufacturing employment since 1940, although the 1960s showed a slower gain in manufacturing employment than was recorded in the two preceding decades. Percentage gains by decade are as follows: 1940–50, 35.6 percent; 1950–69, 44.8 percent; 1960–70, 42.1 percent. This slightly slower rate of growth in manufacturing in the last decade is due to an employment increase in the services sector.

Mississippi has numerous large and medium-sized manufacturing establishments. Moreover, the number of large firms has been on the increase recently. For the period 1968–71, the total number of manufactur-

MANUFACTURING ESTABLISHMENTS AND EMPLOYMENT BY STATE ECONOMIC AREA

U.S. Census Economic Area	(Establishments) Total	With 100 or More Employees	Employees, 1971
1	210	36	14,658*
2	206	44	16,116**
3	284	39	17,386
4	211	52	18,506
5	260	67	28,435
6a	305	47	20,295
6b	255	34	13,529
7	207	26	8,725
8	199	23	24,421
A	247	40	12,000

* Tunica County employment figures are for 1970.
** Benton County employment figures are for 1970.

EMPLOYMENT IN MISSISSIPPI BY MAJOR INDUSTRY

Industry Group	(Thousands) 1950	1960	1970
Lumber & Wood Products	32.1	24.6*	22.7
Furniture & Fixtures	2.4	6.4	13.1
Stone, Clay, & Glass	2.3	4.7	5.9
Primary & Fabricated Metals (Industries)	N/A	3.8	10.8
Machinery, except Electrical	N/A	2.9	7.5
Electrical Equipment (Machinery) & Supplies	N/A	5.3	12.5
Transportation Equipment	1.2	6.5	15.0
Ordnance & Instruments (Ordnance & Accessories)	N/A	N/A	2.2
Miscellaneous Manufacturing	N/A	N/A	3.9
Food & Kindred Products	8.0	16.0	18.7
Textile Mill Products	5.4	5.1	6.4
Apparel & Related Products	14.6	28.5	28.6
Paper & Allied Products	6.5	4.6*	7.1
Printing & Publishing	1.8	2.5	3.0
Chemicals & Allied Products	2.9	3.9	5.5
Petroleum & Coal Products	N/A	N/A	1.2
Rubber & Plastic Products	N/A	N/A	5.2
Leather & Leather Products	N/A	N/A	2.1

N/A   Not available.
* Data not strictly comparable with earlier years.
Source: U.S. Bureau of Labor Statistics, *Employment and Earnings, States and Areas*, 1939–71 (BLS Bulletin 1370–9).

ing establishments in Mississippi remained constant at 2,384. However, the number of establishments employing 20 or more workers rose from 848 to 991, or 16.9 percent, and the number of establishments with 100 or more employees grew from 308 to 408, or 32.5 percent. Additionally, the average establishment's employment increased during this same three-year period from 54 to 74 workers.

Individual counties show considerable variations in number and size of plants and employment. These variations reflect differences in the type of manufacturing common to diverse areas of the state. Mississippi also has experienced significant changes in employment by major industrial groups during the period 1950–70.

Apparel and related products had replaced lumber and wood products as the largest manufacturing employer in the state by 1970. Also, a number of industry groups not sufficiently important in 1950 to merit separate classification had become major sources of employment. Notable among these were transportation equipment, primary and fabricated metals industries, and electrical equipment and supplies.

VALUE ADDED BY MANUFACTURE

Value added by manufacturing and value added per production worker in manufacturing are useful indicators of manufacturing magnitude and worker productivity. Value added by manufacture is calculated by subtracting the value of supplies and materials and of energy required to manufacture a product from the sum of the sales value of finished products. Value added per production worker is calculated by dividing the total value added by manufacture by the number of workers.

Jackson and Hinds counties are the most significant in Mississippi in terms of value by manufacture. Jackson, with nearly $170 million, and Hinds, with about $155 million, accounted for 21 percent of the state's total value added by manufacture in 1967. Lee, Yazoo, Lowndes, Adams, Warren, and Monroe counties—all with value added figures ranging between $69 million and $52 million—ranked behind Jackson and Hinds. The county average for the state was $18.7 million. Manufacturing is well distributed throughout the state, and no single region or block of counties can account for a majority share of the value added by manufacture.

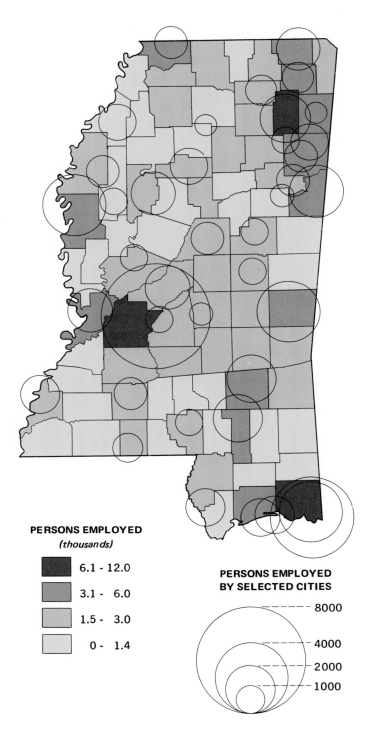

PERSONS EMPLOYED
(thousands)

- 6.1 - 12.0
- 3.1 - 6.0
- 1.5 - 3.0
- 0 - 1.4

PERSONS EMPLOYED BY SELECTED CITIES

- 8000
- 4000
- 2000
- 1000

MANUFACTURING EMPLOYMENT

Source: U.S. Census of Population, 1970

A comparison of value added figures for counties and cities provides some indication of the urban-oriented nature of manufacturing. The city of Jackson accounted for 86 percent of the value added in manufacturing for Hinds County, Pascagoula for 40 percent of Jackson County, Tupelo for 81 percent of Lee County, and Hattiesburg for 93 percent of Forrest County. Even in cities where the value added percentage is small compared to the county figure, the industries are usually in close proximity to the urban areas.

Of the eighteen major industrial groups represented in Mississippi, as reported by the Bureau of Census, eight were in the over $100 million category of value added by manufacture in 1967. During 1967–70, eight industries experienced a larger gain in value added than that shown by the U.S. on the average. Three of these industries—paper, electrical equipment, and transportation equipment—had a percentage gain in value added ranging from almost two to over five times the national gain.

INCREASE IN VALUE ADDED BY MANUFACTURE, 1967–70, MISSISSIPPI AND UNITED STATES

Industry Group	Percentage Change in Value Added Mississippi	United States
Food	21.8	19.8
Textile	24.7	18.3
Apparel	25.0	18.3
Lumber	22.2	22.0
Furniture	17.4	15.6
Paper	81.2	15.7
Electrical Equipment	41.0	21.4
Transportation	31.3	14.1

Although significant progress has been made in manufacturing in Mississippi, the state continues to fall short of national average figures in several important areas. In value added per production worker, for example, the national average in 1970 was $22,008, while the figure for Mississippi was only $14,285. The state's manufacturing sector is increasing in overall size relative to the national sector, but it has not shown an increase in relative productivity. Additionally, hourly pay rates have tended to be less than national averages. Atlhough five industry groups—paper, apparel, textile, leather, and miscellaneous manufactures—exceeded the national average in value added per production worker in 1970, in only one case (that of the paper industry) was this reflected directly in

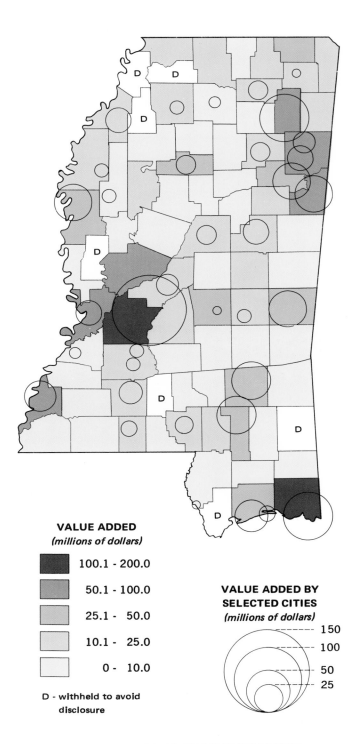

VALUE ADDED
(millions of dollars)

■ 100.1 - 200.0

▦ 50.1 - 100.0

▨ 25.1 - 50.0

░ 10.1 - 25.0

□ 0 - 10.0

D - withheld to avoid disclosure

VALUE ADDED BY SELECTED CITIES
(millions of dollars)

150
100
50
25

VALUE ADDED BY MANUFACTURE

Source: U.S. Census of Manufactures, 1967.

hourly pay data. However, nearly all Mississippi industrial groups with a relatively high value added ratio also have relatively high state-to-nation hourly pay ratios.

VALUE ADDED AND HOURLY PAY, 1970
MISSISSIPPI AND UNITED STATES
(U.S. Average Equals: 1,000)

Industry	MS/US Value Added	MS/US Hourly Pay
Paper	1.238	1.098
Apparel	1.205	.868
Textile	1.111	.955
Leather	1.107	.923
Misc. Manufactures	1.080	.856
Furniture	.930	.867
Lumber	.891	.782
Machinery	.804	.744
Fabricated Metal	.798	.779
Chemicals	.797	.718
Rubber, Plastics	.773	.957
Electrical	.751	.703
Stone, Clay, and Glass	.672	.734
Food	.607	.772
Transportation	.606	.799
Instruments	.482	.618
Printing	.474	.611
Primary Metal	.465	.642
STATE–NATIONAL AVERAGE	.642	.720

DURABLE GOODS MANUFACTURING

FURNITURE AND FIXTURES, LUMBER AND WOOD PRODUCTS—The furniture and fixtures and the lumber and wood products industries accounted for 19.7 percent of the total manufacturing employment in Mississippi in 1970. Separately, employment trends in these two timber-based categories have been in sharp contrast over the past several decades. The lumber and wood products industry has declined sharply since 1950, from 32,100 employees to 22,700 workers in 1970. The decline virtually nullified the rapid employment increase experienced by the furniture and fixtures category which rose from a 1950 level of 2,400 to the 1970 employment total of 13,100. When compared to all other major groups, the importance of these industries has been on the decline, showing a percentage decrease from 34.5 percent of total manufacturing employment in 1950 to 19.7 percent in 1970.

Both the furniture and fixtures and the lumber and wood products categories rank low on state pay scales, fifteenth and twelfth respectively, but this represents their relatively low position nationally rather than being a characteristic only of Mississippi. State

VALUE ADDED BY MANUFACTURE

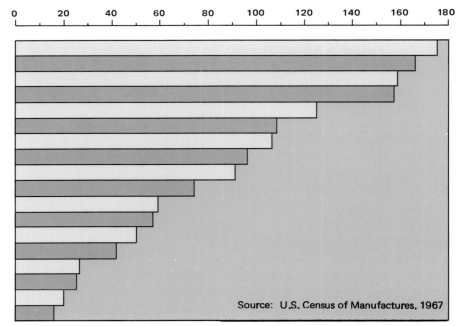

(millions of dollars)

Apparel and related products
Lumber and wood products
Chemicals and allied products
Food and kindred products
Transportation equipment
Machinery, except electrical
Fabricated metal products
Electrical equipment and supplies
Furniture and fixtures
Paper and allied products
Stone, clay and glass products
Textile mill products
Rubber and plastic products, NEC
Miscellaneous manufacturing industries
Leather and leather products
Printing and publishing
Instruments and related products
Primary metal industries

Source: U.S. Census of Manufactures, 1967

data suggest a reasonably competitive performance in both value added and pay by these state industries when compared to the national average.

The timber-related industries are of greatest importance in the industrial structures of SEA-6b (Webster, Choctaw, Winston, Kemper, Lauderdale, Newton, Jasper, Clarke, and Wayne counties), the Mississippi Piney Woods–Eastern Area, and of somewhat lesser importance in SEAs-3 (Pike, Amite, Wilkinson, Warren, Claiborne, Adams, Franklin, Lincoln, Jefferson, and Copiah counties), 6a (Montgomery, Attala, Leake, Scott, Rankin, Smith, Simpson, Lawrence, Covington, Jefferson Davis, Walthall, and Marion counties), and 7 (Lamar, Forrest, Perry, Greene, Pearl River, Stone, and George counties). Furniture, lumber, and wood products establishments are of little significance in SEA-8 (Hancock, Harrison, and Jackson counties), the Mississippi Gulf Coast. Jones County, with 2,174 workers, Madison County with 1,036 workers, and Lauderdale County with 1,018 employed in these industries are the only counties in the state with more than one thousand employees working in this classification.

The lumber and wood products industries have a number of operations, including such diverse activities as pine and hardwood lumber manufacture and weaving of baskets. There are 261 such establishments in Mississippi, employing 22,800 workers. The Anderson–Tully Company, with 700 employees, is the largest plant within this classification. Seventy-two of Mississippi's eighty-two counties have lumber and wood manufacturers. Geographically, the establishments are most heavily concentrated in the southern and northeastern parts of the state where acres of forest land are most numerous.

The furniture and fixtures industries rank fifth in manufacturing employment in Mississippi; there are 95 plants employing 13,000 workers. The heaviest concentration of plants is in the northeastern part of the state. Hinds, Chickasaw, Lee, and Union counties rank highest in number of employees in this category. Two of the larger companies are MPI Industries in Hinds County and Futorian Manufacturing Company in Chickasaw and Union counties. MDI employs 1,700 people, and Futorian provides work for 1,650 workers.

PRIMARY AND FABRICATED METAL PRODUCTS—The metals industries are of minor significance in Mississippi, partly due to lack of raw mate-

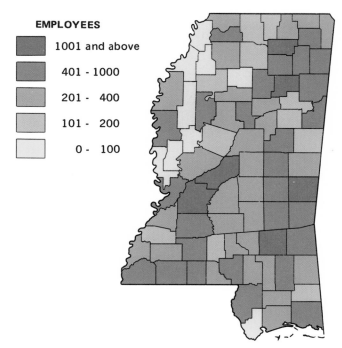

EMPLOYEES

■	1001 and above
■	401 - 1000
■	201 - 400
■	101 - 200
□	0 - 100

EMPLOYMENT IN FURNITURE, LUMBER AND WOOD PRODUCTS INDUSTRIES

Source: U.S. Census of Population, 1970

rial sources of any value in the state. Only 5.8 percent of manufacturing employment in the state was engaged in these industries in 1970. Yet, the 10,800 metal workers in 1970 represent a considerable increase from the 548 total employees in the group in 1940. Only Washington County, in SEA-1, with 1,116 workers, employed over a thousand individuals in these industries in 1970. Both metal industry groups pay above the state's average manufacturing wage. But only the fabricated metals group ranks favorably in comparison with national figures.

The primary metal industries employ 1,900 workers in 20 establishments scattered over a total of sixteen counties. These manufacturers produce castings, extrusions, and electrolytic manganese. The largest plants are in Monroe County and together employ 640 individuals—the American Potash and Chemical Corporation and Cramco Division of Gulf and Western Industries Incorporated. The largest plants producing aluminum extrusions are Craft Aluminum in Pike County (250 employees) and Olin Corporation in Harrison County (200 employees).

Fabricated metal products are produced in 172 establishments by a total of 8,900 employees. The

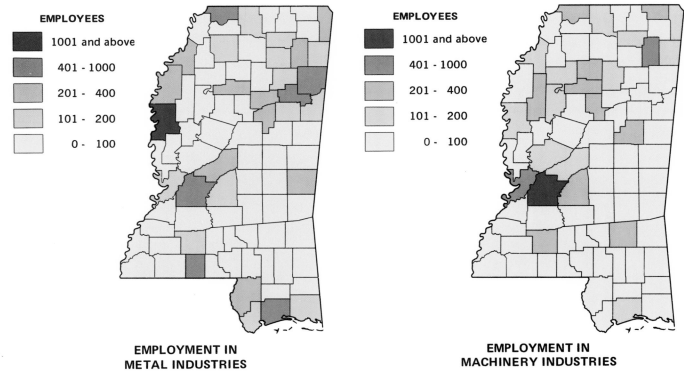

EMPLOYEES

■ 1001 and above

▓ 401 - 1000

▒ 201 - 400

░ 101 - 200

□ 0 - 100

**EMPLOYMENT IN
METAL INDUSTRIES**

EMPLOYEES

■ 1001 and above

▓ 401 - 1000

▒ 201 - 400

░ 101 - 200

□ 0 - 100

**EMPLOYMENT IN
MACHINERY INDUSTRIES**

Source: U.S. Census of Population, 1970

plants are well distributed over the state, but only Clay, Washington, Pike, Bolivar, Lee, and Lauderdale counties employ over 500 workers each in this category. Hinds County has 44 fabricated metal plants, the largest number per county in the state, but none of them employs as many as 100 persons. The largest fabricated metal establishment, Babcock and Wilcox Company, has 1,250 employees and is located in Clay County.

MACHINERY EXCEPT ELECTRICAL— The machinery industry in Mississippi is also unimportant quantitatively in terms of numbers employed in the industry. Only 4.8 percent of total manufacturing employment in the state was devoted to the production of machinery in 1970. As was the case for the metals industries, however, the small total represented a dramatic growth rate over that of previous decades. In 1940 only 600 persons were occupied in machinery industries in Mississippi; by 1970, this figure had risen to 7,500.

Only in the Jackson SMSA (Standard Metropolitan Statistical Area), including SEA-A (Hinds County), is the machinery industry relatively large. Here 11.1 per-

cent of the total manufacturing employment is in the machinery category—a total of 1,504 workers in 1970. Hinds County, which includes most of the Jackson SMSA (Hinds and Rankin counties), was the leading machinery employer by county in 1970 with 1,364 persons.

The nonelectrical machinery industry includes 118 companies situated in thirty-eight counties within the state. These companies manufacture such items as garden tillers, power tools, tractors, hydraulic scrapers, heating–air conditioning–refrigeration products, elevators and industrial lifts, and marine products.

Hinds County is the focus of this industry, having 1,364 workers employed by 31 establishments. The two largest companies in Hinds County, Magna American Corporation and M–R–S Manufacturing Company, employ about 300 persons each. Counties other than Hinds having notable employment in nonelectrical machinery firms are Grenada, De Soto, Warren, Lee, Winston, Harrison, Lincoln, Yalobusha, Alcorn, and Sunflower counties. The largest machinery manufacturer in Mississippi, McQuay Incorporated, employs 835 workers and is located in Grenada County.

ELECTRICAL MACHINERY, EQUIPMENT, AND SUPPLIES—A total of 12,400 persons were employed in the electrical machinery, equipment, and supplies category in Mississippi in 1970. Since only 85 workers were employed in this industry in the state in 1940, its rate of growth has been the highest for any single group over the past three decades.

Employment in the Mississippi electrical industry is most important, relatively, in the Jackson SMSA and therefore makes SEA-A (Hinds County) the most significant of the State Economic Areas. In 1970, Hinds County recorded 1,236 employees, Alcorn County 1,236 workers, and Simpson County 1,120 persons employed in electrical equipment production. Of the 2,202 total manufacturing employment in Simpson County, over half worked in electrical equipment production. Simpson County was one of ten counties in Mississippi in 1970 to have 50 percent or more of its industrial sector dominated by one industry group.

Electrical machinery, equipment, and supplies averages approximately 302 persons in each of the 41 establishments in Mississippi. The industry is spread over twenty-six counties, but only eight counties employ over 500 persons. These are Simpson,

Alcorn, Lowndes, Neshoba, Wayne, Hinds, Warren, and Lee counties. Actually, three major industries located in three counties provide work for over 25 percent of all workers in the industry. Universal Manufacturing Corporation in Simpson County, ITT Telecommunications in Alcorn County, and Ambac Industries in Lowndes County employ over 1,000 workers each.

TRANSPORTATION EQUIPMENT—The transportation equipment industry includes both motor and non-motor vehicle transportation equipment. Nationally, the motor vehicle equipment category is of major importance, but it is not a major one in Mississippi.

The Gulf Coast is the only area of the state where the transportation industry is of significance. Here, ship- and boat-building dominates. Of the state's 15,200 total employment in transportation equipment, 6,925 are located in Jackson County. Numerous other persons working in Jackson County shipyards have residences in adjacent counties. Nearly 58 percent of Jackson County's total manufacturing employment is engaged in the transportation industry. Almost ten thousand workers in the seven closest counties to the

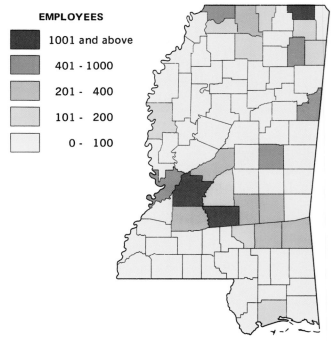

EMPLOYMENT IN ELECTRICAL EQUIPMENT, MACHINERY AND SUPPLIES INDUSTRIES

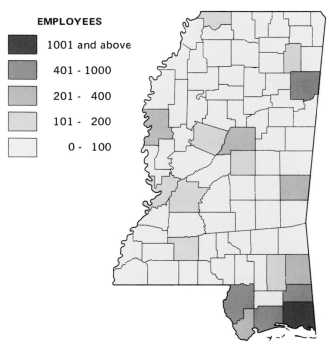

EMPLOYMENT IN TRANSPORTATION EQUIPMENT MANUFACTURE

Source: U.S. Census of Population, 1970

Gulf of Mexico were engaged in producing transportation equipment in 1970. Transportation equipment manufacture ranked second in the state in hourly pay in 1970, with an average wage for production workers of $2.41 per hour.

Transportation equipment manufacturing ranks fourth in total employment in the state with 15,200 workers in 58 establishments. Jackson County dominates the industry group. Litton Industries, Marine Divisions provides work for 13,000 workers on its site in Jackson County. Litton Industries is not only the largest company in the transportation equipment category, but it is the largest manufacturing concern in Mississippi. Nuclear-powered submarines, naval and commercial service ships, and marine facilities are constructed at this large shipyard.

Hinds County with 1,262 employees working in four establishments ranks a distant second behind Jackson County in this category. The Vickers Division of Sperry–Rand Corporation accounts for 900 of Hinds County's transportation equipment employees. In addition Warren, Attala, and Monroe counties each have 500 or more workers in this industry group.

OTHER DURABLE GOODS—In 1970, 16,178 Mississippians were employed in a variety of establishments producing goods not classified in any preceding group. These included such diverse categories as rubber and plastics products; stone, clay, and glass products; leather and leather products; instruments and related products; and ordnance and accessories. Hourly average wages paid in Mississippi in these industries ranged from $3.11 in rubber and plastics to $2.15 in the instruments class. The only county where the aggregate employment in these industries exceeded one thousand was Hinds, with 1,792 workers.

NONDURABLE GOODS

FOOD AND KINDRED PRODUCTS—Food and kindred products manufacturing is one of the state's lowest paying industries with an average weekly wage of $87 in 1969, $8 below the total average manufacturing wage. However, the average hourly wage of $2.14 was close to the national average.

Only eight counties in the state do not have food and kindred products manufacturing establishments. The other seventy-four counties have 399 concerns, employing a total of 18,800 workers. The number of manufacturers in the food and kindred products industry is double that of any other major industry group in Mississippi. Most establishments are small, employing only a few workers each, yet the industry group ranks third in the state in total employment. Moreover, the large number of total workers in the industry represents a doubling of employees since 1940. Nonetheless, a loss of jobs between 1960 and 1970 in the food and kindred products industry did occur. The major concentrations of employees in food-based categories are in Hinds, Jones, Harrison, Clay, and Lee counties.

Major food commodities processed in Mississippi are meat products, poultry, seafood, dairy products, and bakery and confectionery goods. Meat products, poultry, and seafood processing plants number 80 and employ 8,400 workers. The heaviest concentration of plants is in the central and southwestern portions of the state, Scott County being the focal point. The two largest processing plants are Bryan Brothers Packing Company (1,000 workers) situated in Clay County, and Purnell's Pride, Inc., a major poultry producer in northeastern Mississippi. The seafood processing plants are concentrated along the coast; the largest is Cruso Canning Company in Biloxi. The dairy products industry employs some 1,800 workers in 38 establishments. Among these are branches of such national companies as Borden, Pet, Kraft, and Carnation. Moreover, there are several locally owned concerns as well. Thirty-six establishments in sixteen counties provide work for about 1,800 people in the bakery and confectionery industry. The largest bakeries, employing over 100 workers each, are situated in Hinds, Lauderdale, Coahoma, Adams, Forrest, and Harrison counties. Their primary product is bread.

TEXTILE MILLS, APPAREL, AND OTHER FABRICATED TEXTILE PRODUCTS—The textile mill products sector is of less importance than apparel and other fabricated textile products, having only 3.5 percent of total manufacturing employment in Mississippi in 1970. The textile mill industry is the most important employment sector in Clarke County. The average hourly wage rate in 1970 was $2.37, ten cents below the state average for manufacturing as a whole. Both wages and employment in this category have experienced considerable upward fluctuations over the past several decades. The highest employment for any single year was 7,100 reached in 1969.

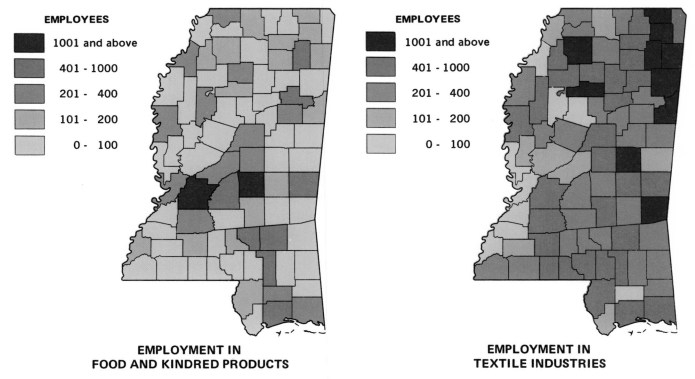

EMPLOYEES

■ 1001 and above

▨ 401 - 1000

▨ 201 - 400

▨ 101 - 200

▨ 0 - 100

**EMPLOYMENT IN
FOOD AND KINDRED PRODUCTS**

EMPLOYEES

■ 1001 and above

▨ 401 - 1000

▨ 201 - 400

▨ 101 - 200

▨ 0 - 100

**EMPLOYMENT IN
TEXTILE INDUSTRIES**

Source: U.S. Census of Population, 1970

Mississippi has 23 textile mills employing about 6,500 people. Over one-third of these workers are employed in hosiery mills. The largest hosiery mill, Round-the-Clock Hosiery, is located in Grenada and provides jobs for some 1,500 persons. Sixteen counties account for the state's 23 textile mills. The largest mills are situated in Clarke and Grenada counties. In addition, Washington, Panola, and Tate counties each employ over 500 workers. The primary products, other than hosiery, are woven fabrics, men's and boy's socks, underwear, knit apparel, and carpets.

In contrast to the textile mill industry, the apparel and other fabricated textile products industry has been the largest single employer of manufacturing labor in the state every year since 1956, when it surpassed the lumber and wood products industry. In 1970, 38,400 employees were being utilized in 175 apparel industry firms—more than one apparel worker for every five manufacturing workers in Mississippi. Apparel manufacturing not only has the distinction of being the largest employer in the state but it also pays the lowest hourly wages. In 1970 the average hourly wage paid to Mississippi apparel employees

was $1.97, less than 8 percent of the state average manufacturing wage. Low as the wage was however, it was not much below the national average for the apparel industry.

The apparel industry is well distributed throughout Mississippi, but a heavy concentration is located in the northeastern portion of the state. Over one-third of the workers in the industry are employed by seven large companies—Kellwood Co., Blue Bell, Inc., Glenn's All American Sportswear, Garan, Inc., Seminole Manufacturing Co., Movie Star, Inc., and Midland Shirt Co. The Mississippi apparel industry produces products ranging from men's and boys' shirts and trousers to gloves and women's lingerie.

Figures for state employment in both textile and apparel show that the composite groups are most important as an employer in SEA-4, the Mississippi Pine Hills, where 34.5 percent of total manufacturing employment falls in this category. Monroe County (in SEA-5) had 3,132 of its 1970 total of 5,937 manufacturing employees working in these industries; Clarke County employed 1,049 of a total 1,975 manufacturing workers in textile and apparel. Lee, Grenada, Ne-

163

shoba, Panola, Prentiss, Itawamba, and Alcorn counties also employed more than one thousand workers each in textile and apparel industries in 1970. Only the latter three counties are located in SEA 4. Additionally, Walthall and Tunica counties had more than 50 percent of their relatively small manufacturing labor force engaged in the two industries in 1970.

PRINTING, PUBLISHING, AND ALLIED PRODUCTS—Printing, publishing, and allied products manufacture is relatively unimportant in Mississippi. Only 4,074 persons were employed in these industries in 1970. Hinds County, containing the state capital and largest urban center, has an employment level approaching the one thousand mark. In 1970, Hinds County showed 933 persons of a total manufacturing employment of 11,256 working in the industry group; the state-employed labor force was 81,833. Twelve of the state's eighty-two counties do not register a single employee in these industries. In 1940, printing, publishing, and allied products accounted for 2.8 percent of total manufacturing employment in Mississippi. By 1970 the percentage had fallen to 2.2 percent, although the total number employed in the industries had more than doubled, from 1,857 to 4,074, during the thirty-year period.

Value added by Mississippi workers in printing, publishing, and allied products represented only 47.4 percent of the average value added by workers nationwide. Correspondingly, the 1970 Mississippi average hourly wage of $2.37 for this category represented only slightly more than 60 percent of the average for all similar employees in the nation.

Printing, publishing, and allied industries have 171 establishments in Mississippi. At least two-thirds of the eighty-two counties have, minimally, one printing or publishing firm. Printing companies employing 50 workers or more are found in Hinds, Lee, Lauderdale, and Alcorn counties. Hinds County serves as the center of the printing, publishing, and allied products industries, having 62 establishments providing jobs for about 1,100 people. The largest printing firm in the state, *The Clarion-Ledger* and Jackson *Daily News*, is situated in Hinds County. Most of the companies in this industry category publish daily, weekly, or biweekly newspapers. In addition, some printing companies are involved in such processes as lithographing, bookbinding, and commercial printing.

CHEMICALS AND ALLIED PRODUCTS— Only the printing industry recorded fewer employees in Mississippi in 1970 than did the chemical industry. A total of 5,888 workers, or 3.2 percent of the employed labor force in manufacturing, were listed in this industry group in the 1970 census. Furthermore, the chemical and allied products labor force was only marginally larger than it had been in 1940, when the chemical industry accounted for almost 7 percent of the manufacturing labor force. The growth rate over the years 1940–70 was 29.2 percent, with only the lumber and wood products industry recording a lower rate of growth.

Hourly wages in Mississippi's chemical industry were slightly above the manufacturing average of $2.77 in 1970. This represented a wage level 28.2 percent lower than the average hourly pay for chemical workers in the nation. Mississippi chemical worker productivity, as measured by relative value added by manufacture, was 79.7 percent of the national average.

The chemical industry is most important in SEA-7, the Mississippi Low Coastal Plains, where slightly over 10 percent of the area's manufacturing employ-

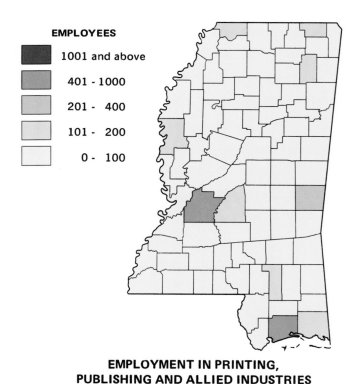

EMPLOYEES

1001 and above

401 - 1000

201 - 400

101 - 200

0 - 100

EMPLOYMENT IN PRINTING, PUBLISHING AND ALLIED INDUSTRIES

Source: U.S. Census of Population, 1970

ment worked in this industry. Forrest County, located in SEA-7, had the largest total chemical employment of any Mississippi county, with 825 persons. Yazoo County is also an important center of the small Mississippi chemical industry. Yazoo County's employment total in chemicals is 35.5 percent of total manufacturing employment for the county, making Yazoo the only Mississippi county where the number of chemical manufacturing workers represents as much as one-fourth of the total manufacturing labor force.

The chemicals and allied products group employs about 5,500 people in 80 establishments. Counties with significant numbers of workers in this industrial group are Bolivar, Forrest, Yazoo, Jackson, and Monroe. The largest firm (900 employees) is Baxter Laboratories in Bolivar County, which specializes in intravenous solutions and disposable hospital devices. The second largest firm is Hercules, Inc. (860 workers) in Forrest County, which makes resin-based compounds. The third largest concern is Mississippi Chemical Corp. in Yazoo County, whose 600 employees are engaged primarily in the manufacture of fertilizers. Jackson and Monroe counties employ over 500 persons each in this industry group.

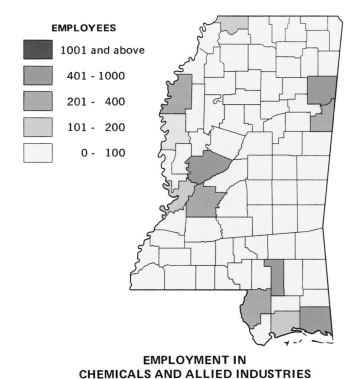

EMPLOYEES

1001 and above

401 - 1000

201 - 400

101 - 200

0 - 100

**EMPLOYMENT IN
CHEMICALS AND ALLIED INDUSTRIES**

Source: U.S. Census of Population, 1970

OTHER NONDURABLE GOODS—Two industries that are not generally listed as separate entities in data collected on the Mississippi manufacturing sector are the paper and related products industry and the petroleum and coal products industry. The petroleum industry employed only about 1,200 people in 1970 and has been so relatively unimportant that federal statistics have only been kept on its employment since 1965, and wage data are still not tabulated. The paper industry, however, is an important industry.

Some 7,100 persons were employed in the paper industry in Mississippi in 1970. They received an average hourly wage of $3.93, the highest manufacturing wage rate in Mississippi. This wage rate was almost 10 percent higher than the national average wage in the paper industry. An important reason for the higher rate is the value added per production worker in Mississippi. The value added is almost one-fourth greater than for the paper industry employee nationwide. This industry recorded an 81.2 percent increase in value added per worker between 1967 and 1970.

Mississippi has 35 paper and allied products plants located in twenty counties. The largest manufacturers of paper and allied products are situated in Jackson, Adams, and Warren counties. These three counties contain the plants of International Paper Company which employs 3,400 workers. This number is over one-half the state's total employment in this manufacturing group. Other important paper-producing counties are Washington, Wilkinson, Lauderdale, Lawrence, Rankin, Forrest, and Itawamba.

Mississippi's smallest major industrial classification is petroleum refining and related industries. Ten counties contain 15 establishments employing about 1,200 workers. The only firm employing more than 350 people is Standard Oil Company in Jackson County. Several other national oil companies have refineries within the state; these are located primarily in Hinds, Lamar, and Warren counties.

The generalized category of "other, nondurable goods" is quantitatively important in only three counties: Jackson, with 2,626 employees; Adams, with 2,220 of a total manufacturing force of 2,954; and Hinds with 1,209 employees.

*James M. McQuiston
Ralph D. Cross*

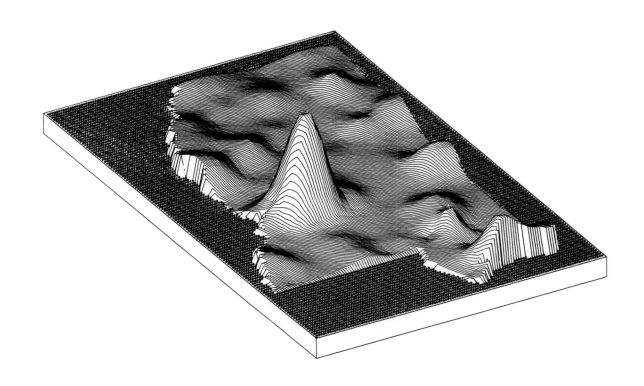

TOTAL EMPLOYMENT IN SERVICES

SERVICES

Service functions may be broadly grouped into six service categories: distribution; transportation, communications, and utilities; financial, real estate, and insurance; government; construction; and other services. These activities, in aggregate, represent the majority of persons in the employment structure of a city, county, or state.

In Mississippi in 1970, over 65 percent of the employed persons were working in one of the many different activities associated with service functions. Seventy-seven percent of the persons employed in services were working in urban areas of the state. By broad categories, in 1970 there were 129,015 persons employed in distribution functions; 42,862 persons employed in transportation, communications, and public utility activities; 81,430 persons employed in government; 23,063 employed in financial, real estate, and insurance services; 53,770 persons in construction; and 141,763 persons employed in other service functions.

A useful index of demonstrating the importance of service activities is income measures. The most utilitarian measure available in the Bureau of Census reports is median income by industry group. In 1969, the median Mississippi income earned by a civilian employee was $5,043. Median incomes for service activities ranged from a low of $3,804 for personal services to a high of $6,625 for financial, real estate, and insurance services. The median incomes for individual service groups in 1970 were $5,214 for construction, $5,846 for transportation, communications, and public utilities, $4,591 for distribution func-

tions, $6,625 for finance, real estate, and insurance, $3,234–$5,936 for miscellaneous services, and $6,592 for government.

It is useful to understand income employment distributions among the various vocational groups in Mississippi, but of slightly more importance is the comparison of certain occupation groups in that state to the national averages. Over 69 percent of persons employed in the United States in 1970 were engaged in service activities, as compared to slightly over 65 percent in Mississippi. An interesting aspect of employment comparison becomes apparent when examining the distribution of service activities contained within urban areas. Mississippi recorded over 77 percent of its urban employment in service activities in 1970 whereas the national percentage was only 73 percent.

The 1970 median income in service activities for the nation was $7,610, as compared to $5,043 for Mississippi. For the various broad categories the median income comparisons were as follows: distribution functions, Mississippi $4,591 to $6,599 for the nation; transportation, communications, and public utilities, Mississippi $5,846 to $8,347 for the nation; government services, Mississippi $6,592 to $8,640 for the nation; financial, real estate, and insurance services, Mississippi $6,625 to $9,130 for the nation; other services, Mississippi $3,234–$5,936 compared to a range of $5,128–$7,978 for the nation; and construction, Mississippi $5,214 to $7,540 for the nation.

James W. Gladden, Jr.

SERVICE ACTIVITIES

Service activities represent the third category of economic production. The first two, primary activities and manufacturing, involve the harvesting of naturally produced commodities in mining, fishing, agriculture, and forest products industries, and the changes in form of the goods gathered. The term "service" embraces those economic pursuits which entail neither a change in location nor an alteration in the form of commodities. Within this sector are included a diversity of occupations—retail and wholesale traders, government employees, plumbers, household servants, bankers, teachers, and a host of others.

Although the range of service-type activities is large, there are relationships among them which permit distinctions to be made. For the purpose of this section, six general service sector headings are recognized—distribution activities, transportation and communication, government, finance, construction, and other miscellaneous services.

Because of the diversity of occupations within the service sector, it is difficult to conceive of them as having an identifiable spatial pattern. The problem of identification is eased, however, since service activities tend to agglomerate. While it is true that an isolated roadside gasoline station constitutes a service-oriented pursuit, the absolute number of single or even small clusterings of services is of relatively little significance. In Mississippi, and elsewhere in the United States, by far the largest number of service establishments are to be found in urban situations; and the larger the urban agglomeration, usually the greater is the number of services and service employment. The role of services and the number of services by category, however, can and usually does vary among urban areas. Thus, it might be expected that a relatively small city housing a university would have a greater proportion of its service employees in teaching, and an administrative center would be high in government employment, while finance or other specialized activities might tend to dominate the function of other appropriate specialized centers.

Compared to the national average, employment in service activities in Mississippi compared to total state employment is low. Of the eight State Economic Areas (see map on page 154), only one SEA exceeds the national average of 63.6 percent of total employment engaged in service activities. Each of the state's

EMPLOYMENT BY MAJOR INDUSTRY DIVISION

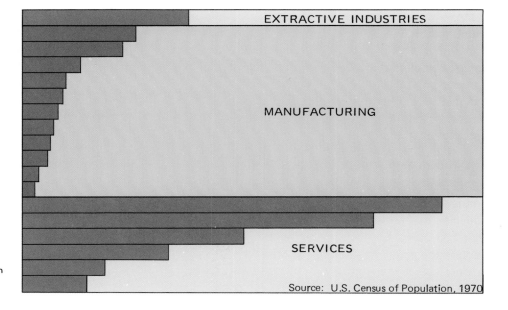

(in thousands)

Source: U.S. Census of Population, 1970

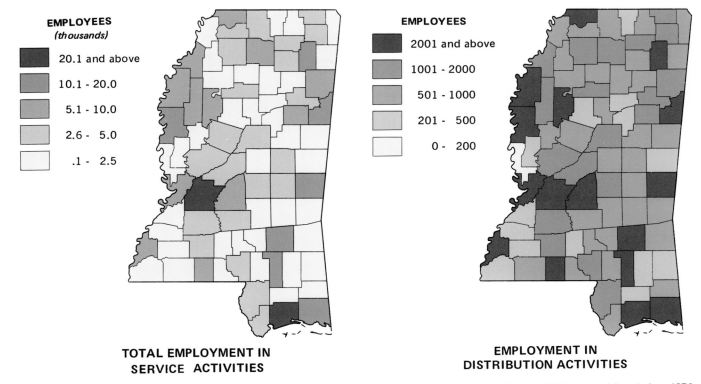

EMPLOYEES
(thousands)

■ 20.1 and above
■ 10.1 - 20.0
■ 5.1 - 10.0
□ 2.6 - 5.0
□ .1 - 2.5

**TOTAL EMPLOYMENT IN
SERVICE ACTIVITIES**

Source: General Social and Economic Characteristics, 1972

EMPLOYEES

■ 2001 and above
■ 1001 - 2000
■ 501 - 1000
□ 201 - 500
□ 0 - 200

**EMPLOYMENT IN
DISTRIBUTION ACTIVITIES**

Source: U.S. Census of Population, 1970

SEAs, however, noted services as the major employment sector in 1970. The leading SEA in service employment, which included the Jackson metropolitan area, recorded 74.9 percent of its working force in services. The second highest service employment area (63.1 percent) included the three urbanized Gulf Coast counties. SEAs 4 and 6a, encompassing much of the northeastern and central parts of the state, had the lowest percentage in this category, with 47.0 and 48.5 percent, respectively. (As might be expected, these are among the state's least urbanized areas.) Hinds led the counties in service employment with 76.5 percent, while Itawamba County (35.2 percent) noted the least relative employment in services.

EMPLOYMENT BY MAJOR CATEGORY

DISTRIBUTION ACTIVITIES—Distribution activities is here defined as all wholesale and retail trade activities in the state. Of the two, retail employment, with 105,069 employees, is by far the more significant, leading in every county in Mississippi. In fact, in only six of the eighty-two counties is wholesale trade (23,946 employees) responsible for as much

as 25 percent of total retail–wholesale employment—Clay, Rankin, Hinds, DeSoto, Adams, and Leflore. Hinds County had the state's largest employment in distribution activities in 1970 with a total of 16,972 persons. The Jackson metropolitan area, lying partially in both Hinds and Rankin counties, must be considered as the nodal point of wholesale–retail activities for the entire state.

As is true of the majority of service functions, employment in distribution activities has grown at only a moderate rate within the state. Over the period 1950–70, distribution activities increased from an employment level of 95,592 to 129,015, or by 34.9 percent.

TRANSPORTATION AND COMMUNICATION—The transportation and communication sector includes employment services in railways, roads, waterways, pipelines, radio, telephone, telegraph, postal systems, and publications. This sector has shown a slower growth rate during the years 1950–70 than any other category of services. The relatively static condition of transportation and communication employment in Mississippi since World War II seems a mere reflection of the nationwide situation, including

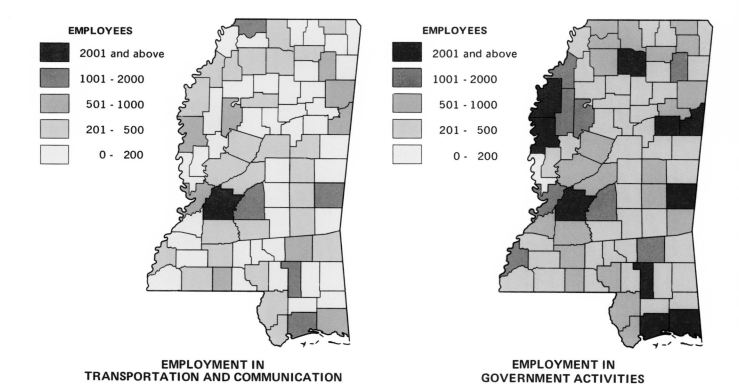

Source: U.S. Census of Population, 1970

**EMPLOYMENT IN
TRANSPORTATION AND COMMUNICATION**

**EMPLOYMENT IN
GOVERNMENT ACTIVITIES**

the rather sharp decline in importance of rail transportation. Whatever the cause, employment in this category of activity was only 30,028 in 1970, an increase of 24.8 percent since 1950. In no county of the state is transportation and communication the major source of service employment. In only six counties—Hinds, Harrison, Lauderdale, Forrest, DeSoto, and Rankin—are one thousand or more persons employed in these activities.

GOVERNMENT ACTIVITIES–Two major categories of government services are noted in Mississippi —public administration and public educational services. Of these two, public educational services has grown most rapidly since 1950, being especially pronounced in the decade 1960–70. For the period 1950–70, total government employment grew by 99.1 percent, from 40,852 to 81,430.

Government employment constitutes the primary service sector activity in Benton, Greene, Issaquena, Lafayette, and Oktibbeha counties. In all five counties total employment is small, however, and only in Lafayette and Oktibbeha are more than a few hundred persons employed in this category. The importance of government employment in these two largely

nonurbanized counties is accounted for by the presence of two of the state's leading universities—Mississippi State University and the University of Mississippi.

Other counties have significantly large government sectors, but are not relatively important owing to high employment in other service activities. Forrest and Bolivar counties, which include the University of Southern Mississippi and Delta State University, respectively; Lauderdale, Lowndes, and Harrison counties, all with Air Force bases; Hinds County with Jackson, the state capital; and Washington and Jackson counties with various miscellaneous activities, each have government employment exceeding 2,000 persons.

FINANCIAL ACTIVITIES—Financial employment in the state includes activities associated primarily with commercial banks, savings and loan associations, credit unions, real estate firms, and insurance companies.

Although the financial sector has shown the greatest percentage increase in employment between 1950 and 1970, it continues to remain among the smallest in total employment of all service activities. Only 23,063 persons were employed in this sector in 1970, and in no county was it the leading service employment category. In only two counties, Hinds (6,424) and Harrison (1,774), were as many as 1,000 persons employed in financial institutions.

CONSTRUCTION ACTIVITIES—Construction employment in Mississippi is third only to retail trade and to public and private educational activities within the service sector. In 1970, 53,770 persons were employed in construction activities, an increase of 34 percent over the 1960 employment figure, and a 65.1 percent increase over the 32,557 persons employed in 1950.

While construction is in progress throughout the state, a large portion of it is concentrated within fairly well-defined areas. Only ten of the eighty-two counties have 1,000 or more persons employed in construction, and together these account for 45.2 percent of the total construction employment. Not surprisingly, these ten counties encompass the state's largest urban agglomerations and areas of rapid industrial growth. Hinds County employed 5,696 persons in construction in 1970, leading all other counties in that category. Next in importance were Harrison, Jackson, and Warren counties, with employments of 4,338, 2,577, and 2,274 persons respectively.

The value of construction contracts in Mississippi reached an all-time high in 1971 at $933 million. (The previous high was $576 million in 1969.) Residential construction is the most important part of the building industry.

OTHER SERVICES— Other miscellaneous service activities not included in the above groups accounted for 154,597 employed persons in 1970. Although significant in total employment, only two of the ten categories included here were by themselves important employment groups: private households and other personal services, employing 53,783 persons, and hospital and health services, with 33,743 employed persons. Other activities of less importance included legal, engineering, and miscellaneous professional services (13,047 persons), utilities and sanitary services (12,834), private educational (10,561), welfare, religious, and nonprofit membership organizations (10,255), and repair services (10,044).

James M. McQuiston
Robert W. Wales

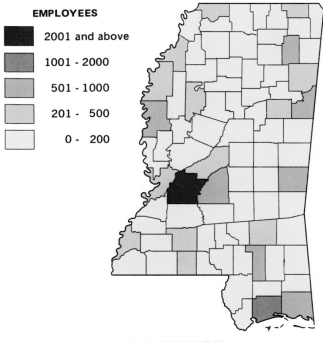

EMPLOYEES

- 2001 and above
- 1001 - 2000
- 501 - 1000
- 201 - 500
- 0 - 200

**EMPLOYMENT IN
THE FINANCIAL SECTOR**

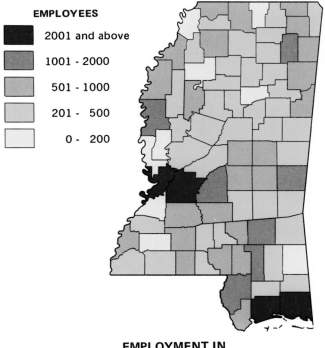

EMPLOYEES

- 2001 and above
- 1001 - 2000
- 501 - 1000
- 201 - 500
- 0 - 200

**EMPLOYMENT IN
CONSTRUCTION**

Source: U.S. Census of Population, 1970

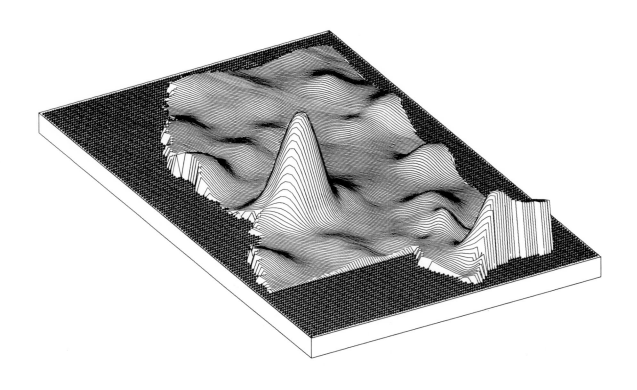

PROJECTED POPULATION FOR THE YEAR 2000

MISSISSIPPI: FUTURE PERSPECTIVE

Mississippi is becoming more like the rest of the United States. The state's economic base is already much like a composite of America, and most of her economic and social trends are in the direction of national norms. Television, transportation improvements, and, perhaps most important, national intervention in the Mississippi economy and society have greatly affected the state and her people. These agents of change will continue their homogenizing influence for the remainder of the century. Neverthe-

less, Mississippi will retain many of her distinctive characteristics.

POPULATION

For many decades, Mississippi's population has been static, with massive outmigration offsetting natural increase. But between 1970 and 1990, a population growth of about 600,000 is expected, due to expanding employment opportunities. This growth would give the state a projected population of about 2.8 million in 1990.

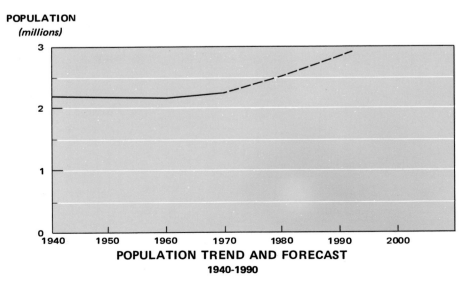

POPULATION
(millions)

POPULATION TREND AND FORECAST
1940-1990

Source: U. S. Census of Population, 1940 - 1970.

URBANIZATION

Urbanization is the process whereby a city increases in size, usually connoting an increase in population. Growth may occur internally as net natural increase or by inmigration. However, both processes most often contribute to a city's growth, and inmigration is usually the more notable of the two. Urbanization has been a prominent trend in the United States during the twentieth century, especially since World War II. Today, the United States is a highly urbanized country with about 72 percent of its population living in urban centers of 2,500 or more. Conversely, Mississippi is one of the nation's most rural states, but it is rapidly becoming more urbanized. The urban population has grown steadily since 1950, and by 1990 it is likely that over 60 percent of all Mississippians will be living in an urban community (2,500 or more). Most of the growth has been in cities over 10,000. These cities in 1950 accounted for 20 percent of Mississippi's population; by 1970 they accounted for 34 percent, and if the current rate of increase continues, they should account for approximately 48 percent of the state's population in 1990.

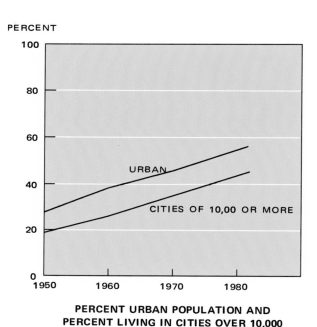

PERCENT URBAN POPULATION AND
PERCENT LIVING IN CITIES OVER 10,000

CITIES WITH POPULATION OVER 10,000

Source: U. S. Census of Population, 1960, 1970.

174

CENTERS OF GROWTH

The major growth centers in the state are the Jackson metropolitan area, the Gulf Coast, the Memphis suburban area in DeSoto County, and certain portions of northeastern Mississippi.

Most of the coastal counties in the United States are gaining population, and the Mississippi Gulf Coast counties are no exception. Although currently dependent on the federal government (Keesler Air Force Base, the Litton Shipyard with its naval contracts, and the Mississippi Test Facility), the area is strengthening its manufacturing and commercial base and should continue to attract population.

The Jackson area is developing into a major trade, service, and distribution center for an area within a 100-mile radius. Jackson will continue to gain population as its economic hinterland develops.

DeSoto County, part of the Memphis metropolitan area, will continue to become more suburban and densely populated, and the rate of growth in this county may well exceed that of any other in Mississippi.

In northeastern Mississippi, Tupelo has become a major trade and service center. Despite the lack of any geographical advantage, Tupelo has grown steadily over the past two decades. This growth ought to continue through 1990, stimulated by highway improvements, by the diversified economy in Lee County, and by the "prime mover" effect of manufacturing plants in adjacent counties. Another growth center in northeastern Mississippi is in the Columbus–Starkville–West Point area, known as the Golden Triangle.

MAJOR POPULATION GROWTH AREAS

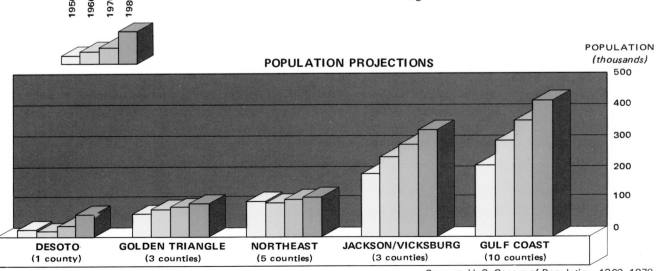

POPULATION PROJECTIONS

Source: U. S. Census of Population, 1960, 1970.

175

DELTA COUNTIES

The Mississippi Delta has been rapidly losing population for many years and the trend is expected to continue. In ten Delta counties total population has declined by about 85,000 people in the last twenty years. The loss has been largely in its black population. The trend will continue over the next twenty years with whites beginning to outnumber blacks in these counties during the 1980s. The total population of the ten Delta counties should decline to below 250,000 by 1990.

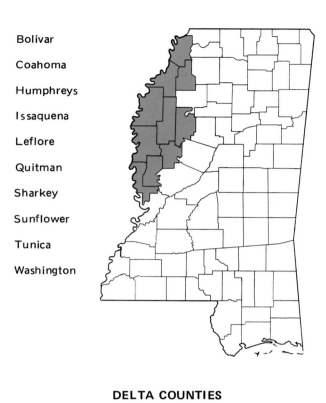

Bolivar

Coahoma

Humphreys

Issaquena

Leflore

Quitman

Sharkey

Sunflower

Tunica

Washington

DELTA COUNTIES

Source: U. S. Census of Population, 1960, 1970.

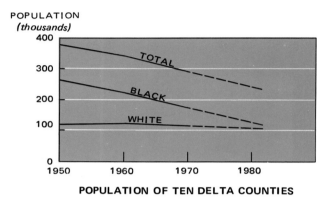

POPULATION OF TEN DELTA COUNTIES

BLACK POPULATION

Mississippi's black population has been declining for several decades, as blacks have sought employment in the large cities of neighboring states and in the North. The chart shows that the nonwhite population has dropped from about 45 percent of Mississippi's total in 1950 to approximately 37 percent in 1970.

Statistics show that better-educated people are more likely to move to a new town or state. This presumably is because they are more aware of employment opportunities elsewhere and have more confidence that they can obtain new employment. Thus, as the average educational level of Mississippi's black population increases, more outmigration ought to result. Blacks should make up 34 percent of Mississippi's population in 1980 and about 30 percent in 1990.

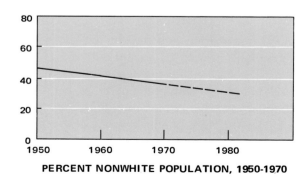

PERCENT NONWHITE POPULATION, 1950-1970

Source: U. S. Census of Population, 1960, 1970.

MOBILITY AND MIGRATION

In the period 1965–70, approximately 157,000 people moved to Mississippi from other states—equivalent to 8 percent of the state population. Of those people 140,000 were white—equivalent to 11 percent of the state's white population. Future inmigration is expected to increase. White immigration will outnumber blacks about six to one.

Outmigration from Mississippi during the same five-year period was almost 200,000. The outmigration rate for whites was slightly higher than for blacks. Better job opportunities in the state will greatly increase inmigration, but if Mississippi conforms to the U.S. pattern, a substantial amount of outmigration will occur regardless of employment opportunities.

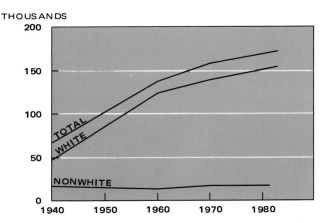

MOBILITY OF MISSISSIPPI POPULATION: RESIDENTS LIVING OUTSIDE THE STATE FIVE YEARS PRIOR TO CENSUS, 1940, 1960, 1970

Source: U. S. Census of Population, 1940, 1960, 1970.

AGE DISTRIBUTION

Mississippi has a large number of children and older people but relatively few young and middle-aged adults. This is particularly true of the black population. The skewed age distribution pattern results from a high birthrate combined with a large outmigration of people in their late teens and early twenties. By 1990, this net outmigration will be diminished or perhaps reversed, and the birthrate is expected to be much lower. These changes will produce a higher percentage of population in the income-earning middle-aged groups. The charts show the present Mississippi age distribution and the expected U.S. age distribution by 1990, which the state should be approaching by that time.

AGE DISTRIBUTION

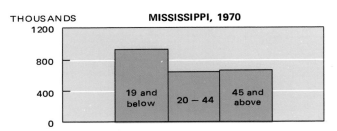

MISSISSIPPI, 1970

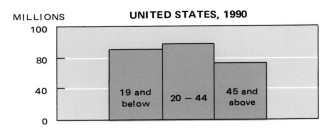

UNITED STATES, 1990

Source: U. S. Census of Population, 1970
U. S. Bureau of the Census, Current Population Reports.

INCOME

Per capita income in Mississippi has more than tripled in the last twenty years and has grown from 51 percent of the U.S. average in 1952 to 70 percent in 1972. Per capita income by 1990 should exceed 80 percent of the national average. If current trends continue, the average Mississippian ought to be nearly twice as wealthy (in terms of purchasing power) in 1990 as in 1970.

Manufacturing, now the largest source of income in Mississippi, should continue to gain in relative importance. Mississippi will remain basically a "small town" state, and this factor will favor development of manufacturing over tertiary or service activities, which tend to cluster in large cities. Mississippi's agricultural output will continue to increase moderately, but the greatest progress in agriculture will be more labor-saving efficiency, enabling the land to produce the same value crop with less employment. Thus, agriculture will provide an improved standard of living for those engaged in it, but the number engaged will decline.

EMPLOYMENT

Employment in Mississippi is expected to increase by 250,000 between 1970 and 1990. This employment increase, which will give impetus to the population growth described earlier, will result from continued growth in nonagricultural employment, combined with the "bottoming out" of employment in agriculture. The state's nonagricultural employment has been expanding rapidly for many years; but until recently the release of agricultural workers because of increased farm mechanization has offset this increase. With farm employment now leveling off and nonagricultural employment continuing its dynamic growth, Mississippi's labor force will need to expand.

As total employment rises, wage rates, responding to the law of supply and demand, will also increase. Lower-wage industries will need to increase wages to compete for labor.

The projected gain in manufacturing will spearhead Mississippi's economic growth. The type of manufacturing in the state will begin to change from

PERCENT

Manufacturing

Federal government   1950
                        1970

Wholesale and retail trade

Property income

State and local government

Services

Farms

MAJOR SOURCES OF INCOME
1950 and 1970

Source: U.S. Bureau of Economic Analysis.

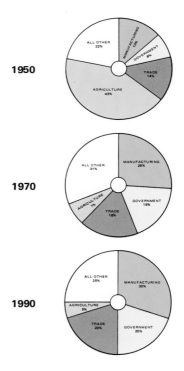

MISSISSIPPI EMPLOYMENT

Source: U.S. Census of Population, 1950, 1970.

178

predominantly labor-intensive operations (such as apparel) to more capital-intensive industries (such as chemicals and metal working). The heavier, more capital-intensive industry will concentrate on the Gulf Coast, on navigable water in the northeast, and at Mississippi River ports. Higher technology industry will concentrate around such growing population centers as Jackson, DeSoto County, the Gulf Coast, and parts of northern Mississippi.

RESOURCE DEVELOPMENT

Petroleum and natural gas will continue to be produced in Mississippi in moderate quantities for the next twenty years. Exploration at deeper levels should accelerate as increased fuel prices make more expensive drilling operations economically feasible.

Mineral deposits—bauxite, iron ore, and lignite—in northeastern Mississippi may prove to have commercial value, but the mineral resources in the state will contribute only modestly to Mississippi's overall economy.

Lumber and pulpwood from the timber grown in Mississippi now provide an annual value of about $1 billion. Through more efficient tree-farming methods, this harvest can undoubtedly be increased without depleting the net growing stock of timber.

Productive soil in many parts of the state and abundant water supplies are perhaps Mississippi's most important natural resources. It is likely that farming in Mississippi will continue to shift from dependence on cotton toward food crops. Food-processing operations will gain in importance. Utilization of marginal land for pasture and crops will increase.

TRANSPORTATION

The outstanding development in Mississippi's transportation system in the next twenty years will be the Tennessee–Tombigbee Waterway, providing barge transportation from northeastern Mississippi to the Gulf, and to the Mississippi River Valley. This waterway will greatly stimulate industrial development along its course. Extensive highway improvements have been authorized throughout the state and will be completed within the next two decades. It is unlikely that the railroad network in Mississippi will be significantly extended; indeed, it is likely that track transport may be abandoned in some areas. Commercial air transportation will develop in the state mainly at Jackson and at a few regional airports. As highways improve, air service between smaller cities in the state will be curtailed.

EDUCATION

Mississippi since 1950 has nearly doubled its percentage of total personal income invested in education. This increase, together with a rapid rise in total personal income, has meant that funds available for public education in the state have risen spectacularly. In 1951–52 the average expenditure per pupil in Mississippi was $96, or 39 percent of the national average. By 1971–72 this figure had risen to $655, 68 percent of the national average. The state will continue to spend increasingly large sums on public education. Educational quality in the state will depend more on the administrators' ability to perceive and meet student needs and less on financial resources.

Vocational education in secondary schools should expand tremendously over the next twenty years. As noted earlier, the state's economy will be heavily based on manufacturing, and, since many Mississippi families are poor and socially disadvantaged, vocational training will be important and attractive to many students. As the high school vocational curriculum improves, the level of vocational courses offered in junior colleges will be upgraded.

SOCIAL CHANGE AND IMAGE

For many years Mississippi has been handicapped by an unfavorable national image—one of racial repression, poverty, and rural ignorance. The state has been changing rapidly, both socially and economically, but the image changes more slowly. However, Mississippi's national image is improving, and by 1980 Mississippi's "poor image" should be not more than a trivial problem in attracting new residents and outside investments.

Irlyn C. Toner
F. John Wade

INDEX

Hurricane Camille, 19

Iberville, Sieur d' (Pierre LeMoyne), 23, 29, 30
Iberville River, 31
Ibitoupa tribe, 25
Ice Age, 11
Illinois Central-Gulf Railroad, 142
Income, 43, 61–63, 178
Indians: tribes, 23–28; captives of, 26; consumer items of, 26; foods of, 26; housing of, 26; games of, 27; moities, 27; contact with Europeans of, 28; life-style/society of, 27–28; marriage, 28; treaties with, 28, 37, wars with, 31; affairs, 32; colonial policy of, 32–33; British relations with, 33; commissioner for, 33; congress of, 33; Spain's relations with, 35; land cessions of, 38; Removal Act of 1832 for, 57; lands of, 24, 27, 46; education of, 73
Industrial Institute and College. See MSCW
Industry: development of, 42; increases in Bourbon era of, 43; growth of, 43, 44, 49
Ingalls Shipbuilding Corp., 48
In migrants, 53
Institutions, Boards for, 66
Interior Flatwoods, types and uses of soils of, 83
Interior Low Plateaus, 4, 8
International Paper Co., 165
Iron ore, 90
Ironwood tree, 20
Isle of Orleans, 31
Issaquena County, 53, 54, 79, 106
Istrouma (Baton Rouge), 29
Itawamba County, bentonite production in, 91
ITT Telecommunications, 161

Jackson, Andrew, 37
Jackson: buried intrusions at, 10; population growth of 1860–90, 44; as population core, 52, 53; as capital and largest city, 60; SMSA of, 60; planning agency for, 71; health facilities in, 79; as growth center, 175
Jackson County: population of, 53, 54; low percentage of elderly in, 57; urban population in, 59; planning agency for, 71; port authority for, 72
Jackson Dome, 11
Jackson Field, 93
Jackson geologic formations, 10, 70
Jefferson College, 73
Jefferson County, 36, 37, 58, 62, 63, 73
Jefferson Davis County, 93
Jet stream, 14
Johnson, Paul B., Jr., 69
Johnson, Paul B., Sr., 77
Johnstone, George, 32
Joliet-Marquette exploration parties, 28
Jones, Lawrence Clifton, 77
Judiciary: structure of, 32; election of, 38; as branch of government, 66–67

Junior colleges, 66, 76
Jurrasic age strata: petroleum from, 89; oil and gas in, 92–93

Keesler Air Force Base, 175
Kellwood Co., 163
Kemper County, 5, 54, 90
Koroa tribe, 25
Kosciusco strata, 93

Laborers: political unrest of, 44
Lake Beulah, 86
Lake Bolivar, 86
Lake Eagle, 86
Lake George/Holly Bluff archealogical site, 134
Lake Maurepas, 29, 31
Lake Pontchartrain, 24, 29, 31
Lake Washington, 86
Lamar County, Baxterville Oil Field in, 93
Land agencies dealing with, 65
Landmarks, 133
La Salle, Sieur de (Robert Cavelier) 23, 28, 29
Lauderdale County: population of, 53, 57–58; health facilities of, 78, 79
Laurel oak, 20
Law, John, 30
Law: Indian, 27; military, 32; Crown colony policies on, 32
Leake County, 5, 58
Lee, Stephen D., defeats Sherman, 41
Lee County: low percentage of elderly in, 57; mean income in, 62
Leflore County, 57–58
Legislature: in antebellum period, 38; enacts 1865 "black code," 42; organization of, 64
Lemos, Gov. Manuel Gayoso de, 35
Lignites, 10, 90
Limestone: and cement, 90; utilization of, 94
Literary Fund, 73
Litton Industries, 162, 175
Live oak trees, 20
Livestock production, 23, 111–15
Loblolly pine trees, 20
Loblolly-Shortleaf Pine, forests of, 96–97
Local government, 68–69
Loess, surface material, 5, 7, 11
Longleaf Pine Belt, 7
Longleaf-Slash Pine, forests of, 96
Longwood antebellum home, 133
Louis XIV, 29, 30
Louisiana Delta, 19
Louisiana Territory, 23
Louisville, 10
Lower Coastal Plain; types and uses of soils of, 84
Lowndes County, 57
Lumbering, 98, 158, 159

MATCOG, 71
MRS Manufacturing Co., 160
Machinery, manufacturing of, 160
Macon, 4
McRaney, Bob, Sr., 150
Madison County, 7, 71

Madison Academy, 73
Magna American Corp., 160
Manchac, 33, 35
Manufacturing, 23, 43, 49, 153–65; persons employed number of, 156; value added by, 157–58
Marine greensands, 10
Marine marls, 10
Marion County: Baxterville Oil Field in, 93; gas production in, 93
Marls, 4, 7, 10, 90
Masonry cement; raw materials of, 90
Mastodons, 11
Matthews, George, 36
Memphis, 7, 71
Meridian, 10, 19, 44, 60, 78
Merrill, 12, 86
Mesozoic deposits, 8
Metal Products, manufacture of, 159–60
Methodist Episcopal Church, 76
Mexican War, 23, 38
Midland Shirt Co., 163
Midnight: buried intrusions at, 10; volcano, 11
Midway group, 10, 90
Migration, projections for, 177
Migratory game birds, 118–19
Milksheds, 113
Millsaps, Reuben W., 76
Millsaps College, 76
Mineral Resources, 89–95
Minorities, population characteristics of, 58
Miocene epoch, 10, 11, 90
Mississippian geologic age, 8, 89
Mississippian cultural complex, aboriginal, 24
Mississippi, admission to Union, 23, 37
MISS/ARK/TENN Council of Government, 72
Mississippi Association for Teachers in Colored Schools, 77
Mississippi Authority for Educational Television (MAET), 151
Mississippi Board of Education, 77
Mississippi Chemical Corp., 165
Mississippi College, 73
Mississippi Company, 30
Mississippi Education Association, 77
Mississippi Embrayment, 8, 20
Mississippi Employment Security Commission, 63
Mississippi Fishing Banks Committee, 124
Mississippi Industrial and Training School, 76
Mississippi or Interior Salt Basin, 89
Mississippi Normal College. See University of Southern Mississippi
Mississippi Power Co., 147
Mississippi Power and Light Co., 147
Mississippi River: Spain's control of, 35; Delta floodplain of, 11; ports of, 145; and throughout
Mississippi Salt Basin, 11
Mississippi School and Colony for the Feeble Minded, 76
Mississippi Sound, 19
Mississippi State College for Women, 76

184